Daughters of Painted Ladies

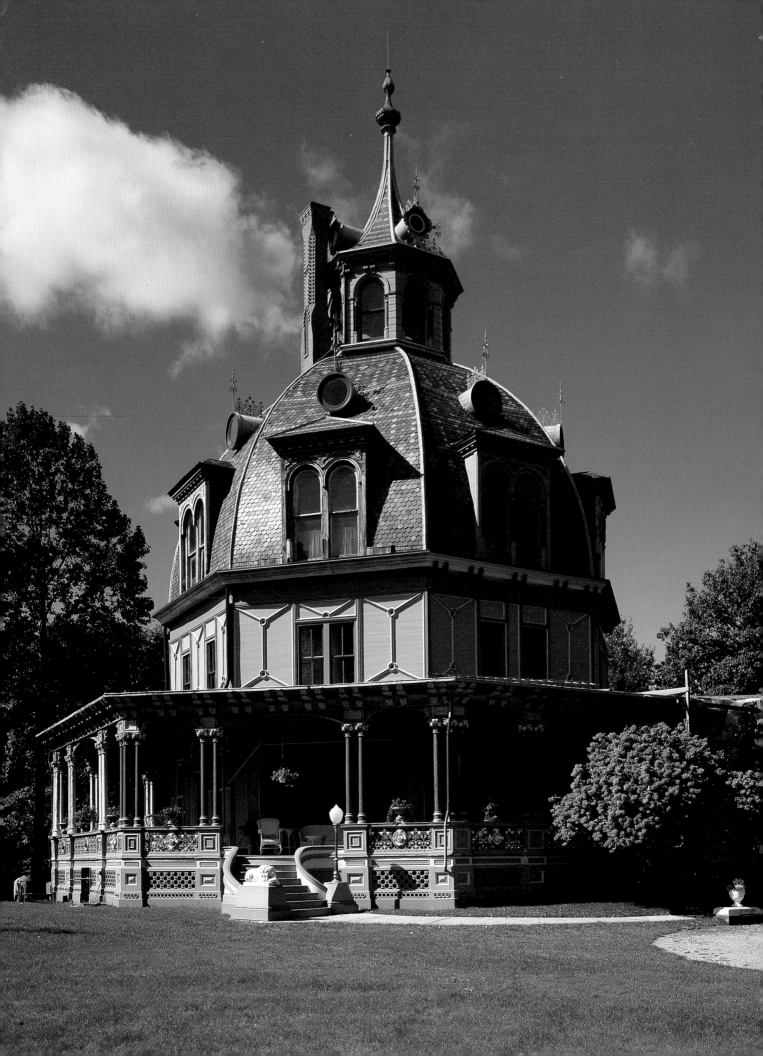

Elizabeth Pomada
and
Michael Larsen

Photographs by
Douglas Keister

DAUGHTERS
of
PAINTED LADIES

America's
Resplendent Victorians

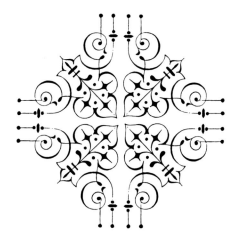

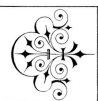

E. P. Dutton
NEW YORK

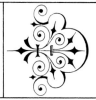

(*Frontispiece*)

IRVINGTON—ON—HUDSON, NEW YORK.
The Octagon House. 1860–1872. Gothic, Second Empire, and Eastlake with Eastern embellishments. Banker Paul Armour built a plain two-story octagon in 1860, inspired by phrenologist Orson Squire Fowler and his book *The Octagon House: A Home For All* (1854).

Most octagon structures were called "Follies" from the French word *folie* or "delight." A folly was any expensive building that was out of sync with its neighbors, and a costly mistake.

In 1872, Joseph Stiner, a New York City tea merchant, added the dome, verandah, and elaborate decorative details on his summer house to remind him of the India and China of his travels and business. Like other follies, this domed octagon—the only one in the world—was meant to amuse. Whimsy was brought indoors along with the theme of eight: eight windows, moldings with eight sides, and an octagon-shaped ballroom. The porch alone, with fifty-six posts, cast-iron railings, and portrait busts of his favorite dog, Prince, framed in the railing of each bay, cost $26,000. (See detail illustration on opposite page.)

Author-historian Carl Carmer lived here for thirty years. After his death in 1976, the house was acquired by the National Trust for Historic Preservation. In need of restoration, it was the first house to be resold by the National Trust to a private citizen, Joseph Pell Lombardi, an architect specializing in restoration and historic preservation.

M. C. Taylor did the microscopic paint analysis to match the ten 1872 colors, including pink, wine, and gray, with a touch of violet. During our visit, craftsmen were still restoring the exterior and interior, working "to hold together the fragile unity of the structure and to maintain the goals of the original builder."

From its richly patterned roof to its intricately designed porch railings, this magnificent, breathtaking building is one of America's most beautiful Victorians. The exterior may be viewed from the private grounds by appointment only.

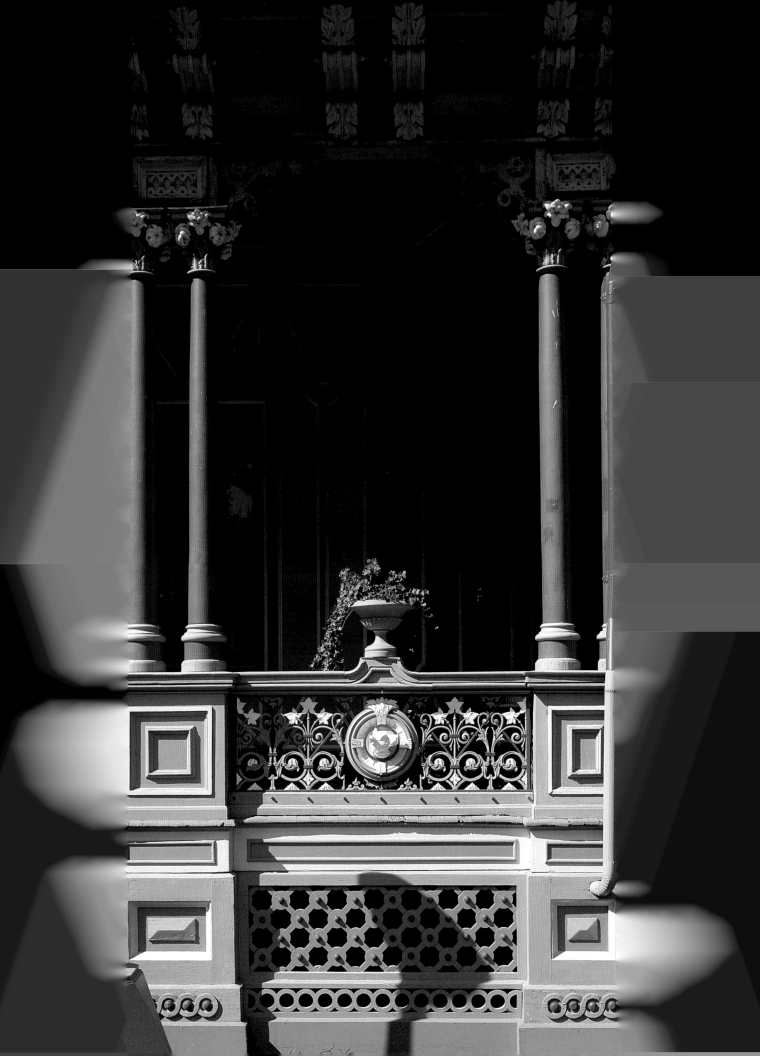

This book is dedicated to
those who fought to save these beautiful buildings,
the Victorian network that enabled us to find them,
the homeowners and colorists whose artistry graces its pages,
and to the readers inspired to bring new life to gray ladies.

Acknowledgments

While there had to be houses to find, it would have been an unthinkable task to find every Painted Lady in fifty states without the generous assistance of the Victorian network. Ever since we started putting *Painted Ladies* together, these American beauties have brought out the best in the people who design, paint, own, and enjoy them. They spontaneously generate a contagious sense of pride, enthusiasm, and eagerness to help. The Ladies have always generated positive energy, and we needed a ton of it.

There were kind souls in almost every state who answered our questions or found answers if they didn't have them; who gave us directions; who knew what houses to guide us to and the fastest way to get to them; who fed and housed our weary bodies after twelve-hour days of driving and searching, most of the time in vain. We could only laugh when friends would comment on how lucky we were to have had such a great vacation.

We were sustained by finding these delightful damsels, especially the unexpected ones, and by the hundreds of people around the country who did what they could for us. To all of you, named and unnamed, please accept our deep gratitude.

The people in the following list gave us leads, sent us pictures and information, and acted as tour guides. They are a Victorian network and we couldn't have done the book without them. Thanks go to:

Deborah Andrews, Portland Landmarks, Portland, Me.; Priscilla Demers, The New Bedford Glass Society, New Bedford, Mass.; Arthur Railton, Duke's County Historical Society, and Ellen Weiss, Martha's Vineyard, Mass.; Kathy McKechnie, Martha's Vineyard Camp Meeting Association; Mrs. R. T. Hall, Providence, R.I.; Mark Dollhopf, New Haven, Conn.; Carolyn Flaherty, *Victorian Homes,* Brooklyn, N.Y., Patricia Poore, *Old-House Journal,* Brooklyn, N.Y.; Cathy Rosa Klimaszewski, The 1890 House, Cortland, N.Y.; Mark and Karen Caulfield, Historic House Parts Shop, Rochester, N.Y.; Cindy Howk, Landmark Society of Western New York, Rochester; Christine Smith, Allentown Association, Buffalo, N.Y.; Peter Levine, Buffalo Restoration and Design; Eugene Kleinhans, Jr., and Trudey Fitelson, Wellesley Island Victorian Village, Thousand Island State Park, N.Y.; Lynn Dunning Vaughan, Albany, N.Y.; Frances Weaver, Lake George, N.Y.; Anne LeDuc and Judy Bartella, Chalfonte Hotel, Cape May, N.J.; Dan Damon and Nat Singleton, *Victorian Accents,* Plainfield, N.J.; Roger Moss, Philadelphia Atheneum; Charles Uhl, Tom Mistick and Sons, Pittsburgh, Pa.; Stephen Delsordo, Historian, State of Delaware, Dover, Delaware; Matt Mosca, Color Researcher, Baltimore, Md.; Kathleen Kotarba, CHAP, Baltimore, Md.; Richard Weiss, National Paint and Coatings Association; Amy Schlagel, National Register of Historic Places, Washington, D.C.;

David Gordon, Historic Staunton Foundation, Staunton, Va.; Angela K. Barnett, Historic Wilmington Foundation, Wilmington, N.C.; Terry Myers, Preservation Administration, Raleigh, N.C.; Laura Phillips and Gwynne Taylor, Winston-Salem, N.C.; Mac Lackey, Statesville, N.C.; Larry McBennett, Historic Preservation, Raleigh, N.C.; John Postum, Preservation Society, Charleston, S.C.; Lyle Certain, Brunswick, Ga.; Ann Horstman, Historic Savannah, Savannah, Ga.; Lynn Meyer, Atlanta Preservation Center, Atlanta, Ga.; Sharon Wells, Old Island Restoration Committee, Key West, Fla.; Larry Hesdorffer, Historic District Landmarks Committee, New Orleans, La.; Joey Dillon, Southern Tours of Selma, Selma, Ala.; Cheryl Nichols, Quawpaw Quarter Association, Little Rock, Ark.; Ron and Brenda Bell, Crescent Cottage Inn, Eureka Springs, Ark.; Sarah Milligan, 1876 Lafayette House, St. Louis, Mo.; Tom Finan, Publisher, *Painting and Contractor Magazine,* St. Louis, Mo.; Deb Sullivan, Marshall, Mich.; Louisa Pieper, Ann Arbor, Mich.; Jacki Jackson and David Eller, Hinsdale, Ill.; Sam Van Hook, Bennett-Curtis House, Grant Park, Ill.; Kurt Bell, Architectural Restoration, Rockford, Ill.; Charles Burnidge and Chuck Hanlon, Burnidge, Cassell & Associates, Elgin, Ill.; Charles Mayhew III, The Painted Lady, Newburg, Wis.; Joyce Grafton, Cedarburg, Wis.; Paul Lusignan, State Historic Society, Madison, Wis.; Dallas Weekley, La Crosse, Wis.; V.J. "Val" Schute, Architect & Planner, La Crosse, Wis.; Charles Nelson, Minnesota Historical Society, St. Paul, Minn.; Loren Horton, Iowa State Historic Society; Patrice Beam, Victorian Society of America, Des Moines, Iowa; Allen Nelson, Executive Vice President, Chamber of Commerce, Red Oak, Iowa; Jane Slightam, Council Bluffs, Iowa; Barbara Metzger Apple, Toledo, Ohio; Stanley Blersch, Victorian Society of America, Cincinnati, Ohio; Bob Richmond, Terry Marmet, and Martha Hagadorn, State Historic Society, Topeka, Kansas; Lynn Meyer, Landmark Council, City Planning, Omaha, Neb.; Joyce Fletcher, Landmarks, Inc., Omaha, Neb.; Ed Zimmer, Historic Planner, Lincoln, Neb.; Jim Wilson and Paul Putz, State Historic Preservation Center, Vermillion, S.D.; Alan Richard Demster, Arch. Inc., Sioux Falls, S.D.; Tom Van Arkle, Manitou Springs, Colo.; Shirley Martin, Tigerrrrrags, Breckenridge, Colo.; Steve Berstein, Historic Preservation Planning, Aspen, Colo; Ramona Markalunas, Aspen Historical Society; Chuck Murphy, Colorado Springs, Colo.; Debbie Abel, Colorado Springs, Colo.; Mary Davis, Pikes Peak Library District, Colorado Springs, Colo.; Ellen Ritacco, Victorianne's, Leadville, Colo.; Dave Hughes, Colorado City, Colo.; Roger Roper, Salt Lake City, Ut.; Jennifer Attabury, State Historical Preservation Officer, Boise, Idaho; Janet Ore, Preservation Officer, Butte, Mont.; Pat Bic and Lon Johnson, State Historical Preservation Officers, Helena, Mont.; Larry Kreisman, Seattle, Wash.; Larry Nickel, Ellensberg, Wash.; Richard and Mary Sauter, John Palmer House, No. Portland, Ore.; Richard Lucier, Nunan House, Jacksonville, Ore.; Scott Clay, Medford, Ore.; Rosalind Clark Keeny, Historic Preservation, Albany, Ore.; Mark Siegel, Historic Preservation, Salem, Ore.; Naomi and Joe Stokes, Portland, Ore.; Larry Jacobson, Historic Officer, Eugene, Ore.; Max Kirkenberg and the Victorian Alliance of San Francisco, Cal.; Judy Hilberg and Jerry Grulkey, Heritage Foundation, Vallejo, Cal.; Michael Nicholette, Monterey County Historical Society, Salinas, Cal.; Rick and Dyan Beguelin; Mary Ann and Ramon Otero, Monrovia, Cal.; Barry Herlihy, Bill Cooper and Marilyn Callendar, Cultural Heritage Foundation of Southern California, Los Angeles, Cal.; Carl Lyungquist and Gary Conway, Morey Mansion, Redlands, Cal.

These color consultants have been a great help: John Burrows, Herbert Kramer, John Crosby Freeman, Annette Conti, Joe Adamo, James Jereb, David Irvin, John Lough, Mike Lyster, Neil Hiedeman, James Martin, Kepa Askenasy, Bob Buckter, Don Buckter, Jill Pilaroscia, and Robert DuFort.

Robert DuFort, Jull Pilaroscia, and Bob Buckter were also kind enough to review the text.

Thanks also to the more than one hundred proud homeowners around the country who sent us photos of their homes to consider.

Special thanks to Rita Pomada, Alberta Cooper, Charles Pomada, Susan Sheeley, Carolyn Sheeley, Ray and Maryann Larsen, Carol Larsen and Don Kosterka, Diana and Denny Nolan, Karen LeClair and Buck Welleck, Ernie and Phil Germain, and Fran Ames.

Thanks to our editor, Cyril I. Nelson, for his encouragement, his taste, his knowledge of the Victorian world, and his faith in us. Our agents, Charlotte Sheedy and Peter Skolnik, were always there when we needed them.

For his fourteen-hour days, his 21,000 miles, his craft, his good spirits, and his magic eye, thanks to photographer Doug Keister for helping to create one work of art out of many.

Contents

Introduction

Welcome to the Revolution

Painted Ladies, a book about San Francisco's Victorian houses, sparked a revolution: The Colorist Movement. The weapons are paint brushes and the ammunition is paint and imagination.

The winners are America's architectural heritage, the homeowners, their neighbors, and new generations of admirers who take an old gray Victorian for granted but enjoy, learn from, and are inspired by a Painted Lady.

The only casualties of The Colorist Movement are the wounded sensibilities of traditionalists aghast at "those victrocious colors!"

Nine years after its publication in 1978, the words "Painted Lady" have become generic for a multicolor Victorian. Bright multicolor paint jobs are called "San Francisco Style." Homeowners and color designers around the country use the book as an essential reference when deciding about colors. "Color Consultants" is a new listing in the yellow pages.

The opening sequences of several popular TV series featured Painted Ladies: "Too Close for Comfort" in San Francisco, "Mork & Mindy" in Boulder, and "The Mary Tyler Moore Show" in Minneapolis. One of the famous row houses on Alamo Square in San Francisco was the setting for the movie *Invasion of the Body Snatchers*. Other television shows, movies, and advertisements have brought Painted Ladies into living rooms across the country.

Stores and magazines now specialize in Victoriana, and the images of Painted Ladies grace posters, sculpture, needlework, ceramic teapots, cookie jars, and knickknacks in Victorian profusion.

The true victory is that homeowners are thinking seriously about color, and not just accepting gray or white "because it's always been that color." House owners from around the country have visited San Francisco and returned home determined to create a Painted Lady of their own. Painted Ladies now adorn forty-six states.

This explosion of color fits into a major architectural trend away from simplicity in design and color toward an eclecticism that embraces strong colors and ornamentation. When Philip Johnson tops New York's AT&T building with a salute to Chippendale, something's in the air. The orange and blue State of Illinois building in Chicago and the rainbow apartment buildings in Miami done by Arquitectonica are vivid proof of the exhilarating revitalization of modern architecture.

St. Paul color consultant Neil Hiedeman, who synthesizes the old with the new by using Victorian colors in a modern way, explains that each cycle, or movement, is a reaction to what came before it. The Art Deco cycle followed the Arts and Crafts Movement and was in turn followed by the bare-bones International Style—now followed by the present decorative cycle. Since we have done everything, we are now reaching back and replacing stark black and white with color. Neil plays the recorder and has found the musical equivalent for the renewed interest in color and ornamentation in that baroque music is more popular now than it has been for years. He credits the old-house movement with the impetus for change and showed us a new St. Paul skyscraper garnished with two colors of stone and decoration.

Another sign: after decades of neglect, the jewel boxes created by Louis Sullivan in St. Louis, Chicago, and Owatonna, Minnesota, have been spruced up and hailed as a "color symphony."

Ironically, this is happening at the same time that, in another cyclical trend, homeowners, even in San Francisco, are choosing more conservative colors than those used by the pioneers of The Colorist Movement in the 1970s. In the 1970s, earth tones like oranges and greens were popular. Today, rosy sunset tones are in favor.

Today's baby boomers are proud of their houses, and want to share their pride and joy with their neighbors. Their homes have become the "Daughters of Painted Ladies."

What Makes a Painted Lady?

Although we prefer bright colors to placid ones, we have not let our tastes dictate the houses chosen for this book. We aimed for as much variety as possible in color and architecture. As with *Painted Ladies*, the criteria were:

—that the Victorian building be a balanced, felicitous blend of color and architecture;

—that the house be painted in three or more contrasting colors;

—and that color be used to bring out the decorative ruffles and flourishes.

The small octagon house in Barrington, Illinois (see p. 71), is an excellent example of a lovely building enhanced with charming decorative elements captured in vivid yet traditional colors.

Some exceptions proved irresistible. Although the only color restrictions on the houses we chose were our fallible judgments, we were limited by time, money, and problems such as poles, trees, wires, and the condition of the house and paint. Also, with miles to go before he slept, Doug Keister was obliged to shoot the houses whether or not they were spotlighted by sunshine.

In our journeys to 128 cities and forty-one states (see map, pages 132–133) we found a treasure trove that might have suited this description in an 1887 issue of the *San Francisco Chronicle*: "houses with no two sides alike, houses of chaste and rigid outline, and houses all angles and florid garniture, houses eccentric and scrappy as a crazy quilt, apparently pieced together from the leavings of other houses." We selected houses in ninety-five cities in thirty-four states. Houses to which we are pleased to give Honorable Mention are listed on page 134.

The Grand Tour

Discovering outbursts of color on Victorians around the country was an inspiring experience for us, and it will be for you, too. From Fairbanks, Alaska, to Key West, Florida; from below sea level in New Orleans, Louisiana, to Leadville, Colorado, at 10,000 feet; from Portland, Oregon, to Portland, Maine, homeowners are having fun with the most human, glorious, varied, playful, and outrageous style of architecture on the planet.

On our 36,000-mile journey, we found the richness and variety of Victorian decoration combining the elegant, lacy intricacy of a Bach piano partita with the breathtaking exuberance of an Art Tatum piano solo.

We thought that because many Victorian houses had been ordered from mail-order catalogues, we would find the same houses in different parts of the country and so it would be possible for us to compare how color designers across the country had approached the same building. But one revelation of our travels was the amazing variety of Victorian architecture. You won't see the same house twice.

San Francisco remains unique in its collection of 16,000 redwood Victorians and the individualism with which its homeowners and color designers select and apply colors. The Painted Ladies in San Francisco have an unfair advantage over the competition: they were designed more flamboyantly than their sisters elsewhere, so they wear more ornamental finery.

But the city was divided into 25- by 100-foot lots. Most Victorians there either are row houses or are so hemmed in by surrounding houses that only the facades are painted in more than one color. This simplifies the task (and reduces the cost) of painting them. However, almost all of the houses in this book are free-standing, enlarging the possibilities for color.

They are more spread out, giving them a horizontal look rather than the vertical look of San Francisco's row houses. Roofs, some of them artfully designed with colored slate, are another architectural constant in the *Daughters* around the country, while city row-house roofs are usually hidden by false fronts.

The houses vary in size from the "shotgun" cottage in Leadville, Colorado, to the stunning Carson mansion in Eureka, California. Victorian homeowners were determined to make their houses unique. To this end, they used decoration with abandon and an endearing spirit of playfulness.

Regional Variations

There are surprising regional variations in color and architecture. Easterners are more concerned than westerners about tradition and about what their neighbors will think.

Pioneering westerners are bolder than their East Coast cousins in choosing blazing colors.

Several cities or districts have preservation boards that have control over the paint colors that householders are allowed to use. This practice is more prevalent in the East than in the West, but many of the ruling voices on these boards are becoming more educated about the historical authenticity of color and are slowly accepting new ideas. The historical commission in Key West, Florida, for example, has fought the use of pastel "conch" colors used by the Caribbean or Bahamian inhabitants. Under the influence of a young, bright preservation officer, the stark whites are slowly turning tropical. In New Orleans, the preservation board of the French Quarter has the final say over colors, but they are open to any selection as long as it harmonizes with the neighboring houses.

There are also regional variations in preparation and painting techniques and the period of time a paint job will last. Freezing winters and boiling summers weather paint faster than California's moderate year-round weather. In the East, painters balance on ladders; in the West, they drop on suspension hangers, swing stages suspended by block and tackle, or erect pipe scaffolding. Some painters strip old paint with chemicals; other use a gas blow torch.

States and color designers around the country have distinctive "signatures." In Aspen and Leadville, Colorado, gables are painted in colorful stripes. Among the color designers, John Lough in Milwaukee, Wisconsin, likes to embellish his houses with pinstripe accents; Neil Hiedeman in St. Paul, Minnesota, favors shingled gables with patterns of color. San Francisco's Bob Buckter makes Painted Ladies sparkle with gold leaf.

As you will see on page 68, Chicago designer James Jereb's signature is—literally—his signature. And why shouldn't these artists sign their works of art? Their artistic vision, immortalized in this book, if not renewed by future owners, will continue to be a source of delight when much of what now passes for art has mercifully passed into oblivion.

Preserving the Past for the Future

The Painted Ladies have made what is old new again. In a world changing faster than we can possibly comprehend, Victorians provide a continuity with our past that is needed more than ever. They are a response to the dehumanization caused by the monoliths, technology, and institutions that dominate our culture. They are a response to the interchangeable skylines, franchises, and shopping malls that mar our vast, gorgeous landscape.

We are the restoration generation. What was innovative in San Francisco fifteen years ago is now a new tradition. And since young professionals want to be downtown, inner cities that degenerated into slums are being restored to painted and polished splendor. Victorian row houses are now among the most sought-after homes in America.

Today, "resource conservation" is a new phrase used by preservationists who have learned that progress can destroy a valuable, irreplaceable past. There are more than one thousand Landmark Commissions and boards.

Victorians, perennial victims of architectural caprice, are now regarded as treasures worth preserving. Enterprising owners are giving Victorians a new lease on life by adapting them for commercial use as B & B's (indeed, one is called The Painted Lady), stores, offices, museums, apartment houses, and restaurants. This both assures their survival and provides an added incentive to keep them in top condition to impress customers.

In 1966, the Victorian Society of America was created to study the nineteenth century in depth and to encourage appreciation of its achievements. Americans are learning that Victorians were not as staid and conservative as they had been led to believe.

Also in 1966, the National Register of Historic Places was established under the auspices of the Department of the Interior. This official list of the cultural property of the American people encompasses national, state, and city landmarks; single structures; and blocks of buildings constructed by nineteenth-century mass builders. "Districts, sites, buildings, structures, and objects significant in American history, architecture, archeology and culture" can now be permanently protected.

Founded in 1949, The National Trust for Historic Preservation fights to preserve historically significant sites, buildings, and objects through its headquarters in Washington, D.C., and through regional offices. The Trust is more active and more influential today than it has ever been.

The National Preservation Program was dedicated in 1986 to "Main Street U.S.A." Daughters of Painted Ladies now beautify many Main Streets, from Ithaca, New York, to Ventura, California.

Matching government grants for reconstruction, rehabilitation, and restoration help make groups and individuals aware of our heritage. By accelerating the restoration of neglected neighborhoods, these grants also improve the economy of cities across the country. Neighborhood Housing Services created to administer the funds and encourage rebuilding are changing transitional neighborhoods in more than 150 cities.

The National Trust's successful Main Street project has reversed the decline of inner cities across the country. Whole streets have blossomed. Slums have turned into historic districts, then into prosperous neighborhoods. One challenge is how to revive life in run-down neighborhoods without evicting old neighbors.

Protective neglect has, at the same time, made the existence of these neighborhoods and newly beloved *grandes dames* possible. If the neighborhood hadn't fallen on hard times or stayed out of harm's way, many of the houses in this book would have been victims of the wrecker's ball.

There are several examples of neighborhoods surviving in what we call protective neglect along the Mississippi and Missouri Rivers. A city on one side, such as Minneapolis, Minnesota, or Omaha, Nebraska, would be the commercial or modern one, demolishing its architectural heritage. On the other side, in St. Paul, Minnesota, or in Council Bluffs, Iowa, life has proceeded at a gentler pace, preserving the old.

In Bridgeport, Connecticut, a "Love Your House— Paint It!" campaign offered to pay homeowners to take off their siding and repaint their homes—if they'd do it in Victorian colors. If the homeowners did their own painting, they were paid 100 percent of the cost; if they paid to have the work done, the city paid 50 percent of the cost.

The 1890 House museum in Cortland, New York, sponsored a "Painting the Town" program to encourage people to paint their Victorians. In a 17-by-22-inch self-mailing poster that explained architectural styles and color history, The 1890 House offered to help homeowners discover the original paint schemes or to select new hues.

Monrovia, a town in southern California outside of Los Angeles, didn't have an official program, but when one woman painted her dream house, her neighbors caught the urge. Neighbors started working together and formed a Heritage Alliance. To help raise funds for the celebration the Alliance sold "Painted Ladies" cloisonné-enamel stickpins.

The success of Cape May, New Jersey, Ferndale, California, and Port Townsend, Washington, as places to visit is based on the appeal of their Painted Ladies. As this was being written, Oxnard, California, was starting to restore a residential area with seventeen homes for which San Francisco colorist Bob Buckter will do the color schemes. Also, Heritage Squares in Los Angeles and San Diego and the Genesee County Museum in western New York have saved stately Victorians from the wrecker's ball and turned them into popular attractions.

A Is for Albany

The people in Albany, Oregon, call themselves "house proud." A small town south of Portland, Albany was founded in the late 1840s by Walter and Thomas Monteith, who bought land for $400 and a pony. Their quickly growing river-town, named after their hometown in New York, prospered until after World War I, when progress drew residents away, leaving three downtown districts intact but forlorn. Today, Albany is blessed with the most varied collection of historic buildings in Oregon: one hundred square blocks encompassing three historic districts listed on the National Register.

In 1978, the town's preservation officer, author Rosalind Clark, convinced the Department of Housing and Urban Development (HUD) that paint could revive the community. With HUD's help, homeowners received free paint and color advice. *Painted Ladies* was used, not as a color guide, but as inspiration, to show that colorful paint was authentic.

Albany's preservation effort stands as a model for other towns to follow. Individuals who care restored their own homes, and worked together to renovate the town and then to show it off.

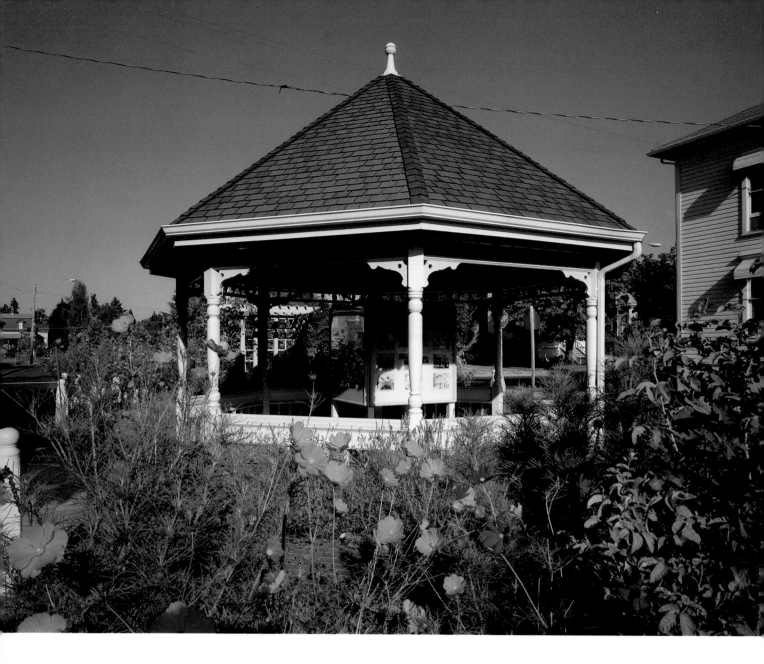

Friends of Historic Albany built this gazebo themselves as an information center and starting point for walking and horse-and-buggy house tours. The gazebo, a copy of the pavillion porch on a nearby Bed & Breakfast, was hand-made. Even the decorative spools were turned by hand. The garden—designed, planted, and maintained by volunteers—bursts with Victorian flowers: lavender, asters, hollyhocks, and authentic rose varieties. The lavender stalks and rose petals are harvested and combined with the bordering thyme and rosemary to make potpourri, sold at Friends' fund-raisers.

A tabloid with walking-tour maps, the town's history, and information is free for the taking at the newspaper rack in the gazebo. It was written, typeset, and published by the journalism and photography classes in the local college, who received class credit for the project. The Friends of Historic Albany have a lot more than their houses to be proud of!

Debutante on the Beach

The Chalfonte Hotel in Cape May at the southern tip of the New Jersey coast is another model for preservationists fighting time and a lack of money. Cape May's oldest operating hotel was built in 1876 for Civil War veteran Colonel Henry Sawyer, whose life was saved when he was exchanged for the son of Robert E. Lee. The Satterfield family ran the Chalfonte, a National Historic Landmark, from 1911 to 1983.

Innkeeper-schoolteachers Anne LeDuc and Judy Bartella are saving this huge white wonder with love and imagination. Anne and Judy had been helping out at the hotel for years—Anne had visited there every summer since she was two—and they vowed to keep Mary Satterfield's traditions alive. They came up with two ingenious ideas to help them: Work Weekends and the University of Maryland Chalfonte Program.

On Work Weekends, families pay a nominal fee for food and come to work: to clean, wash, sew, wallpaper, panel, paint, quilt, garden, and help in the office. They return to "their" hotel every summer.

Each spring, David Fogle, Professor of Urban Planning and Preservation, and thirty University of Maryland students spend a month at the hotel dividing their time between lectures and hands-on restoration experience. One year, they worked on the Chalfonte's foundation. Another year, they restored the dining room, using 600 pounds of Spackle, and chose a color scheme of cream, beige, and rose rather than the original dark brown wainscoting, dark green walls, and fire-engine red ceiling. A small cottage in back of the hotel was restored and painted in polychrome during another stay.

Modest Proposals

On our journeys to capture the revolution in progress, we saw many extraordinary Victorians, parched and crying out for paint to be applied with love and imagination. To save Victorians in the shadow of the wrecking ball, how about starting an electronic bulletin board or SOS line linking national, state, and local preservation groups by computer? This early-warning system will enable individuals or organizations from all over the country to generate legislation-producing letters, ideas, volunteers, supplies, or money to keep up the good fight.

David Hughes, a computer missionary who has been hailed as "the poet laureate of the network nation," has already started a Victorian Bulletin Board: The Old Colorado City Electronic Cottage. The Cottage is a free, advertiser-supported service that allows anyone with a modem to call (303) 632-3391, so as to see color sketches of Victorians in Old Colorado City, and to ask questions about them and the town. May it be the first of many.

Preservation organizations ought to consider adopting historically or architecturally important structures and offering them for public use. In Vallejo, California, for instance, the town heritage association saved a derelict, had it moved to land leased from the city for one dollar a year, and then pitched in to reconstruct, paint, and powder the place with their own elbow grease. The little red, tan, and cream-color cottage is now used as a meeting hall for local groups. A group might turn such a house into a museum, with paint donated by a paint store or manufacturer, then supported by visitors.

The phrase "adaptive reuse" should also mean "adoptive." The Valley Guild in Salinas, California, succeeded with another alternative. They turned part of the John Steinbeck house into a restaurant, which funds the house.

What about creating a photographic inventory of every worthwhile structure, starting with those that are historic or endangered?

Another fantasy: annual local, state, and national Painted Ladies contests sponsored by media, organizations, or suppliers. This will stimulate the painting and repainting of houses by rewarding outstanding work.

Historical or Hysterical?

"It's *always* been like this" is still the unenlightened excuse to mummify white elephants.

One earnest, well-meaning city preservationist we encountered prescribed timid two-color schemes for the Victorians in his town. Yet he proudly showed us an architectural rendering by the town's most renowned nineteenth-century architect, hand-colored by the architect himself with five sparkling, contrasting colors.

Boston's Victoriana merchant John Burrows became a believer when he discovered a black-and-white photograph of an intricately detailed Queen Anne painted in at least twenty different shades while he was serving as state preservation officer of South Dakota.

Traditionalists were quick to denigrate Painted Ladies, comparing them to garish circus wagons. Historian Roger Moss still protests in his book *Victorian Exterior Decoration* that "these 'painted ladies' are best not transported across state lines."

Alarmed neighbors tried to prove this in Wilmington, North Carolina, when they took a brave soul who was painting his house in pink and purple to court. The newspapers argued "This is Wilmington, Not San Francisco," but the judge ruled otherwise.

At the same time, these same historians jumped on the color bandwagon to prescribe "correct" colors, citing historic and modern paint company catalogues.

Too often authentic colors are determined by scraping a building to get down to the original colors. Yet you can't always believe what you see: these scrapings are dark because they've been smothered with paint for a century. Left in daylight, they lighten up to become truer to the original colors. Historians still disagree about the validity of this technique.

However, traditionalists and the color consultants using contemporary or "boutique" paint schemes agree that white is out, polychrome is in.

In 1883, the authors of *Modern House Painting* cautioned against "picking out small members in brighter color than the rest, in order to enliven the whole." They also disliked "the custom of painting chamfering, mouldings, and ornamentation in a positive color—frequently bright red . . . the emphasis of shadow is quite good enough without recourse to more violent methods." Obviously, color designers yesterday and today have chosen "more violent methods."

American Victorian housebuilders were imitating English architecture and materials. Shingles, for instance, were painted terra-cotta in imitation of clay roof tiles. Many buildings were built in classical styles, then altered to suit the place and display the creativity of their designers or builders. Must today's Victorian homeowners imitate the imitators and refrain from individualizing their homes as their ancestors did?

In their choice of colors, Victorians were following the fashions of the day. Why shouldn't today's homeowners have the same freedom? Why shouldn't they be allowed to enjoy the same spirit of play, pride, and individuality that their predecessors reveled in?

A Painted Lady owner in Ohio wrote "...this gives the home the feeling of being trimmed with lace. I chose these colors by looking at interior paint samples, as they had a much broader selection.... We are thrilled with the results. I would encourage anyone, no matter what style the house, to consider more original choices in painting. A 'Victorian,' though, is shortchanged whenever the paint scheme does not bring out her details and gracefulness."

Color: A Black and White Issue

Does it make sense that Victorian architects would go to the trouble and expense to gild their houses so luxuriantly with decoration only to white them out or shroud them in gray?

Queen Victoria reigned from 1837 until 1901. Today, "Victorian" often means pompous, stuffy, prudish. Yet the good queen danced, drank whiskey in her wine, and exclaimed "my nature is too passionate, my emotions are too fervent."

Flowers adorned richly decorated Victorian walls, floors, and ceilings. Five layers of window covering on one window were fashionable (shutters, blinds, muslin curtains, velvet draperies, and tasseled valences). Bric-a-brac, fretwork, and whatnots enhanced the irrepressible fancy and exuberant color of Victorian homes.

Victorians regarded their buildings as symbols and worked hard to make them "fitting." They are perfect symbols of an era given to excess, an era of flamboyant art, elaborate clothes, ornate furnishings. Today, a house enables a homeowner to make a creative personal statement on the largest scale available to most people. Homeowners and color designers regard a house as a canvas, asking themselves: "How can I make my house beautiful and unique?"

Learning from the Past

"There is one colour...frequently employed by house painters, which we feel bound to protest *against* most heartily, as entirely unsuitable, and in bad taste. This is WHITE, which is so universally applied to our wooden houses of every size and description...(and) unpleasant to an eye attuned to harmony of coloring." Andrew Jackson Downing, one of America's most influential architects, wrote this in 1842. He was a Hudson River romantic who sought to unite people with nature, and recommended natural earth tones.

Until the middle of the eighteenth century, Colonial houses were left unpainted or perhaps whitewashed with crushed oyster shells, white lead paint, or blueberries crushed in milk, which resulted in Colonial blue-gray. Until

Downing came along, stylish American homes were Greek Revival white, with green shutters, emulating the marble temples of Greece. The irony is that the temples of ancient Greece were painted in vivid colors.

The Industrial Revolution opened up a wealth of possibilities for the emerging middle class. Wood was plentiful and cheap. The cheap, light balloon construction invented in the 1830s in Chicago, in which pieces of lumber were nailed together and covered with boarding to cover an outlined frame, speeded up the building process—as did the invention of machine-made nails. By 1840, houses could be personalized to suit the buyers' needs and tastes. Indoor plumbing, heating, running water, dumbwaiters, and electricity made new houses a necessity for the new bourgeoisie.

As an 1898 editorial in *American Homes* explained the American Dream, "All over America, the idea is spreading that a new building must be original, not thereby meaning a freakish departure from well known principles of design, but one planned originally for the owner. This is right, and will do more toward the growth of an artistic state and the establishment of content in the homes of the people than any factor which can be employed."

Romantic Gothics Emerge

Downing's Gothic cottages, with their steeply pitched roofs, flamboyant bargeboards, varied windows, and board-and-batten siding reminded romantic Victorians of broken castles or abbeys in ruin. It was Downing who introduced bay windows and informal gardens to Americans. He believed that "the features confer the same kind of expression on a house that the eyes, eyebrows, lips, etc., of a face do upon the human countenance." The colors he preferred ran the gamut from earth, stone, and rock to grass, brick, and clay. Downing's pattern book, *Cottage Residences*, inspired Gothic Revival buildings in the East until about 1850 and in the Midwest until 1870. Later examples were painted in warm gray with blue trim or fawn with brown and green, or light pink and brown combinations like The Gable House in Baraboo, Wisconsin (see page 75).

Stately Sticks and Italianates

Early Italianates, with their hipped or flat roofs, projecting eaves with decorative brackets, columns at the sides of windows and stone-like corner quoins were built to emulate the stone villas of Italy. In the East, Italianates were built from 1840 to 1860. Builders in the West and Midwest created dignified Italianates until about 1885. They were usually painted in light colors, with contrasting trim and dark doors and sashes. Two or more colors were used to pick out the decorative details.

James Renwick, a New York practitioner of historic revival styles, favored the High Victorian Italianate in dark, vivid, contrasting colors, with such an abundance of ornamentation that his buildings looked encrusted with jewels.

Stick structures, popular in the East from 1865 to 1885, and in the West from 1870 until 1885, were of wood made to look like wood, with sticks outlining the building. Body and trim in contrasting colors heightened the decorated trim and exaggerated the architectural structural support. Later, Eastlake embellishments—knobs, sunbursts, latticework, columns, and spindles on the square bays, towers, and gables—created additional inviting surfaces for color.

Wedding Cakes in the Landscape

The French Mansard, or Second Empire, style flourished in America after 1850, when Louis Napoleon added a new west wing to the Louvre, using a mansard roof with dormers named for the seventeenth-century architect François Mansart. This classical, symmetrical "wedding cake" style was so popular in the post–Civil War 1870s that it was called the General Grant Style.

Built of wood, stone, and red or yellow brick, Second Empire homes were usually stuccoed and, whether box-plain or awash with gingerbread, ironwork, quoins, and patterned roof shingles, they were painted in many colors.

Describing a favorite mansardic villa in 1886, author E. C. Hussey explained that dark trim on a tricolor house makes it smaller, and recommended iron cresting painted in a deep sky blue, with all the tips gilded. He prescribed other polychrome combinations of two body colors and three trim colors: for example, mustard yellow body; dark green corner boards, cornices, and panels; dark red roofs; finials and cresting, and dark brown sash.

Architectural Caprice

In 1854, Orson S. Fowler wrote *The Octagon House: A Home For All*, introducing what was basically an eight-sided Italianate frame or stone dwelling designed for comfortable living. Fowler proclaimed: "Nature's forms are mostly spherical. She makes 10,000 curvilinear forms to one square form. Then why not copy her forms in houses?" Although Octagons were a short-lived fad, Fowler's legacy endures in some of America's most remarkable Victorians.

Then, at a time when more was more, Oriental and Moorish villas, elegant residences with architecturally illogical details, and eclectic styles mixed Stick/Eastlake, Second Empire, Queen Anne, and shingle styles to suit each owner.

Delicious Excess

But the quintessential Victorian home is the Queen Anne, everyman's dream castle, a tossed salad of Elizabethan, Jacobean, Oriental, Indian, and classical styles. Towers and turrets, arches and gingerbread, palladian and bay windows, and chimneys vied for attention with texture: fishscales, shingles, siding, brick, stone, shutters, and patterned ornament. Sometimes the shingles, made by bandsaw, were laid in wavy patterns so that the whole surface seemed to undulate as porches projected and

receded, and finials reached for the sky. One's palace could make a social statement, reflecting its owner's social status, while expressing his personal fantasies.

British architect Richard Norman Shaw is said to have created the Queen Anne style to remind the English of the good days under Queen Anne, when the Empire began the journey to its imperial destiny and the craftsman's workmanship was more important than the architect's. The English Queen Anne dwelling was modeled on medieval or Elizabethan country houses.

America's Victorians added ostentatious ornamentation, and fashionable colors, until the style was so overdone it was later called a "vile concentrate" of all that was bad about Victorians.

First exhibited in America at the Philadelphia Centennial Exposition of 1876, the Queen Anne style had been written about by Henry Hudson Holly in *Modern Dwellings* in 1873. Most of the designs in the new pattern books dominating America's architectural styles until the end of the century were of eclectic Queen Annes to which the builder could add any interior or exterior detail he could dream up.

The exterior paint colors frequently reflected the colors in the stained-glass and leaded-glass transoms. Usually the body, trim, shutters, and sash were different colors, with up to five harmonious, contrasting shades. Sometimes, as with The Hale House illustrated on the cover of this book, the body of each floor was different and the trim on each floor could pick up the colors of the others.

The French jewel tones of the 1870s yielded, after the Franco-Prussian War, to darker, deeper reds, browns, ochres, and greens in the 1880s, dubbed "the Berlin motif," but always, the many architectural details, the massing of various shapes and textures and horizontal decorated bands were celebrated with color. Shutter colors usually matched the roof and frame colors.

As the pale romantic tones did at mid-century, and the pastels, creams, and whites of the Colonial Revival style which referred back to Greek Revival simplicity did at the end of the century, exterior colors reflected the spirit of the day.

In George F. Barber's design #59 in his *Cottage Souvenir Book #2*, a different color scheme was recommended for each floor in "an orgasmic display of pattern, ornament, texture."

In the American Renaissance of the 1880s and 1890s, money was lavished on homes, and architects H. H. Richardson and Richard Morris Hunt reflected the new delight in the use of materials when they played colors and textures against each other, using terra-cotta, faience, mosaics, colored bricks, tiles, and metal in rich, restless patterns. Richardson's stunning Trinity Church in Boston is red, pink, gray, cream, and black—and all done in brick or stone. The British art critic John Ruskin proclaimed the mixed red and yellow brick "streaky bacon" Venetian Gothic the greatest style of all. A "streaky bacon" Venetian Gothic bank is still open for business in Key West. Even

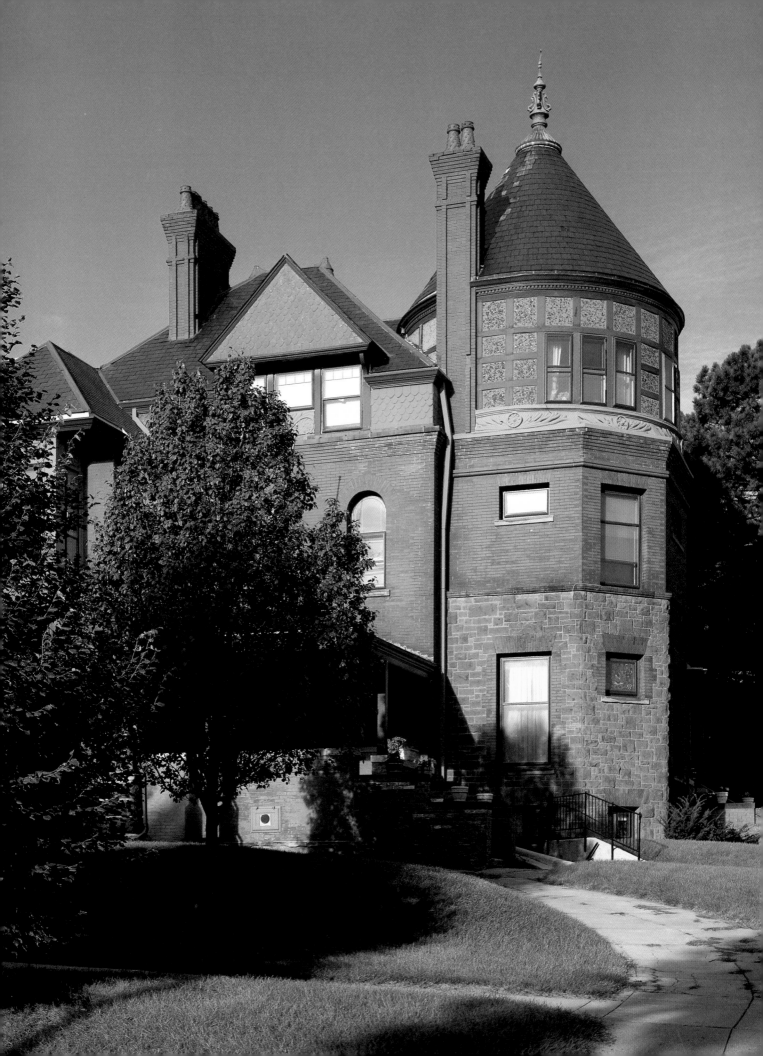

when they were building with stone, Victorians thought in polychrome.

This massive Queen Anne, in Lincoln, Nebraska, at 910 South 20th Street, built in the 1890s by F. Clark Leonard, is all one color. But it's an excellent example of how much can be done with *just* one color. There are two different tones of red brick, a red stone base, red-orange terra-cotta trim, and a crown of red broken glass and stucco on epoxy conglomerate material. The pressed metal on the bay of the porch is made to look like terra-cotta. Red paint is used for trim and black paint on the window sashes adds definition.

When stones didn't glisten enough to please a homeowner, crushed glass mosaic or real jewels were used. In Portland, Maine, the Libby Morse Mansion had sanded paint in the window frames, as did many houses. But in this instance, garnets were mixed in with the beach sand. At the same time, lintels of brick buildings in Boston were sanded to look like marble.

Inside, wallpaper was bronzed, gilded, and silvered to reflect light—to glow. Outside, linseed-oil paint glistened darkly in the light. If their tastes changed on occasion, Victorian housepainters added extra turpentine to the paint to lessen the gloss.

A Sunflower in Every Lapel

In the mid-1800s, John Ruskin and William Morris founded the Aesthetic, or English Arts and Crafts, Movement to combat the ugliness of mass-produced furnishings and bring art into every facet of everyday life. The American middle class, intoxicated with its discovery of art, quickly became followers, reveling in an orgy of form and color indoors and out. No surface was left untouched.

Sunflowers, the dominant motif of the Arts and Crafts Movement (see page 27)—along with other "unsentimental" flowers chosen for form, not feeling, such as the lily, iris, and cattail—bloomed on walls, floors, ceilings, stamped velvet, plush, prints, curtains, cast iron, tiles, and embroidery. Queen Victoria put sunflowers on her curtains at Windsor Castle. Oscar Wilde wore them in his lapel during his American tour in 1882.

Cincinnati's Rookwood pottery, with its bold floral treatments and highly sophisticated crackled glazes, became America's most famous art pottery. The dark rich colors were quickly reflected in paint. Louis Comfort Tiffany's opalescent glazes and John La Farge's boldly outlined luminescent stained-glass windows were the epitome of an art period soon swamped by excess. A hundred years later, architect Richard Monastra was inspired by a Tiffany exhibit to use Tiffany tones in designing the colors on a Chicago cottage.

The Spirit of Play

The spirit of play is an essential element of Victorian architecture. The brackets under a cornice don't hold it up.

Like most decoration, they were added for form, not function.

Victorians took immense pleasure in their homes. An 1884 issue of *Our Homes and Their Adornments* proclaimed, "Home" was "embalmed in song, cherished in the memory, and enshrined in the heart." The Queen Anne house was a symbol of pride, accomplishment, and playfulness.

The ultimate example of this playfulness is an imposing lady named Lucy (see page 40). Lucy is an elephant on the beach in Margate, New Jersey, whose eyes contemplate the Atlantic. Built in 1883 as a twelve-room home, Lucy is the last of her breed. A three-star detour on the way to Cape May, Lucy is now a museum, which will guarantee her longevity. On page 32 is a modern descendant of this playfulness, The Crayon House in that traditional town, Providence, Rhode Island.

A century ago, poet Gelette Burgess, of "I-never-saw-a-purple-cow" fame fulminated: "The Ideal Queen Anne should have the conical corner tower, it should be built of at least three incongruous materials, or better, imitations thereofs, it should have its window openings completely haphazard; it should represent parts of every known and unknown order of architecture; it should be so plastered with ornament as to conceal the theory of its construction; it should be a restless, uncertain, frightful collection of details, giving the effect of a nightmare about to explode."

One Taste Is Not Enough

And what was there never enough of? Gingerbread. Named after the Medieval French *gingimbrat*, for preserved ginger, English gingerbread was ginger-flavored cake in fancy shapes and ginger sugar candy in scrolls, spirals, and curlicues. The word was then used on the carved, gilded decoration of sailing ships, then on lacy architectural ornament. In Germany, then the Midwest, *Lebkuchen Häuschen* were little gingerbread houses with icing and candies for doors and windows, still a Christmas tradition.

In America, the fanciful Gothic designs of A. J. Downing, created for stone, were translated into wood to become, with the advent of the jigsaw, scroll saw, and band saw, the confections of the era. Driven by steam or foot treadle and a free-wheeling imagination, these gadgets produced ornaments for eaves, brackets, porches, and gates, with incised holes and patterns, added-on frills and furbelows. Any wood left over from the construction of the house could be quickly transformed into lavish lacework. Any standard farmhouse could bloom with a new facade. And any pattern-book creation could be decorated to taste.

By 1900, *The Overland Monthly* magazine complained of "misuse of ornament…we have a front loaded with endless repetitions of the same detail; the same scrawny scroll looking at us from a hundred window-heads; the same little panels stuck in every corner; strings of vegetables, all alike, hanging from every column; and wreaths and cornucopias, badly carved, dangling between every projection, as if to leave a bit of plain surface anywhere were to break an 11th commandment."

An 1883 issue of the *California Architects and Building News* noted that the best way to present a showy house was "by a liberal plastering on of gingerbread work and by engaging the services of painters who are expert in the mixing of fancy colors." Today's Victorian homeowners continue to follow this advice.

The Books that Built America

Before the Civil War, there was a twenty-year time lag in styles from East to West. Afterward, in the "first age of mass communication," news reached everyone at the same time. Mail-order pattern books and magazines sent blueprints and actual prefabricated houses across the country by rail. Pattern-book publishers Andrew Jackson Downing, Alexander Jackson Davis, William T. Comstock, A. J. Bicknell, George Palliser, and George F. Barber had a more direct impact on the way Americans built their homes than the architects of the time. The Italianates were usually copied from English pattern books, which were in vogue during the first half of the century. Downing's *Cottage Residences* (1842) quickly spread the news about the Gothic cottage, ranging in price from $800 to $4,000.

The pattern-book king, ruling from Fort Scott, Kansas, was George F. Barber. He advertised that his variations on the Queen Anne could be changed to meet individual needs. You'll find examples of Barber's fantasies on pages 110 and 117.

Color plates in *Scientific American's Architects and Builders Edition* (1884–1905) captured the exciting contrasts of light and shadow, the projections and recesses, the colors and compositions that were the most appealing qualities of Victorian buildings. The pattern included in each issue could be easily followed by any carpenter.

The new ready-mixed paint and new printing systems inspired paint companies to print colorful brochures, showing their new products and giving handy hints for their use. In 1871, Harrison Brothers and Co. offered fifty-two colors. H. W. Johns Co. explained that the "new dark body and trimming colors" were added to their cards "in consequence of the constantly increasing demand for the new styles of decoration" and pointed to "the laudable & rapidly growing tendency to the free use of color...the 'white house with green blinds' is a thing of the past."

In 1887 the *San Francisco Chronicle* noted that "when the present esthetic movement began...it first manifested itself in a growing aversion to gray paint. Cautiously at first, and then more and more boldly, houses appeared in browns, yellows, greens and even reds, all sorts of unorthodox colors."

New Directions

There were and are more lavish details on California houses, so there were and are more lavish colors. Historians have also come to accept as fact the so-called "beach mentality" of gaily colored, lacily bedecked cottages in places like Oak Bluffs on Martha's Vineyard, Thousand Islands, New York, and Ocean Grove and Cape May, New Jersey. And, although some "boutique" colors don't suit the tastes of traditionalists, they are paying attention to detail when they paint. Picking your teeth—highlighting dentils, cornices, and rings on porch spindles—is finally acceptable.

After decades of whiteout, the Morey Mansion in southern California, shown on pages 124–125, now proudly wears the fifteen-color coat of paint originally chosen by its shipbuilder creator.

As Denver colorist James Martin explains, "We live so fast today, we seem to need to have the fine detailing brought to our attention a little more than the Victorians did." Homeowners frequently report that their neighbors had not been aware of sunbursts or wheat rays on their gables before their new paint job. And even historian Roger Moss, who disapproves of the Painted Ladies, particularly their white lacy trim and color placement, applauds the painters who are "creating street art, something that's an artistic, if not an authentically historical, creation."

Today, the media has made everyone more aware of and more accepting of color in every part of our lives. "Miami Vice" colors automatically suggest a hot neon palette. A fashion writer described kids who "dressed MTV but with the color knob turned slightly down." Color creates an aura of youth, fun, desirability. Even old black-and-white movies aren't safe from colorization.

Color is an essential part of life for the television and computer-graphics generation, and the relentless, inescapable onslaught of impersonal technology makes the preservation of America's heritage more imperative and appealing than ever.

John Crosby Freeman, color specialist for *Victorian Homes* magazine, feels that the house has always been the most important thing a family could own. A century ago, he explains, Victorians proved themselves by outdoing their neighbor in exterior embellishment. People still think color, when, for example, they say, "I live in the pink house on the corner." And now, as it was a century ago, chromatic monotony is just not fashionable.

A national Color Marketing Group of representatives from the paint, wallcovering, fashion, automotive, plumbing supplies, textile- and interior-design, and advertising worlds meets twice a year to discuss "the next trend." The color specialists, who pay for the privilege of joining, have workshops and then present upcoming color palettes to their members.

Spurred by Painted Ladies, a remarkable revival of interest in Victorian interiors as well as exteriors is taking place. The raspberry-and-gold Victorian palette has shown up in restaurants and hotel lobbies across the nation. Crafts such as wallpapering, stenciling, ceiling design, plastering, woodworking, furniture and furnishings design are springing back to life.

Modern color designers are using interior colors and

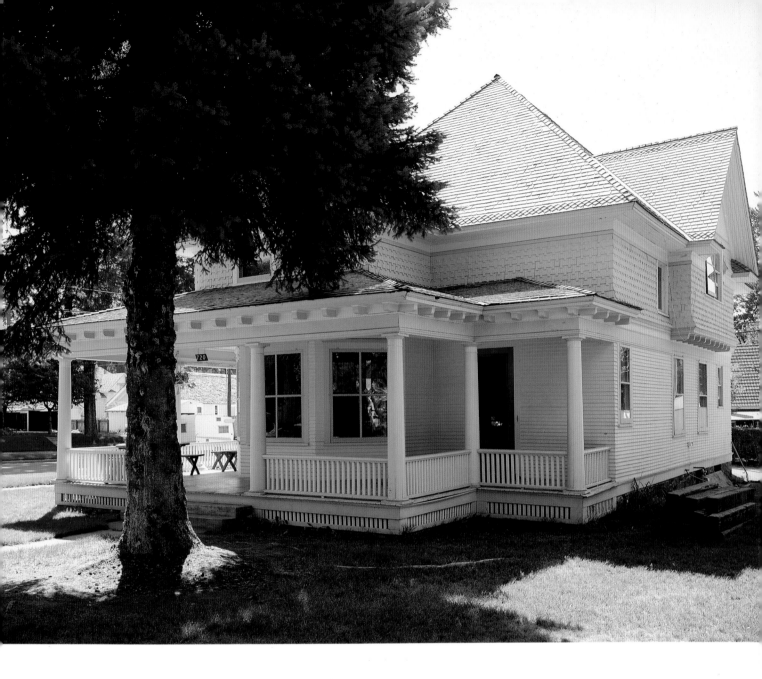

design techniques such as splattering and marbleizing floors, sponging columns in the shades of the house, *faux* finishes, and rubbed and varnished ceilings on exteriors. Jill Pilaroscia of San Francisco has used trompe-l'oeil stencils. Susan Moore of Minneapolis, a leading experimental designer, is always "looking for clients who are willing to take that leap off the edge, into the future."

Painted Ladies has inspired owners of non-Victorians to spurn bland color tones. This 1907 Craftsman Cottage at 720 Foster Street in Coeur d'Alene, Idaho, has won city restoration awards for its "Miami Vice" color scheme. The owners handcut each of the 2,000 roof shingles to get the right diamond design.

Neo Is Now

Neo-Victorians, buildings built today using Victorian style and color design, are increasingly popular. Not every town has something they can restore, so builders are answering the yearning for houses with character by building new homes and condominiums with Victorian accents.

Ken Cummings in Reno, Nevada, at 2375 Kinney Lane, salvaged parts of a torn-down Victorian in New Orleans to trim the porch on his new "old" house. His neighbors, used to plain ranch homes, protested his rose, white, and grape palette, but the neighborhood architectural committee ruled in his favor. Even Neos are better than impersonal boxes, and color enhances anything.

Condominium builders in Alexandria, Virginia; Houston, Texas; Atlanta, Georgia; Little Rock, Arkansas; Los Angeles and San Francisco have used color designs by San Francisco colorists to attract buyers.

The gaily painted Victorian ski resort of Breckenridge was praised by many as *the* place to find Painted Ladies in Colorado. With one diminutive exception, most of the main

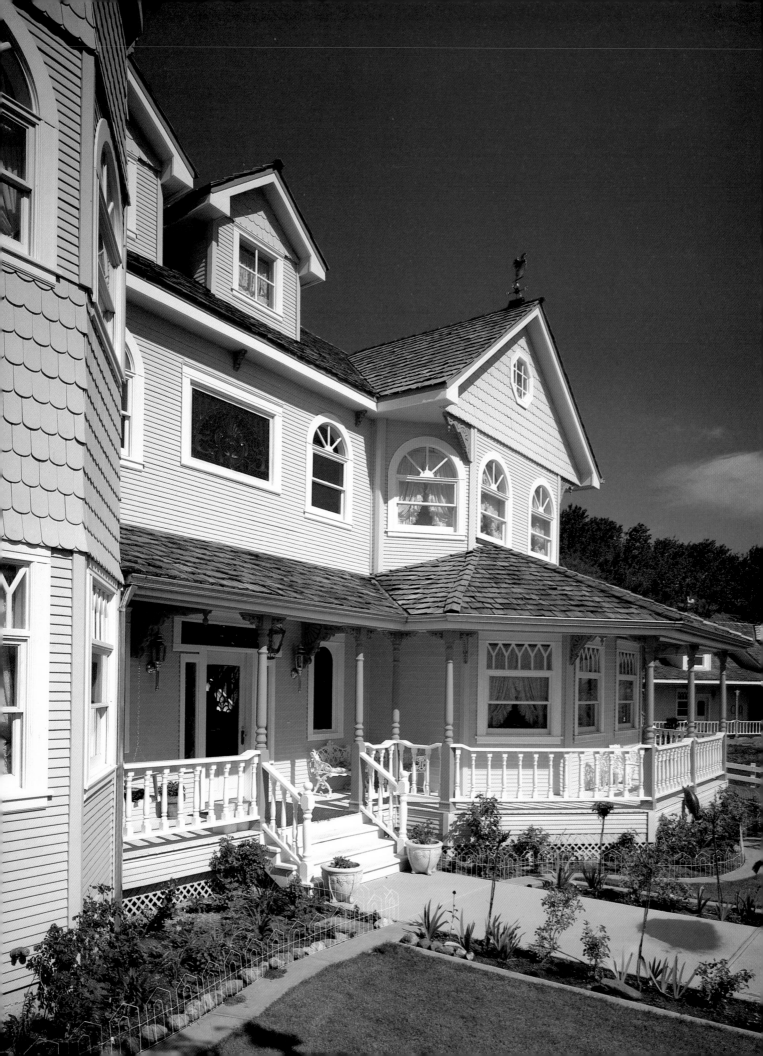

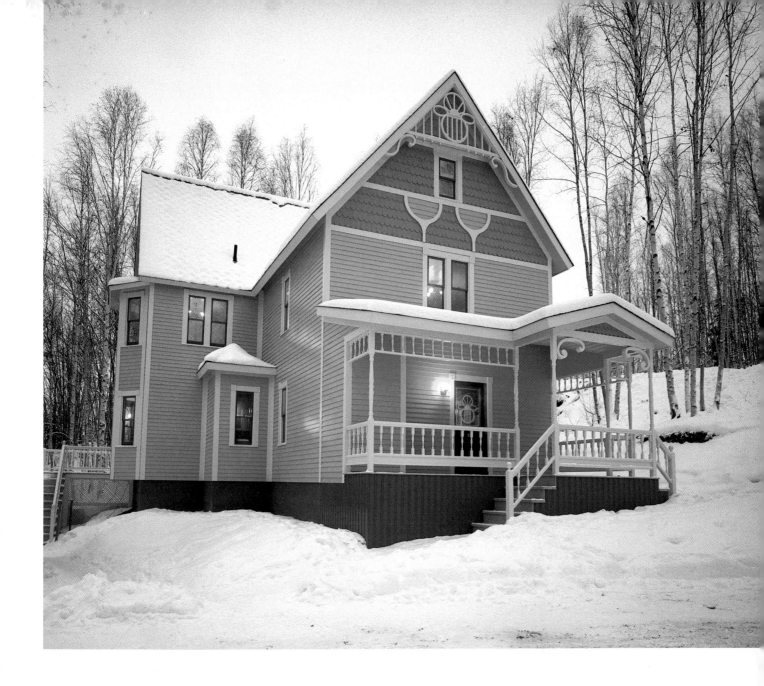

street's Victorians were built in the 1960s to attract tourists.

Catalogues and floor-plan pattern books are again a thriving business. In 1980, D. Scott and Trudy Hugie and Denise and James Trainor formed the THAK Company to "reproduce an architecturally correct Victorian style home" in Fairbanks, Alaska. They wanted a house with the architectural appeal of a Victorian and the added benefit of new materials, insulations, and up-to-date plumbing and electricity. They made most of the gingerbread in their own millshop and tried to achieve an authentic flavor in the interior furnishings as well.

A Home or a Museum?

Victorian homeowners must ask themselves "Am I painting a home or a museum? Should my house be painted in a traditional color scheme or should I use whatever colors please me, and create a design that expresses my taste and personality?" Should they honor the past or be a prisoner of it?

Three perspectives must be considered: scientific, historic, and artistic. The period of the house and the owner's personal feelings are also important.

Certainly, the integrity of a Victorian's exterior architecture should be safe from the desecration of misguided modernization. Even the purest traditionalists accept the right to enjoy a microwave oven in the kitchen and a Jacuzzi in the bathroom. Yet they are appalled if the colors applied on a house a century ago aren't used in perpetuity.

Homeowners should remember that it's *their* house, that they have to pay for the paint and the painters, and then have to live with the results. We think they all should feel about their homes like the woman in Ithaca who wrote, "Thanks to you two, I have a house I'm thrilled with.... I do have five colors which I would never have had if it weren't for your book.... Many, many thanks to you for saving me

23

from having just another white house... I'm sure your book has been an inspiration to many people and I'm happy for all of them, but I'm positively gloriously delighted for me. Thank you."

A Paint Job Is Not Forever

Havelock Ellis believed that civilization is the art of holding on and the art of letting go. Painting a Victorian provides an opportunity to do both. Paint should be looked at as a suit of clothes, to be changed as needed. Homeowners can let their imaginations take flight, knowing that they can change their mind and their palette the next time the house needs to be painted. One proud householder had painted her darling cottage in warm browns and beiges, but she was already looking forward to a new paint job, when everything would be changed to rosy pinks to reflect the newly redone interior.

At the same time, paint is not permanent, and every time a house is repainted, it costs money, a primary consideration for most homeowners. At the beginning of this century, when porch balusters were eight cents each, and gable ornaments four feet long were seventy cents, a fifty-gallon barrel of paint was seventy-two cents. A gallon of paint now costs between twenty and thirty dollars.

Ultimately, painting your Victorian is a labor of love, but then again, so is owning one. The rewards come when strangers knock on your door to tell you how happy you have made them. As a Chicago couple remarked: "Painting a house is a great way to meet people—people knock on the door to talk about it. A Painted Lady can change your whole life!"

We hope that these Daughters of Painted Ladies will bring out the best, not only in the people who create them but also in those who stop to admire them. An environment that lifts our spirits will lead to a new sense of optimism and openness, and a renewed certainty about the value of beauty and tradition in our daily lives.

Regardless of where you live, we hope that this collection of Painted Daughters will make you decide to join the color revolution in its renaissance of the American Spirit.

THE NORTHEAST

The older a city is, the harder it is to drive in it, and the greater the value placed on tradition. Easterners are more concerned than Westerners about tradition and about what their neighbors will think. Yet within the confines of century-old palettes, revelations abounded.

The capital of East Coast color is the lovely town of Cape May, New Jersey, with its gorgeous bevy of seaside beauties. This wonderful collection of Victorians shows the heights it is possible to attain with care and imagination while trying to be faithful to traditional colors.

Another triumph for tradition is The Octagon House in Irvington-on-Hudson, New York. Designed to amuse, it is a stunning tour-de-force thanks to the enormous eight-year restoration job by Joseph Pell Lombardi, the restoration architect who owns it.

Also designed to amuse are The Crayon House in Providence, Rhode Island, and Lucy the Elephant in Margate, New Jersey. And the sprightly couple on Martha's Vineyard proves that when it comes to painting summer homes, caprice rules the day. So despite its being the bastion of tradition, the Victorian spirit of play is alive and well in the Northeast.

On the East Coast's West Coast, Michael Foglia picks his colors as he paints and has created lovely ladies in Buffalo.

There are also regional variations in preparation techniques and how long a paint job will last. Eastern painters prefer ladders to scaffolding, and the Northeast's extreme temperatures mean that they have to repaint more often than their West Coast colleagues who enjoy a moderate climate.

Although the Puritan tradition of Colonial white still reigns, dark barn red has been used as an insulator for two centuries. New Yorkers, especially those in Rochester's South Wedge, have used crushed stone in their gables for color and texture.

And from Providence to Pittsburgh, it was heartening to find Victorians in neglected neighborhoods being restored and bringing new life to their communities.

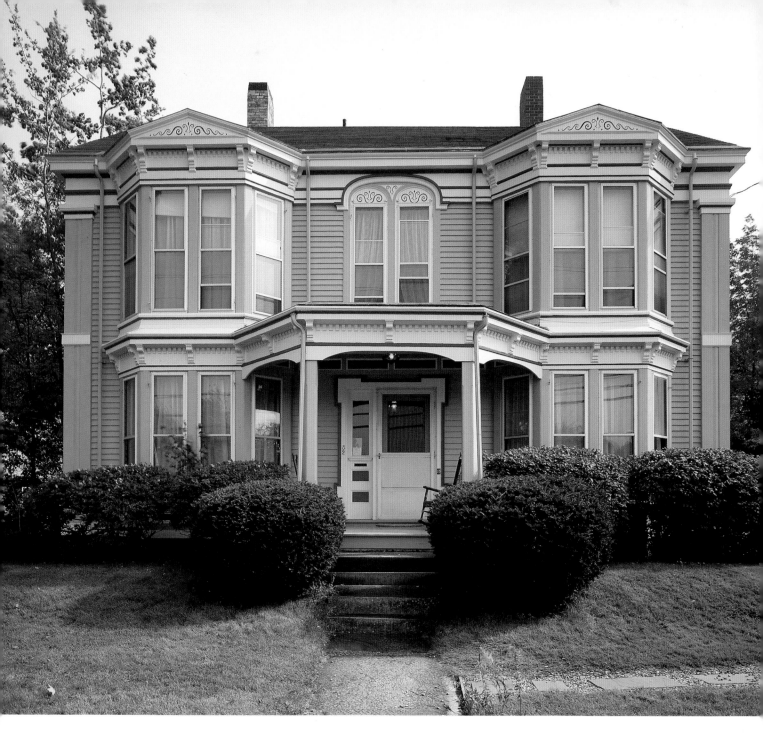

MAINE

CAMDEN

(Above). Blackberry Inn, 82 Elm Street. 1860. Italianate. Inn-keepers Vicki and Edward Doudera worked with Mills Painters to select a color design that would please Job and Elizabeth Knight Montgomery, who built this dignified home, and their neighbors in this windjammer seaport. Work was still in progress when we discovered the place, and a copy of *Painted Ladies* was on the mantel, next to the ladder. The result is a contrasting, pleasing blend of white and gray with a fillip of (what else?) blackberry.

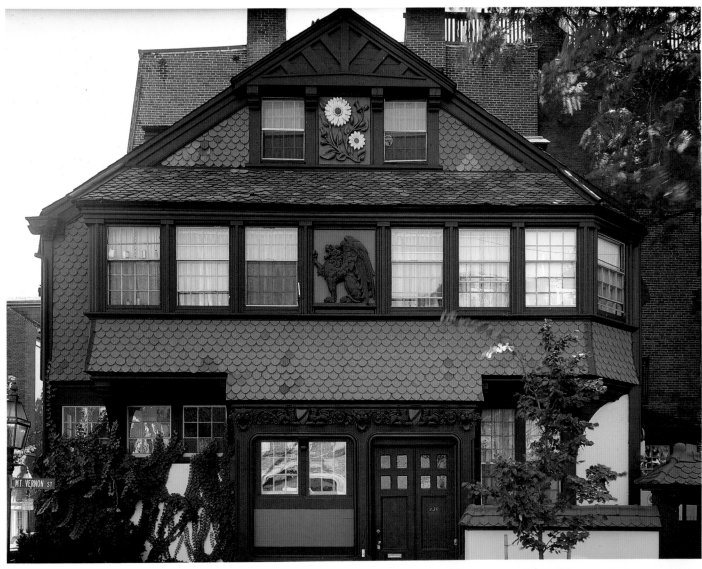

MASSACHUSETTS

BOSTON

(Above and right). 130 Mt. Vernon Street. 1840–1887. This is one of the rare English Queen Annes in America. A forerunner of America's flamboyant Queen Anne style with its turrets and towers, this style reflects what houses were like in early eighteenth-century England, during Queen Anne's reign. Architect Henry Luce redesigned the present exterior in 1887. The Hill-Smith family lived here from 1840 to 1904; the Bourne family has lived here ever since.

As part of the revival of eighteenth-century architecture, shingles were painted vivid pink, to look like the clay tiles popular in England. England was also the inspiration for the vivid yellow. An artist who lived here saw it on the houses she found while traveling in the Cotswolds.

It is said that Oscar Wilde, who liked to wear a sunflower in his lapel, stayed here on a speaking tour. Wilde introduced the Aesthetic Movement, whose symbols were sunflowers and griffins, to America. Oliver Wendell Holmes used to pass by the house and he christened it "Castle Sunflower."

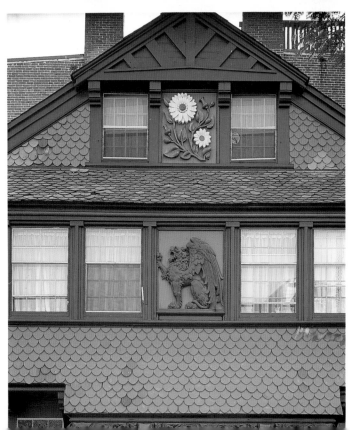

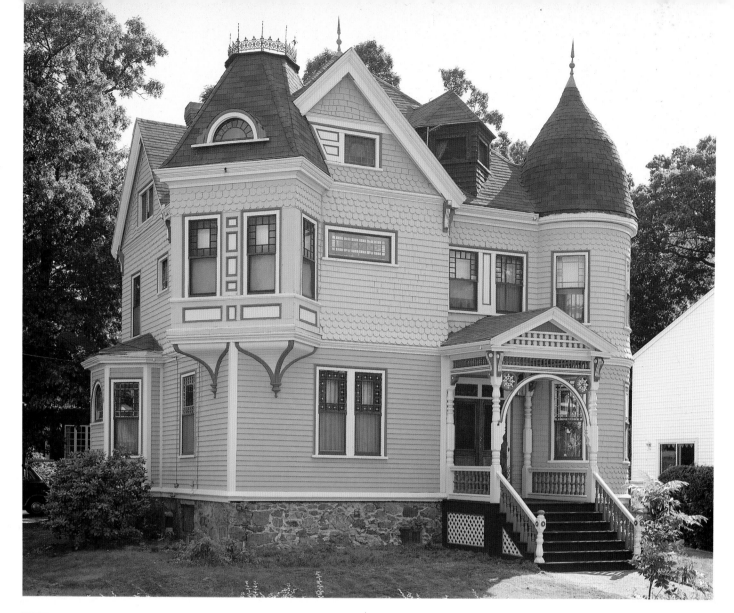

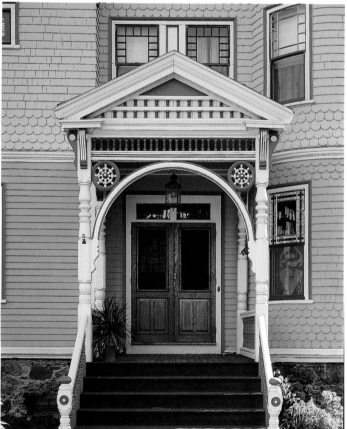

MALDEN

(Above and left). 107 Dexter Street. Queen Anne. 1882. Inspired by the Rose Victorian Inn on page 122, owner Gary Mackiewicz has spent three years painting this charming home in three shades of rose and a dark red.

Note how the imaginative use of color in the detail steers the eye to the diminutive ship's wheels above the entrance arch, the builder's artful bow to New England's seafaring past.

HUDSON

(Opposite). 76 Park Street. Queen Anne. 1893. Working with the inspiration of *Painted Ladies* after consultation with a paint historian, the owner painted this stately house in seven colors in 1981 "to appreciate the beautiful things the Victorians left us. Neighbors have told us that when they drive by, the house lifts their spirits."

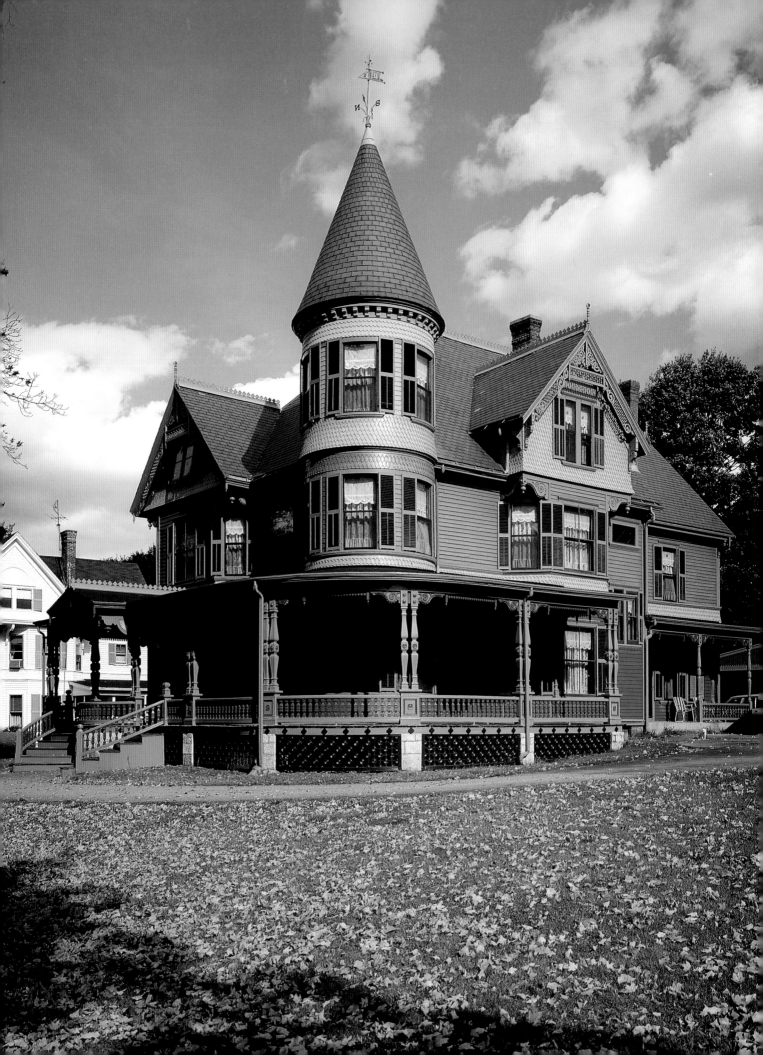

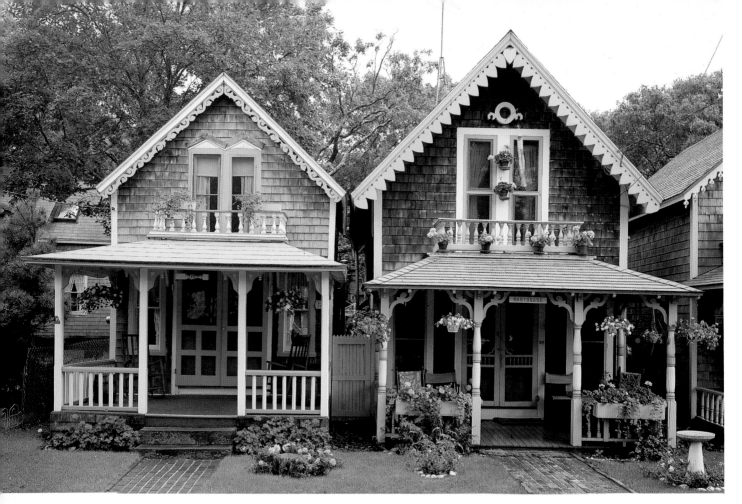

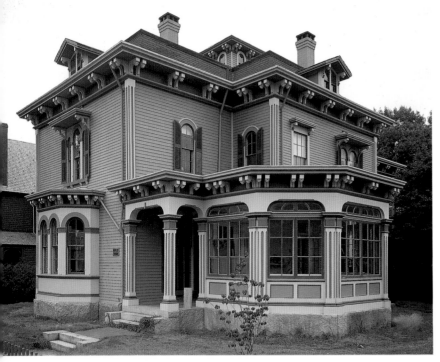

MARTHA'S VINEYARD

(Above). Methodist Campground, Oak Bluffs. 57 and 58 Trinity Park. The streets of this century-old beach town are lined with shingle cottages, like Oops (left, built in 1867) and Hartsease (right, built in 1864), shown here. The 350 houses in this community were tents when the Campground was founded in 1835. After the Civil War, Carpenter-Gothic cottages replaced the tents and in each one, the bargeboards copied the tent trim. Oops and Hartsease face an open park called the Tabernacle, which serves as an open-air meeting place and church during the summer. The Campground cottages are all brightly bedecked with gingerbread and flowers, recalling the carefree fancies of the good old summertime.

NEW BEDFORD

(Left). Abby Tabor Hunt House, Morgan and Orchard Streets. 1855. This stately Italianate was the home of Herman Melville's sister, Katherine, when this whaling capital boasted the highest per-capita income of any city in the world and had its own wallpaper and glass factories. Now the library for the Swain School of Art and Design, this is an outstanding example of how even traditional colors can make a Victorian sing.

Melville, in *Moby Dick*, called New Bedford "the dearest town in all New England." After several decades of decline, downtown New Bedford is being revitalized by WHALE, the Waterfront Historic Area League. Preservationist Anton G. Souza and color designer Bruce Yenuin worked together to return this house to its original resplendence.

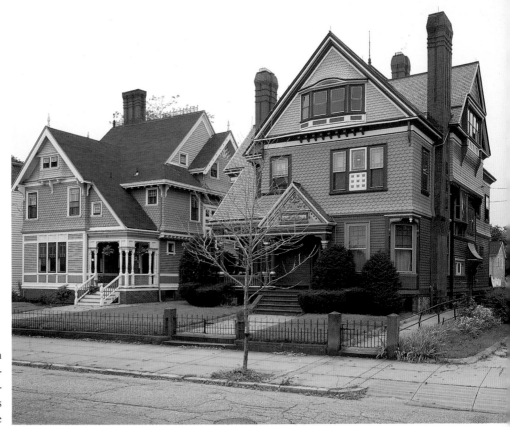

RHODE ISLAND

PROVIDENCE

Developed after the Civil War as an urban residential neighborhood, Providence's Broadway-Armory District became a crowded inner-city area after World War II, with many buildings becoming vandalized and vacant. In 1974, the area was entered on the National Register of Historic Places, and the Providence Preservation Society Revolving Fund has worked with the HUD to restore its architectural heritage and create harmonious streetscapes.

PROVIDENCE

(Above, right). 81 and 77 Parade Street. Queen Annes. 1882. 81 Parade Street was designed by architect E. I. Nickerson for Joseph C. Hartshorn, treasurer of the Providence Steam & Gas Pipe Company. One hundred years later, Kirk Williams created a color design of pinks, creams, turquoise, green, gray, and black. The iron and brownstone railing shared with 77 Parade is original.

Hartshorn built 77 Parade Street for his daughter, Mary, and her husband Frederick W. Hartwell, a bookkeeper, in 1883. In 1985, the new owners restored the house through Providence's SWAP (Stop Wasting Abandoned Properties) Program and painted it in five colors to highlight the many textures.

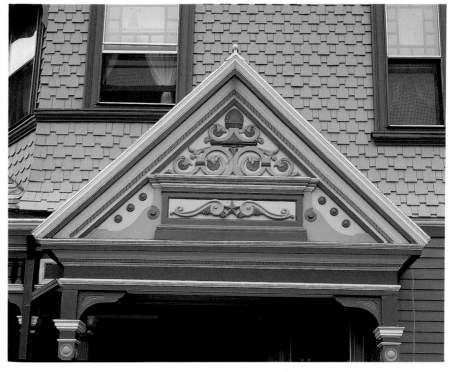

PROVIDENCE

(Below, right). 77 Parade Street. This gable is an exquisite jewel: a lovely design unified and enhanced by a quiet yet endearing choice of colors.

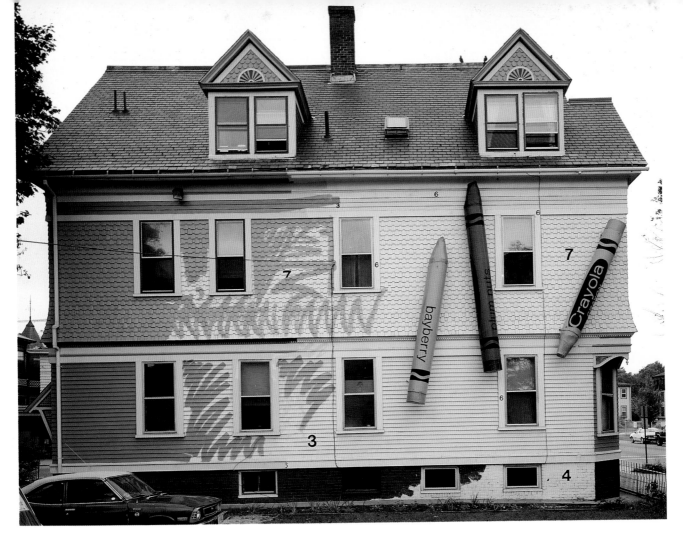

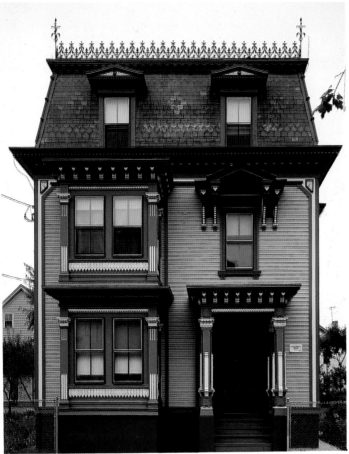

PROVIDENCE

(Above). 1440 Westminster. Queen Anne. 1890. The Victorian spirit of play in architecture is given a new dimension in this apartment house, built as income property by Oscar Burgess. Now called "The Crayon House," it looks like just another Painted Lady from the front. But by the time the owner got to the back, he decided to have fun and show his colors: bayberry green, plum nuts, and taupe pink.

PROVIDENCE

(Left). 78 Hudson Street. Mansard. Businessman Alfred E. Tenney built one of Rhode Island's most distinguished dwellings in 1877. Owner Robert E. Dupré preserved the authentic cast-iron cresting and detailed the portico and bay windows. This is another delightful example of how subdued colors can make a house pop.

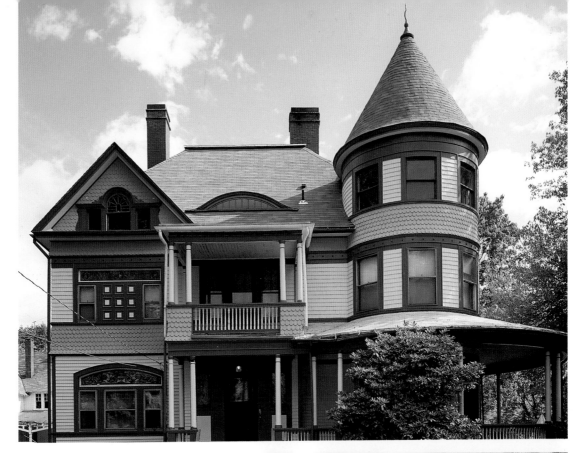

CONNECTICUT
MOODUS

(Above). The Fowler House. Plains Road. Queen Anne. 1890. Originally red with green trim, this inn was a bland white when the present owners bought it. They chose a restrained four-color palette to give it elegance.

NEW YORK
BUFFALO

(Right, above). 95 Hodge Street. Queen Anne. 1883. The unusual design on the gable and swirled columns on the porch of this Medina-stone-and-brick residence brightens the house with dark terra-cotta, blue, and cream.

BUFFALO

(Right, below). 415 Ashland Avenue. Craftsman. 1906. In June 1985, a tree fell on the porch of this simple frame dwelling during a thunderstorm. When the owners took it down to repair it, this fanciful gable was discovered under clapboard. Michael Foglia used seven colors to bring the design to life.

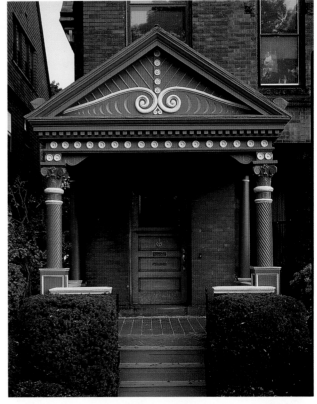

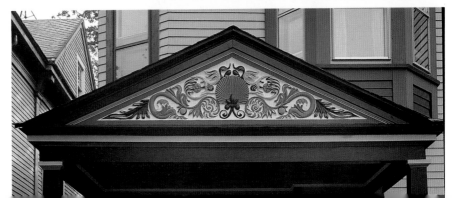

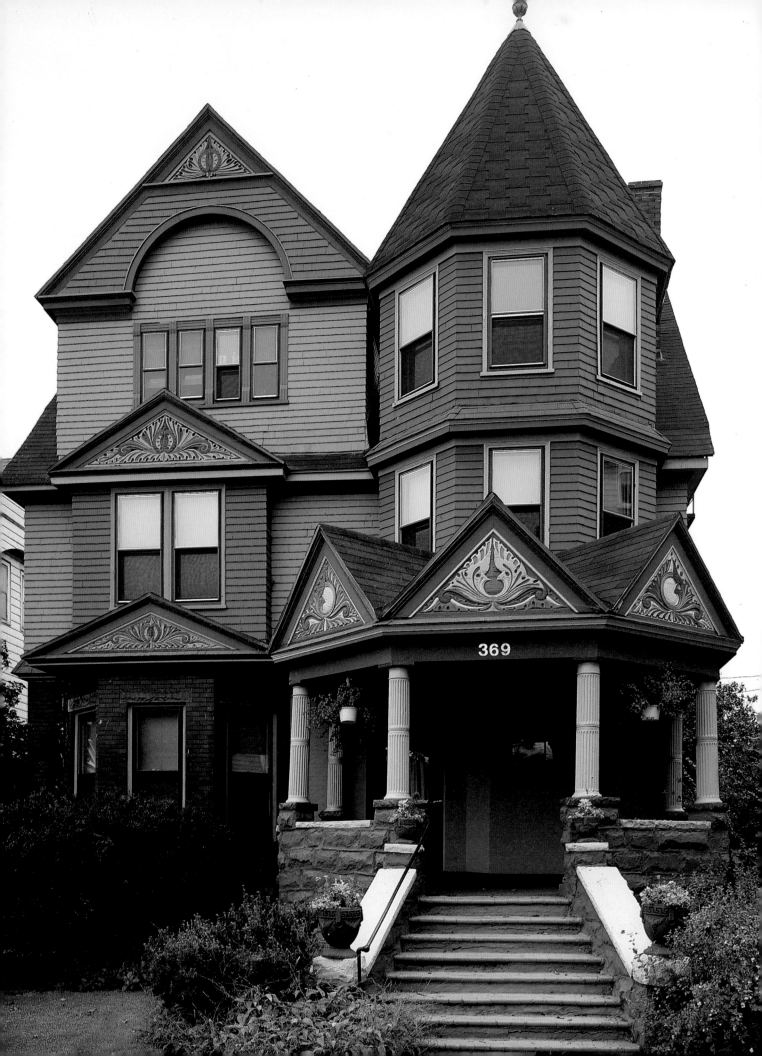

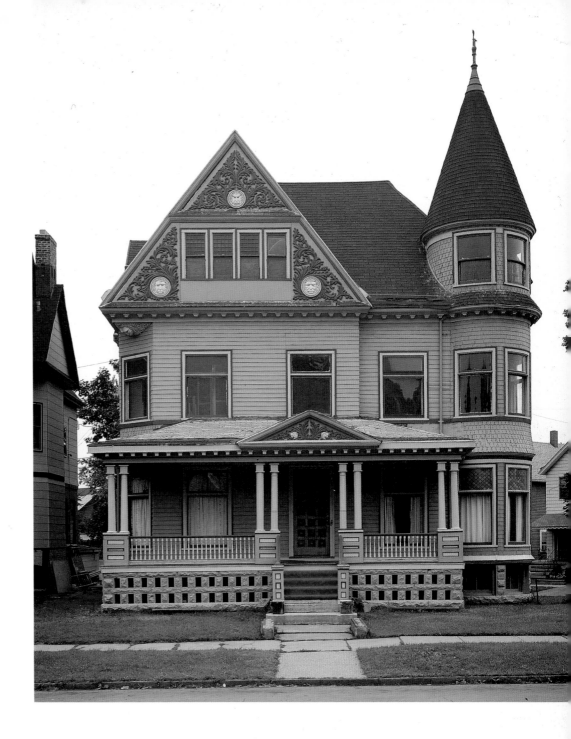

BUFFALO

(Opposite). 369 Porter. Queen Anne. 1896. Encouraged by the Preservation Coalition of Erie County and the Allentown Association, Michael Foglia used eighteen colors—from plum and three shades of lavender to greens, grays, and three shades of terra-cotta—to restore this house of many gables to its original splendor. After talking to the owner, Foglia picks the colors as he paints, bringing quarts to test on the house.

BUFFALO

(Above and right). 412 Porter. Queen Anne. 1893. Inspired by *Painted Ladies*, the owners were guided by a 1920s photograph in restoring their house. Each of the six lion faces has a different expression. In the closeup, you can see the golden mane, blue eyes, and rosy cheeks of this ever-vigilant watchman.

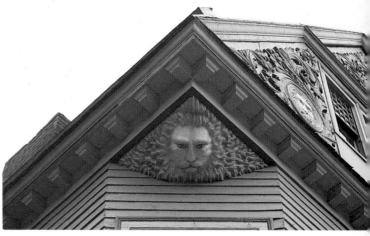

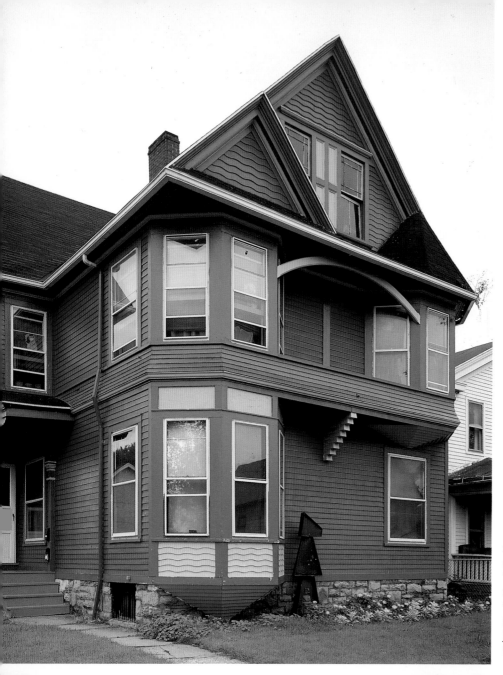

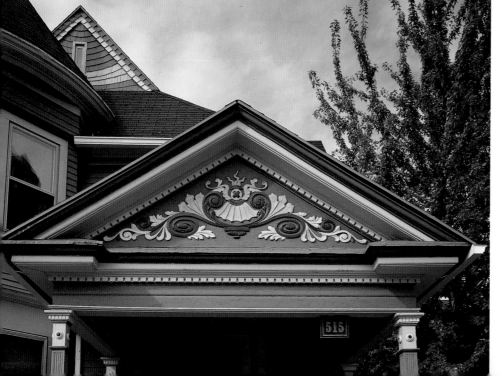

ROCHESTER

(Left, above). 121 Comfort Street. 1890–1892. This Queen Anne cottage, painted barn red, mustard yellow, and bright blue has been called a "Loud House" in the local paper, but it is a traditional Northeast color scheme. Note how the judicious use of yellow accentuates the design of the house.

ROCHESTER

(Left, below). 515 South Avenue. Queen Anne. 1888. The week before their wedding, the former owners, Mark and Karen Caulfield, bought this house, scheduled to be torn down, for $700. They went to San Francisco on their honeymoon, and returned to invest $45,000 in refurbishing and painting.

From 1980 to 1986, this was the first house people saw as they entered a newly revitalized section of town called the South Wedge and the house was called "The Purples and the Pinks." The Caulfields own the Historic House Parts Shop across the street. Their motto matches that of the South Wedge Historic Office: "Preserve the Fruits of Your Labor." In speaking for other Painted Ladies owners in the neighborhood, they explain, "Before we painted them, nobody knew we were there." A new owner kept the design but changed the palette to blues and cream.

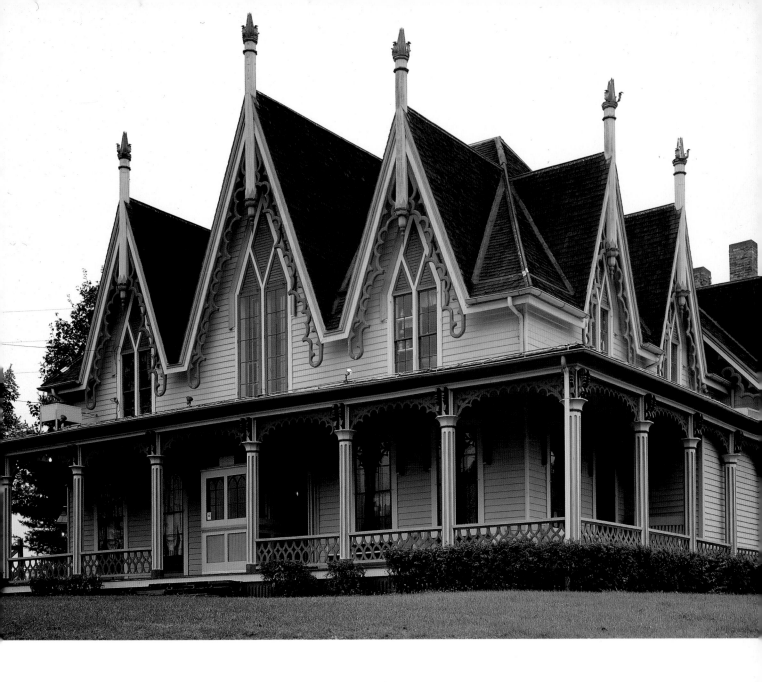

ITHACA

(Above). Turback's. 919 Elmira Road. Gothic Revival. 1851. Tobacco farmer Thomas Jefferson Williams hired local carpenters to build Sunnyside from local pine trees costing $1.50 each. The gingerbread was made by hand. When the house was redecorated in 1875 for Williams's second wife, the first bathroom in Ithaca was installed.

Cornell graduate Mike Turback bought the place in 1968 and restored this imposing Gothic fairy-tale house. The color design by Susan Mallery highlights its airy elegance. Turback's Restaurant specializes in locally produced ingredients and potables.

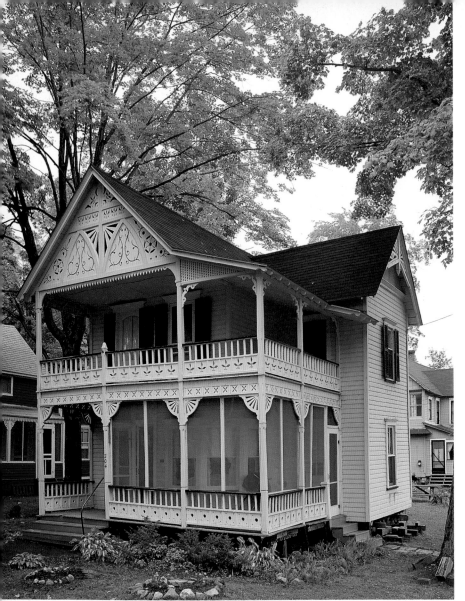

THOUSAND ISLAND PARK

(Left, above). 204 Ontario. Eastlake cottage. 1870s. A privately owned corporation, Thousand Island Park has been a popular summer community since the middle of the nineteenth century, when, as at Martha's Vineyard, a camp meeting colony of tents was transformed into wooden cottages.

In celebrating its centennial, a local historian wrote, "All of the architecture and decorative arts of the 1870s responded to the public's appreciation for what was lively, spritely, or, to use a term of the time, 'piquant.'...its rather disarming, engaging quality derives from a certain ingenuous, joyous quality—almost childlike—which may yield some understanding of what our ancestors were talking about, when they referred to simplicity and purity." This richly decorated cottage, with its lacy, intricate gable, proves his point.

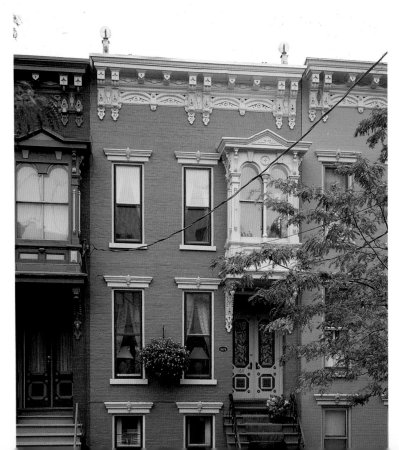

ALBANY

(Left, below). 164 Jay Street. Italianate. 1875. The owner used colors he liked in the stained glass on the door. The gaslights on the rooftop of this row house, built by bankers Olcott and King, still work. The white accents are icing on the cake. Neighbors on either side also used three colors to help rejuvenate this colorful block. Albany surprised us with its banners celebrating the city's 150th birthday and its growing collection of lovingly restored Victorians.

NEW JERSEY

WEST END

(Opposite). St. Michael's Roman Catholic Church. 800 Ocean Avenue. Italianate. 1886. A new paint job helped celebrate this church's 100th anniversary. The white accents on this vivid red edifice gleam in the sun. Although you have to stretch a point and include the gold cross as a third color, we couldn't resist including this glorious edifice in which to make a joyful noise unto the Lord, caught by our photographer on a perfect day.

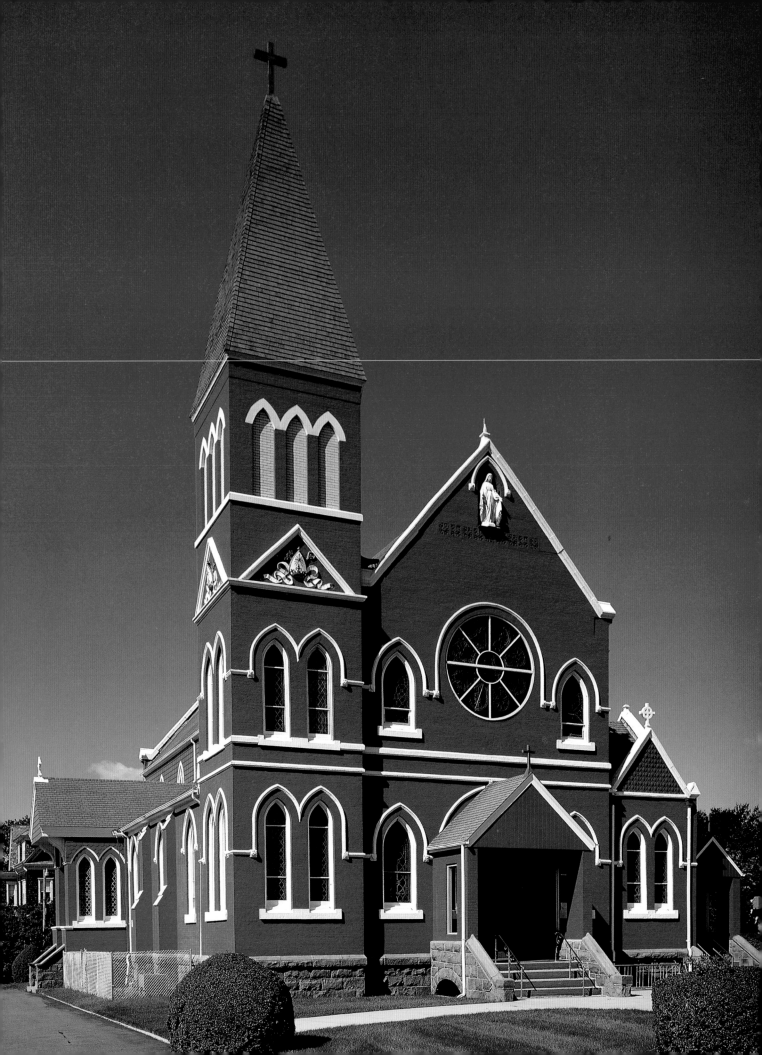

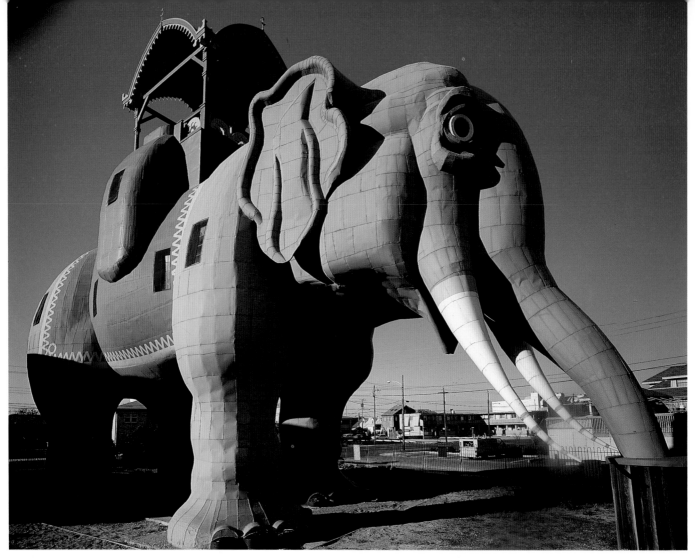

MARGATE

(Above). Lucy, The Margate Elephant, is an architectural "folly" built in 1883 by real-estate developer James V. Lafferty after designs for Louis XV's *"L'Elephant Triomphal"* were published in the *American Architects and Builders News.* An Elephant Hotel 122 feet high was also built on Coney Island, New York.

In the patents for his plans Lafferty lauded the salubrious effects of the design: "The elevation of the body permits the circulation of air beneath it and removes it from the dampness and moisture of the ground.... Furthermore, the body is exposed to light and air in all sides, wherefore it provides a healthy and suitable place of occupancy for invalids & others."

Although Lucy shows how playful the Victorian could be, this twelve-room house, now a museum, was meant to be lived in. From her toenails to the top of her howdah, Lucy is six stories high, built of one million pieces of wood and covered with 12,000 feet of brightly painted tin at a cost of $38,000.

One climbs stairs to reach the living room, dining room, bedrooms, and closets. You can see the ocean from the windows in the eyes. Although Herbert Kramer of Cape May fondly recalls sliding down the trunk while playing hide-and-seek in the trunk as a child, the trunk was used for the laundry, garbage, and ash chutes. Lucy has been designated a National Historic Landmark. Funds are still needed to restore her.

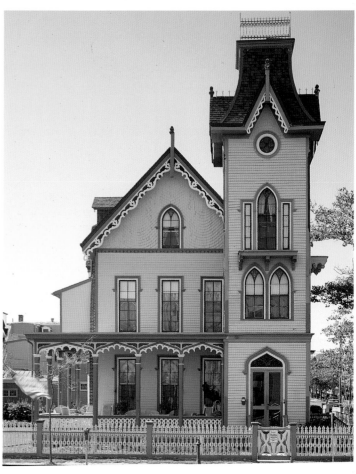

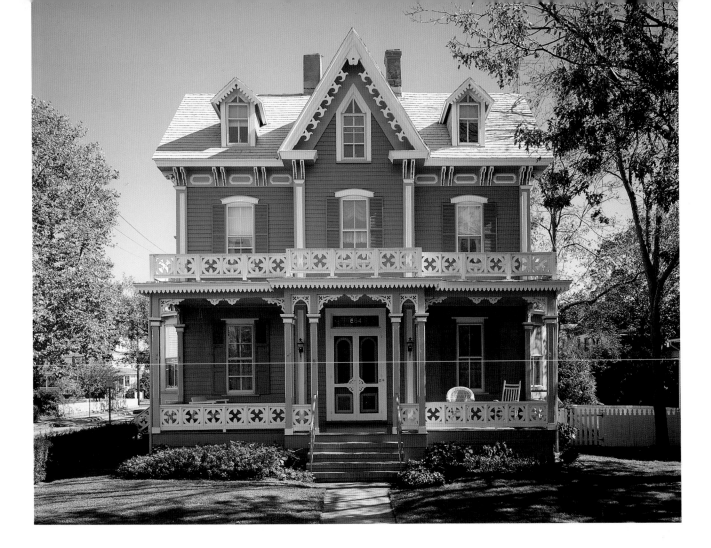

CAPE MAY

Cape May, America's oldest seashore resort, was named for Dutch explorer Cornelius Jacobson Mey who came ashore in 1621. Cape May first became popular in the early 1800s and by the 1870s builders could barely keep up with the hordes of Philadelphia Mainliners and politicians pouring in by rail, steamboat, and coach from North and South. (Cape May is below the Mason-Dixon Line.) A white flag on the beach signaled that women could bathe freely, while the red flag meant "men only."

A fire destroyed thirty downtown blocks in 1878 and in their haste to construct hotel rooms for visitors, builders used every kind of gingerbread and floor plan easily purchased by mail order. The owners of summer "cottages" were, according to a Cape May historian, soon "exuberantly competing with the most lavish ornamentation—lattice work, scrolls and frets, brackets and bargeboards. Each architectural detail was painted a different color, to accentuate the skillful craftsmanship—and to dramatize the decoration insisted upon by their *nouveau riche* owners."

Fires destroyed many of the largest hotels near the turn of the century, and after 1910, the town fell into a long period of protective neglect. But in the early 1970s, some historical buildings were torn down for a shopping mall and Victorian hotels were razed for high-rise motels. This galvanized preservationists who soon had the town listed on the National Register of Historic Places and designated as a National Historic Landmark City, one of only five in the country. This means that all of the town's 600 structures must retain their original form and design, creating a picturesque town that stands as one of the country's finest and most colorful collections of Victorians. Today, visitors stay in restored B & Bs and enjoy a taste of yesteryear all year round.

CAPE MAY

(Opposite, below). The Abbey. Columbia Avenue and Gurney Street. Gothic Revival. 1870. Designed by Stephan Decatur Button as a summer villa for Philadelphia coal baron John McCreary, this elegant B & B is notable for its 60-foot tower, the arched ruby-glass windows, and because no two sides of the house have trim in the same style. Paint purveyor and preservationist Herbert Kramer created the color design, using a sea-green paint named for The Abbey. Note the wavy effect on the gable and how the yellow and terra-cotta pick out the details that make this *grande dame* a gem.

CAPE MAY

(Above). 664 Hughes Street. Gothic. 1883. The owners of this enchanting confection studied *Painted Ladies* and created their own color design of pinks, white, and blue-gray. They also carved the fascinating dove-and-dolphin motifs that decorate the gable. This scrumptious house looks good enough to eat!

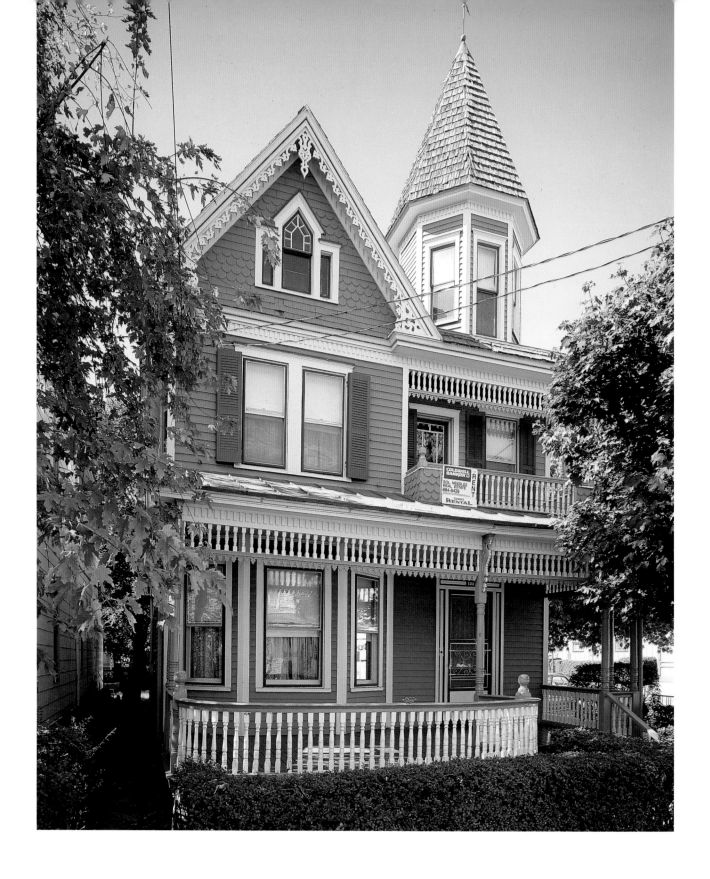

CAPE MAY

(Above). 132 Decatur Street. Queen Anne/Steamboat Gothic. 1895. The Aaron Roseman House, still a private residence, has a stained-glass window, a facade filled with intricately turned spindles, and an octagonal tower. Turquoise, cream, and terra-cotta reflect The Merry Widow Inn down the street. This demure lady wears her lacy cream bargeboard like a scarf to protect her from sea breezes.

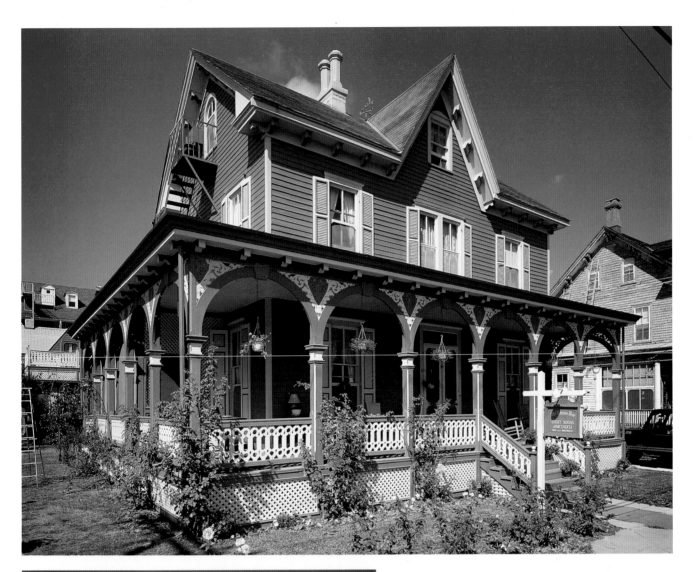

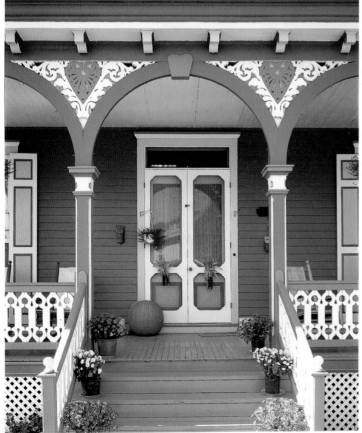

CAPE MAY

(Above and left). The Victorian Rose. 715 Columbia Avenue. Gothic. 1872. The owners used blues, cream, and red to create a Victorian valentine framed by a rose garden. If you look carefully and compare the two photographs, you can see the last kiss of color added to the fluting on the right column as these pictures were being taken.

PENNSYLVANIA

PITTSBURGH

(Right). 1323 Liverpool Street. Italianate. 1876. The owners chose their colors after talking to their painter and reading his copy of *Painted Ladies.* "We liked the new attention to detail, and now I have a rex over the door who is visible, and now you can see the rosettes. Inside, I even painted one pink stripe all along the baseboard of the main floor and down the stairs and that's what I call an inside Painted Ladies influence."

Three sections of Pittsburgh—Manchester, Allegheny West, and the Mexican Wars Districts—once lined with VOV (Vacant, Open, and Vandalized) buildings, are coming to life with the help of Tom Mystick & Sons, a development and construction company that has made a specialty of rehabilitating Victorian period buildings in inner-city neighborhoods. Working with HUD, NHP and neighborhood groups, they've given new life to 350 houses.

DELAWARE

DOVER

(Below). 5 State Street at Division Street. Second Empire. 1868–1885. Salome Edgeworth worked on the color design for The McCosh House, which was saved from desolation under the auspices of the Department of the Interior. The painted brick exterior has been restored to its original look. The cast-iron fence has been painted to match the house.

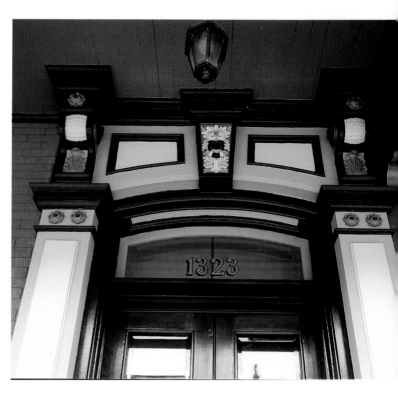

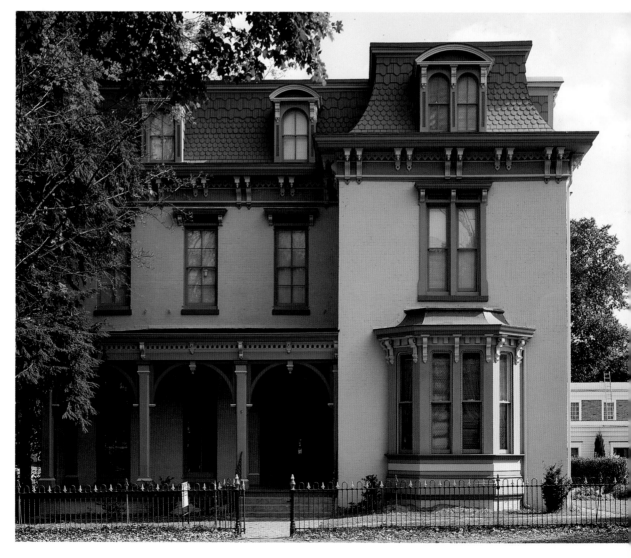

THE SOUTH

Southerners prefer white and pastels because of the heat and of their fond memories of the grand Greek Revival plantations of days now "gone with the wind." Homeowners in steamy climes paint the ceilings of their verandahs a cool sky blue.

Eastern conservatism prevails in the South. Indeed, in a world that divides time as before or after "The War," the Victorian era is just coming into its own. A Charleston, South Carolina, preservation officer remembered that some residents were thankful that "the poverty after the Civil War spared the city the scourge of Victoriana." A century later, Charlestonians are proud of their "rainbow row" and their Victorians, just now breaking into multicolor.

Yet the Painted Ladies in Raleigh, North Carolina, and Eureka Springs, Arkansas, would do any part of the country proud. The Rosalie House in Eureka Springs is a gingerbread dream house, as is the amazing Gingerbread House in Savannah, Georgia. The South also boasts the most colorful Octagon in the country: The Folly in Columbus, Georgia.

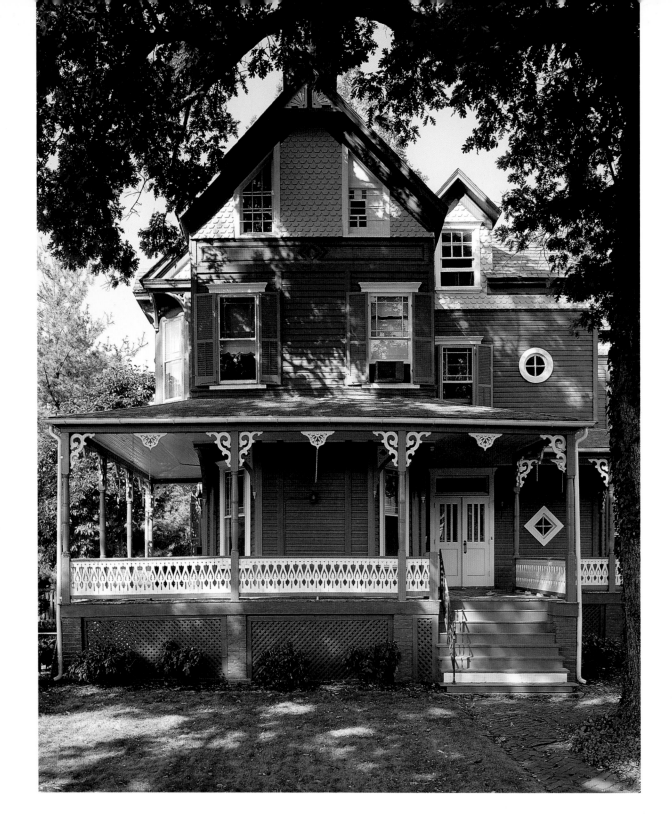

MARYLAND

ROCKVILLE

(Above). 117 West Montgomery Avenue. Eastlake/Queen Anne. 1887. At the turn of the century, Rockville was built up as a resort for Washingtonians seeking to escape mosquito-filled swamps. This house was built by a retired Marine Corps captain, who saluted his career with the porthole windows. His Marine Corps friend, John Philip Sousa, used to bring his band to give concerts on the porch. The owners found this vivid purple, pink, rose, and white color scheme in *Painted Ladies*.

46

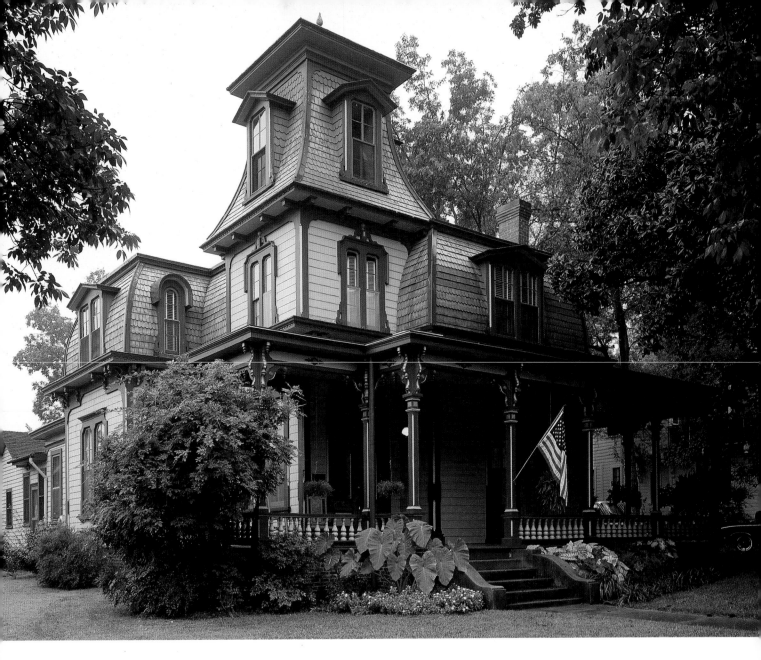

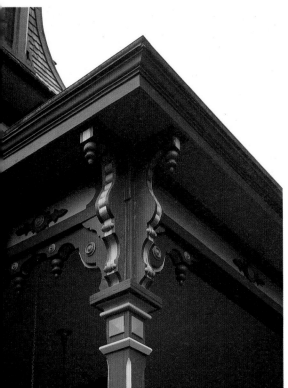

NORTH CAROLINA
RALEIGH

(Above and left). 503 East Jones. Steamboat Gothic with Mansard Second Empire roof. 1872–1873. This imposing design evokes a paddle-wheeler plying the Mississippi. S. H. Applegate designed this formidable residence for J. M. Hack in the Victorian Oakwood section of Raleigh, which was part of the Mordecai Plantation before "The War."

47

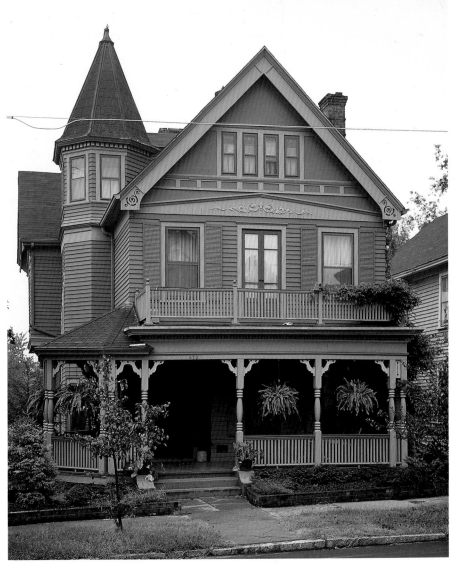

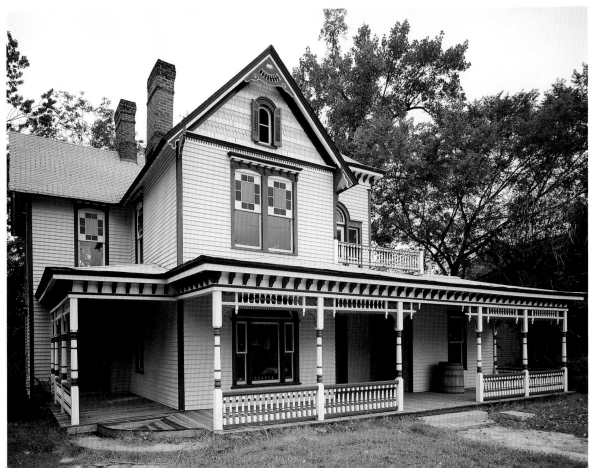

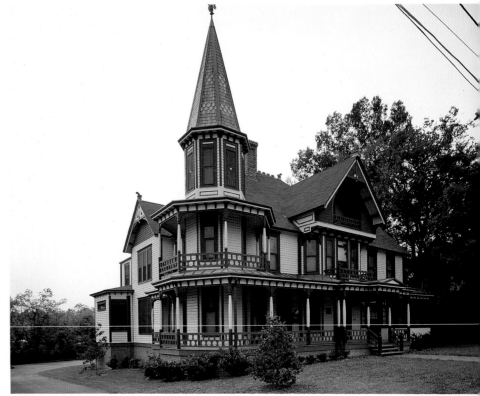

RALEIGH

(Opposite, above). 412 Oakwood Street. Queen Anne. 1897. Chris Yetter, who has been a driving force in restoring and saving his Oakwood neighborhood, used four muted but complementary colors on The Charles B. Hart House.

WINSTON-SALEM

(Opposite, below). The Brock-Horn-Malin House. 857 West 5th. Gothic Revival. 1890s. Red and green, picked up from the stained glass in the windows, give this house a Christmasy feeling that lightens up the street in a section of this college town now being restored. Note the three-color spindle work that gives zest to the fine redesigned porch.

STATESVILLE

(Right, above). 223–231 Walnut. Queen Anne. 1893. Preservation specialist Mac Lackey worked with the owner to restore The Lowenstein-Henkle House, which is on the National Register. The yellow, chocolate, and terra-cotta red apartment building is crowned by one of the most graceful "witch's hats" we found.

GEORGIA

ATLANTA

(Right, below). 105 Druid Circle. Queen Anne/Gothic Revival. 1899. The lacy gingerbread and rainbow of pinks in the pediment fans on this teal-blue home, once called "the Gingerbread House," have perked up the neighborhood. Jim and Jane Kourkoulis tested fifteen colors over a two-week period, checking them at different times of the day, and asking passersby for their opinion. The final seven-color solution was based on a friend's shirt—and the Kourkoulises even took the sleeve of the shirt with them to the paint store.

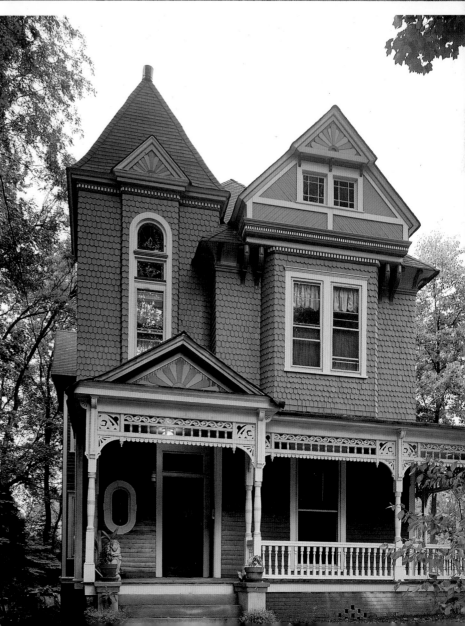

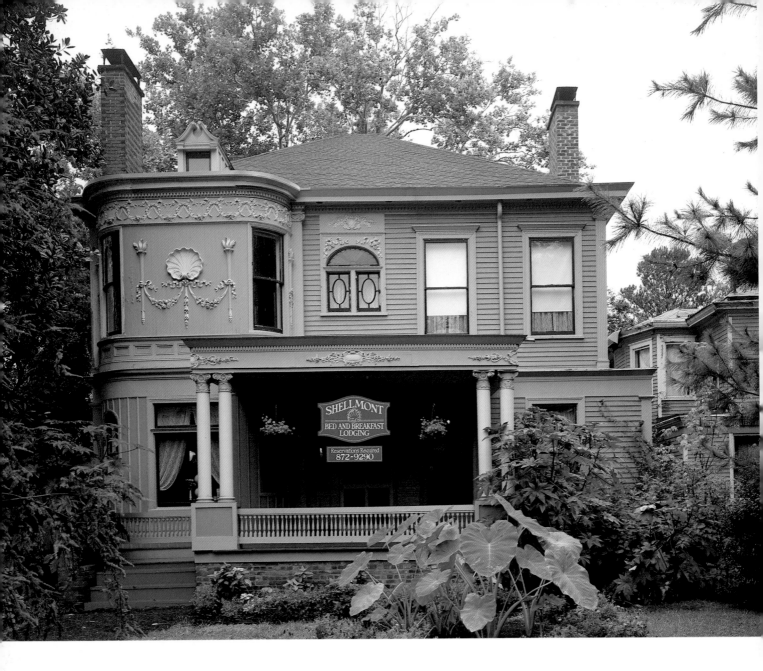

ATLANTA

(Above). 821 Piedmont Avenue, Northeast. Colonial Revival. 1891. Ed and Debbie McCord worked to restore this gracious bed-and-breakfast inn, The Shellmont, by hand. They chose their color design to go with the Louis Comfort Tiffany stained-glass window in the stairwell. It also complements the building's verdant setting. The Adamesque shell, festoon, and ribbonwork, evoking the Federalist Greek Revival era, make particularly handsome decorations.

NEWNAN

(Opposite). 155 Greenville Street. Stick-Eastlake/French Mansard. 1840/1885. The Parrott-Camp-Soucy Home, built by one of the first settlers in Coweta County, was modernized in 1885 when purchased as a wedding gift for Callie Bigby Parrott.

By 1984, it looked like a stale, sagging wedding cake to its new owners, who received an award from the Georgia Trust for Historic Preservation for their loving restoration work. With its nine original colors, this B&B is a polychrome symphony punctuated by outbursts of intense ornamentation.

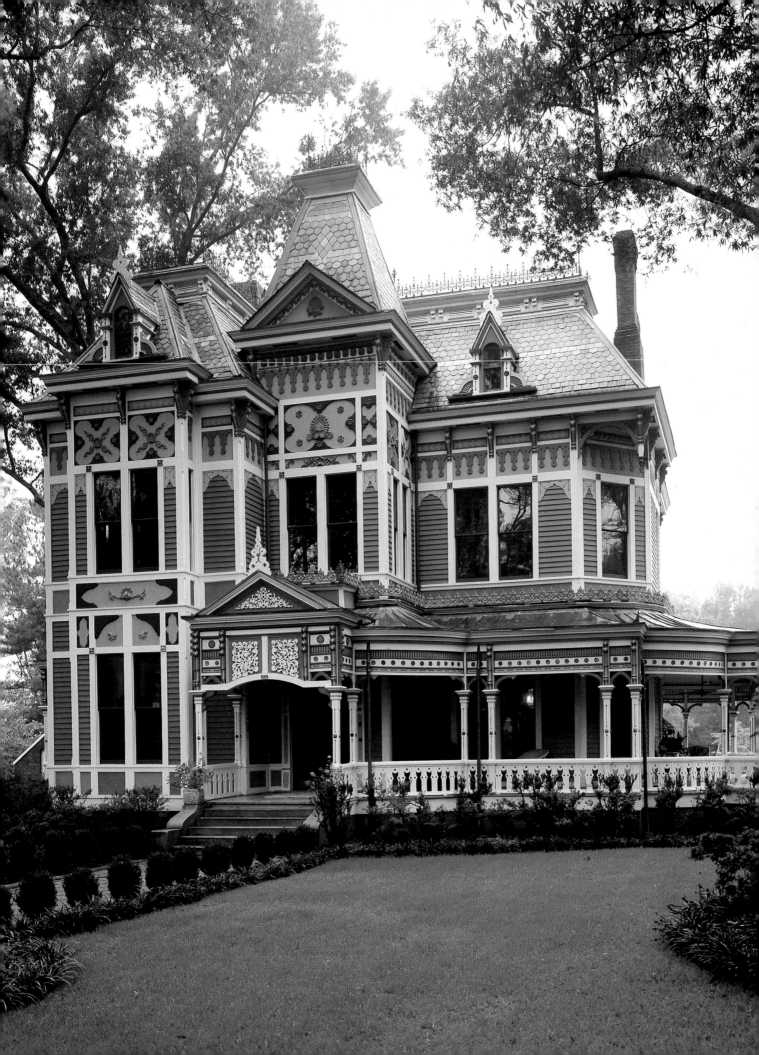

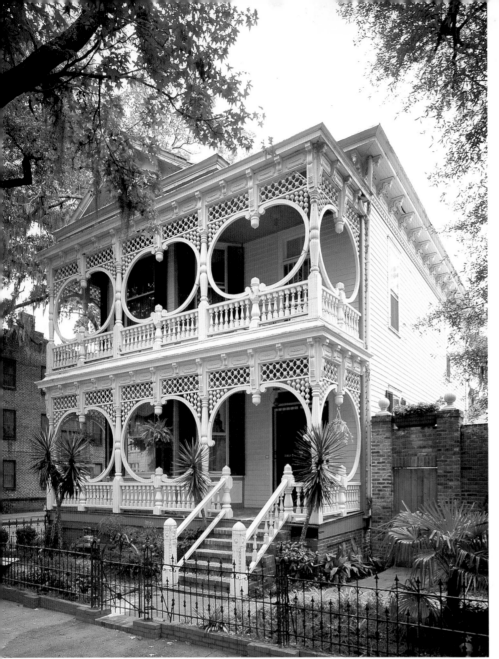

SAVANNAH

(Left, below left, and below right). The Ginger-bread House. 1921 Bull Street. Steamboat Gothic. 1899. Cord Asendorf, a Savannah merchant, had this subtly colored house built to "out ginger-bread" everyone else in town. He designed all of the gingerbread spindles and bric-a-brac himself. His daughter lived in the house until the early 1970s and protested vehemently when the new owners painted the house in three soft colors, insisting that it "had always been white." The new owners, who now give tours and rent the restored house for special occasions, shared this black-and-white 1904 photograph with us. It shows the young Miss Asendorf on the porch with her family—and a home painted in at least three colors.

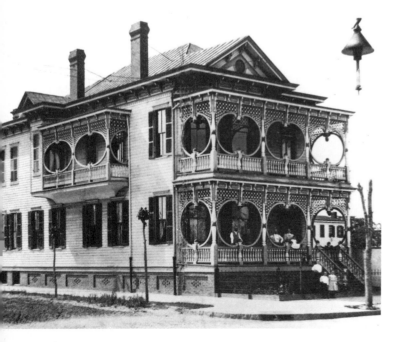

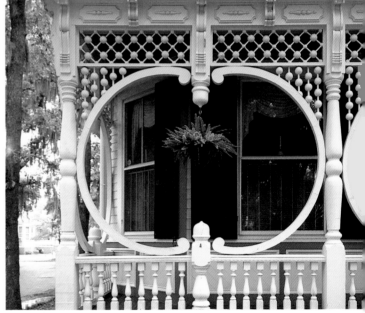

52

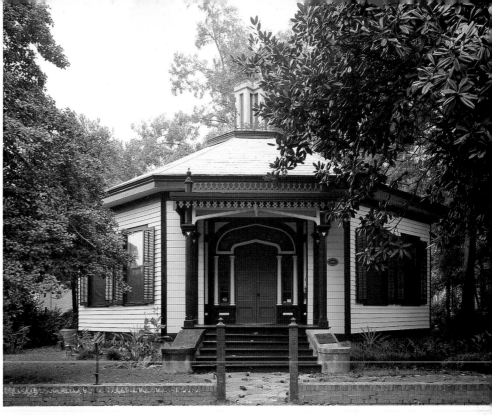

COLUMBUS

(Right, above). 527 First Avenue. Octagon. 1830/1863. The Folly, a National Historic Landmark, is the world's only double one-story octagon. In 1862, Leander May built an octagonal four-room addition around a simple frame structure, the Iverson house, around a central chimney. Instead of building "up," he built "out." He was following the philosophy and floor plans of Orson S. Fowler, author of *The Octagon House: A Home For All* (1854). The vivid green, bright yellow, and Chinese red are the original colors.

LOUISIANA

NEW ORLEANS

(Right). 2846 St. Charles Avenue. Eastlake. 1840/ 1878. Spotlights at night add a glow to the lavender, pink, white, and heliotrope on this splendid New Orleans home. The owner picked the colors to show up the detail of the house. Two non-threatening certified male ghosts live there as part of the family.

New Orleans has a tradition of updating the facades of houses to conform to current styles and we presume that this house was modernized again near the turn of the century. It's too bad the ghosts can't give us its history.

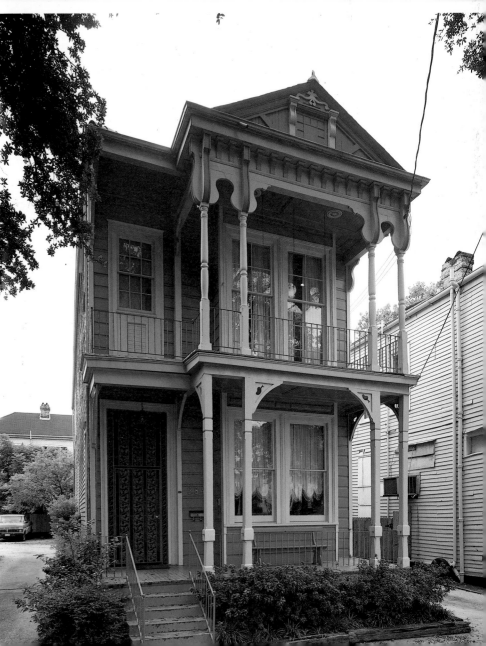

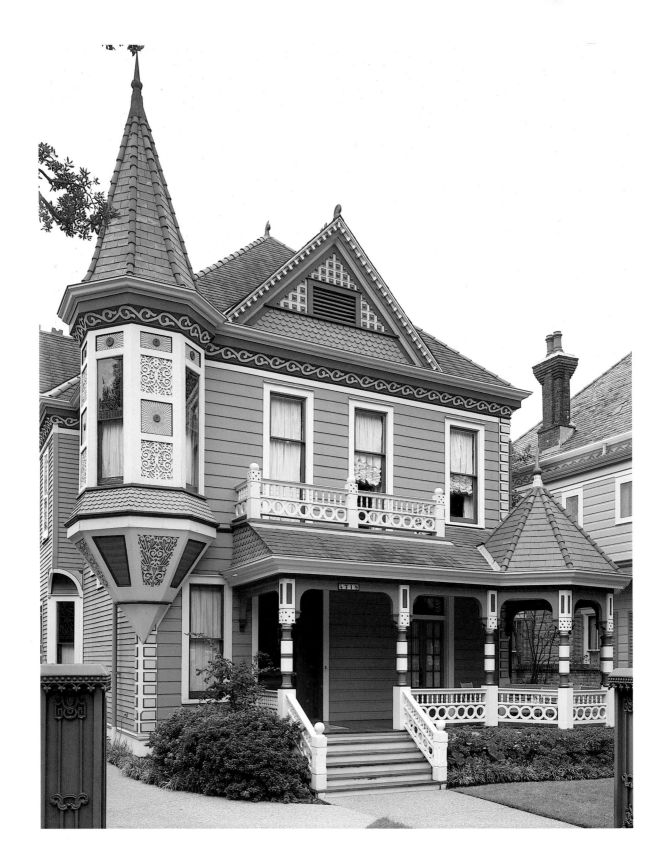

NEW ORLEANS

(Above). 5718 St. Charles Avenue. Queen Anne. 1889. The St. Charles Avenue Street Car makes special stops at this splendid home, and it was on the St. Charles Avenue Street Car's 100th Anniversary poster. The blue and cream color design was created by San Francisco colorist Bob Buckter. Note the unusual seven-sided bay window with its stunning panels of wooden lace.

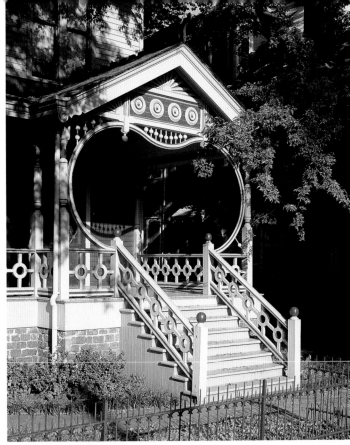

ARKANSAS

LITTLE ROCK

(Left). The Hanger House. 1010 Scott Street. Queen Anne cottage. This 1889 remodeling of an older structure is a sweetheart. Although there are only two colors, the work was done with such devotion to detail that we couldn't resist it.

LITTLE ROCK

(Below). The Ragland House. 1617 Center Street. Queen Anne. 1890. This turquoise, red, and tan combination picks up the colors in the stained-glass windows in the tower and radiates warmth. The house is one of many that have been restored to their original sparkle in the Quapaw Quarter of Little Rock, named after the Native Americans who used it as a meeting place.

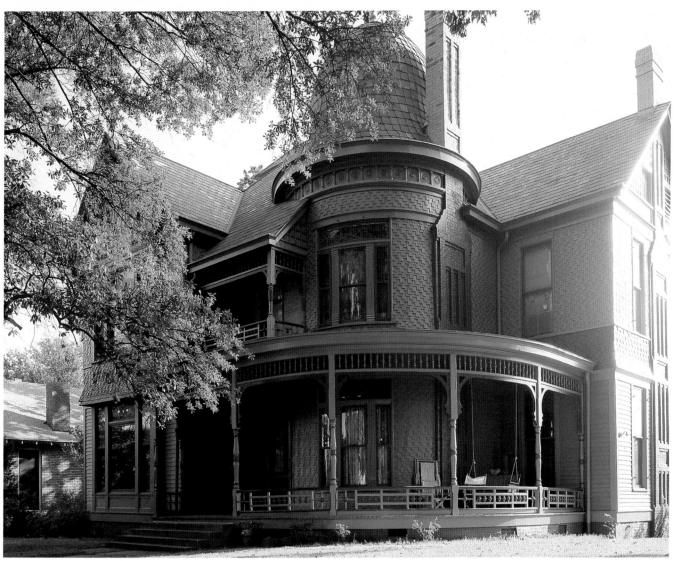

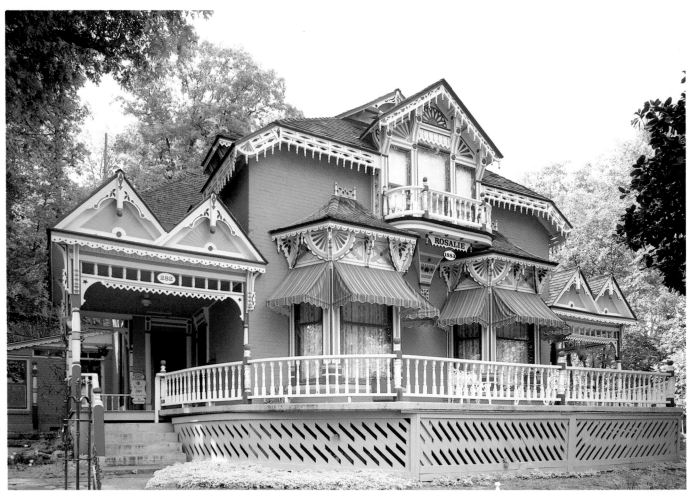

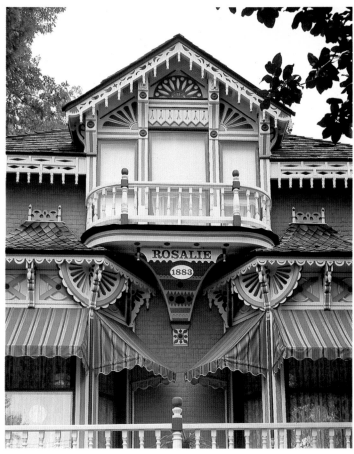

EUREKA SPRINGS

(Above and right). The Rosalie House. 282 Spring Street. This dreamboat steamboat gothic was built in 1883 by livery owner J. W. Hill shortly after the town was founded. The Rosalie House was intended to be "the best and the fanciest" in town. The free-wheeling luxuriance of decoration helps the building look larger than it is.

Bernice and Erwin Pereboom and their son Don restored what had become a white elephant in 1972, using colors found under many coats of white. Now a National Historic Register Site, The Rosalie House is one of the town's leading tourist attractions.

The healing powers of the local springs and the area's natural beauty drew tourists by the trainload until the Depression. Today, tourists are drawn to the artists, craftspeople, musicians, and a living museum of gingerbread houses and rustic turn-of-the-century hotels perched precariously on steep Ozark hillsides. Eureka Springs uses the slogan "Moving forward and reaching back" to describe their approach to progress, which combines historic restoration and good business.

THE MIDWEST

"It was altogether a prospect so variegated and romantic that a man may scarcely expect to enjoy such a one, but twice or thrice in the course of his life," wrote Zebulon Pike in 1805, after climbing one of the bluffs on the Mississippi near La Crosse, Wisconsin.

Today's travelers through the Midwest will compare their experience favorably with Pike's, whether it's that first glance across the Mississippi or the first look at the newly restored Hickory Street in St. Louis. Both natural and created beauties abound from the Smokies to the Rockies.

For the first settlers in the Midwest, the nineteenth century was their colonial period. They, too, left the familiar for a brave new world, but they brought with them the Industrial Revolution, and the Victorian arts to delight in. Rich, rolling farm country where the corn is as high as Lucy's eye and that spirit of seeking out the new are still in evidence from Ohio to Nebraska.

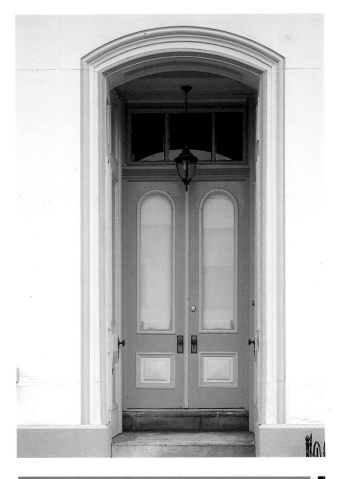

Joe Adamo, the color laureate of "The Gateway to the West," left San Francisco's competitive arena for St. Louis in the late 1970s. Here he found a city on the verge of interest in restoration.

The spectacular $135 million restoration of the Union Street Station, a National Historic Landmark well worth the trip, was just about to get underway. New buyers were purchasing row houses in the Lafayette Square area (some of them Vacant, Open, and Vandalized) for $10,000 and restoring them.

When Adamo started his first house on Whittimore Street, cars lined up to see it. Since then, he's led the Lafayette Square Restoration Committee in fixing up the town. His creativity has turned Hickory Street into one of the loveliest streets in the country.

In working on a house, Adamo explains that he can be an artist, chemist, carpenter, mason, tinworker, and painter. He envisions a house as a canvas and offers follow-up preventive maintenance. "I like to accent every detail on a house. A carpenter didn't hand-carve an intricate rose so that it would be lost in a solid coat of paint." Adamo asks his customers whether they want colors that are busy and exciting or muted and calm. Craftsmanship and authenticity are his main concerns. When his work was lauded in the Sunday paper, Adamo responded with a poem:

> "People here are putting a lot of trust in me
> for a person they don't know.
> I'm being handed a city that needs its charm awakened
> again after a long sleep.
> If I'm to be the prince, then I'll gladly kiss St. Louis
> on the lips and stand back and watch her open
> her eyes to look at the beautiful *Lady* she is."

Because of his artistry and perseverance, Adamo has had a greater effect on his city than any other colorist has had on any other city. Here are our Adamo favorites.

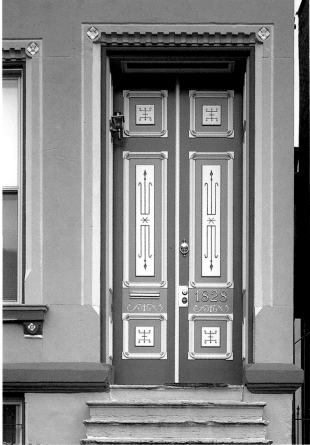

MISSOURI

ST. LOUIS

(Left, above). 1219 Mississippi. Italianate. 1870. The owners put together a combination of such bright blues and pinks that their neighbors call this The Care Bear House. In sunlight, it's dazzling.

ST. LOUIS

(Left, below). 1828 Hickory Street. Second Empire/French Mansard. 1871. Adamo's carpenter made fold-in exterior doors to match the interior ones. In St. Louis, double doors are necessary in winter. With Joe's lovely colors, they're works of art in themselves.

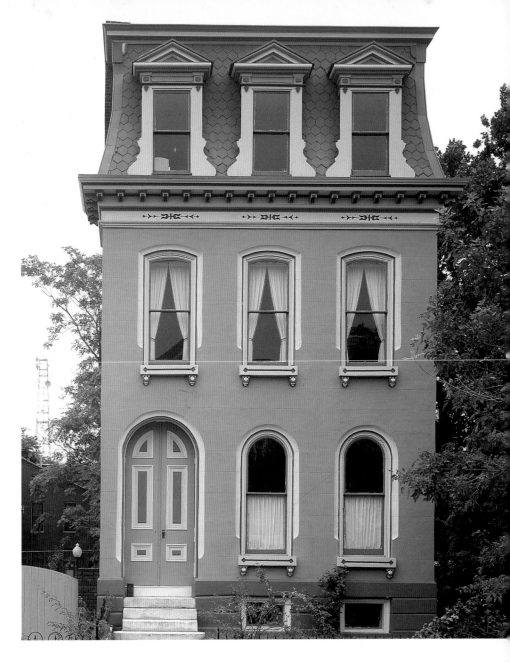

ST. LOUIS

(Right, above). 1901 Hickory Street. Second Empire/French Mansard. 1875. The tracery framing the windows in three-dimensional concrete was highlighted by paint. Three cheers for red, white, and blue, especially when it is balanced with such elegant precision.

ST. LOUIS

(Right, below). 2006 Lafayette. Second Empire/French Mansard. 1878. Adamo and his crew were on the scaffold painting while the leaves in the park across the street changed colors in their autumnal dance. Inspired by nature, Joe's planned colors changed to autumn golds and greens. Now the neighbors call this "The Autumn House."

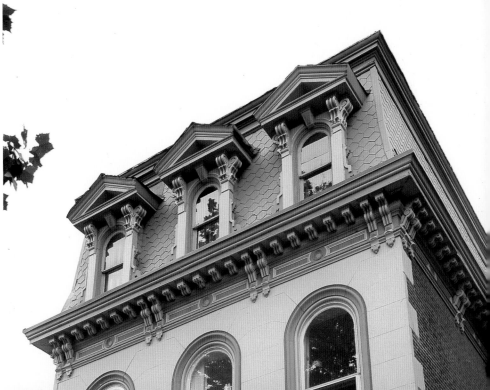

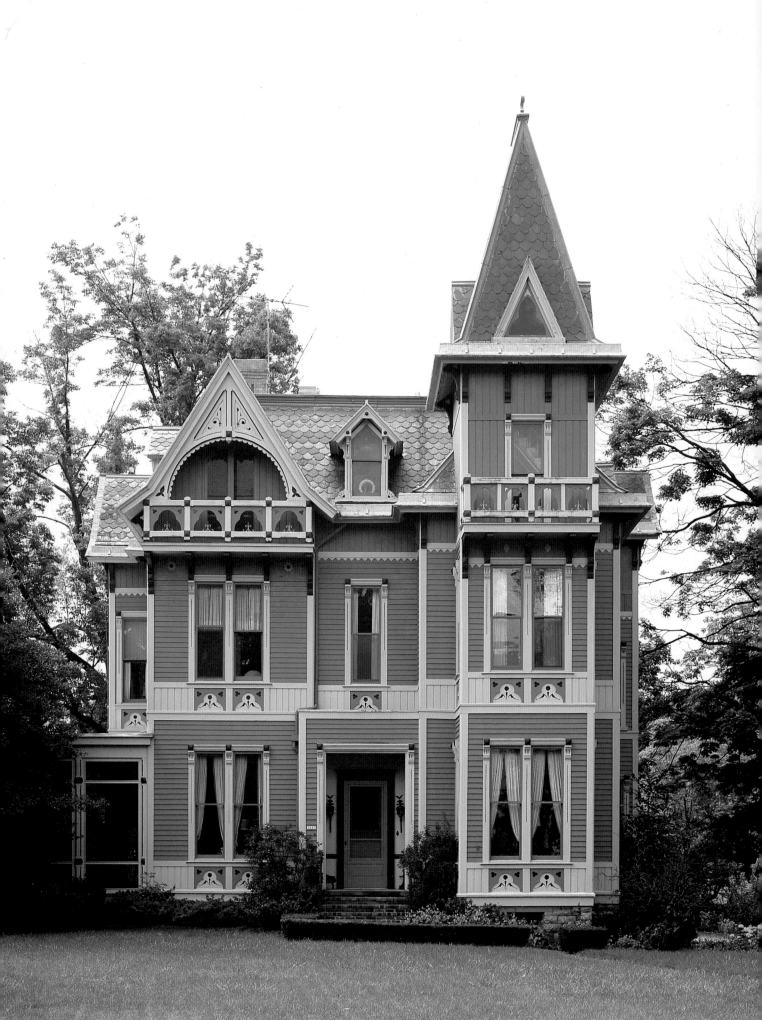

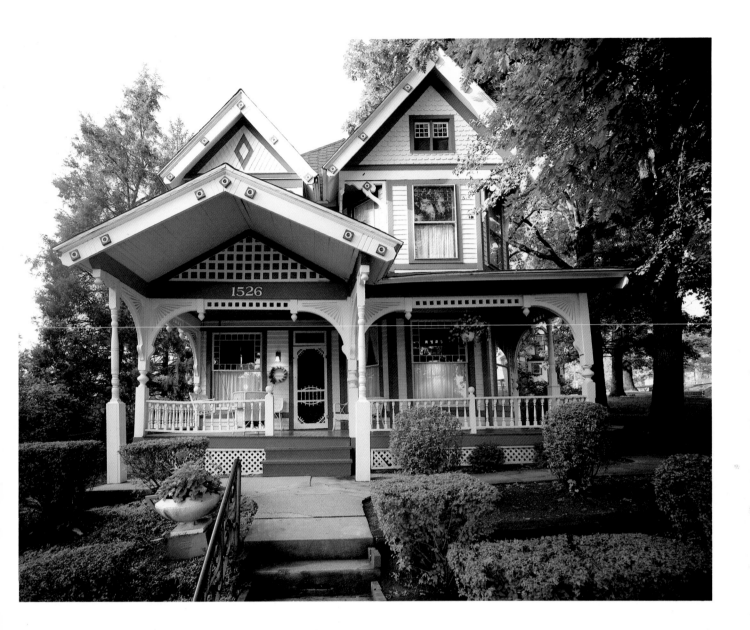

OHIO

CINCINNATI
(Opposite). 3023 Observatory Avenue. Gothic Revival. 1888.
Salmon-pink trim and gingerbread really enliven the grays and teal
blues that complement the shingled roof of this majestic house.

INDIANA

LAFAYETTE
(Above). 1526 Cason Street. Stick/Gothic. 1893. Inspired by the
Bicentennial, the designer-owner of this colorful home painted it in
patriotic red, white, and blue.

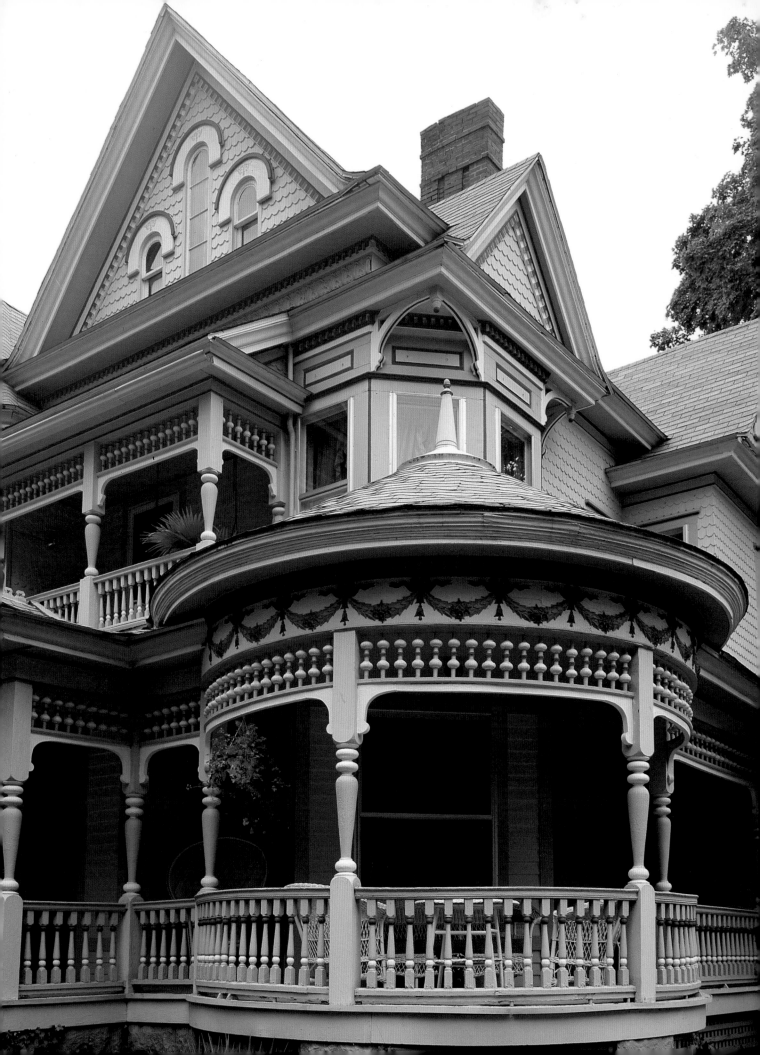

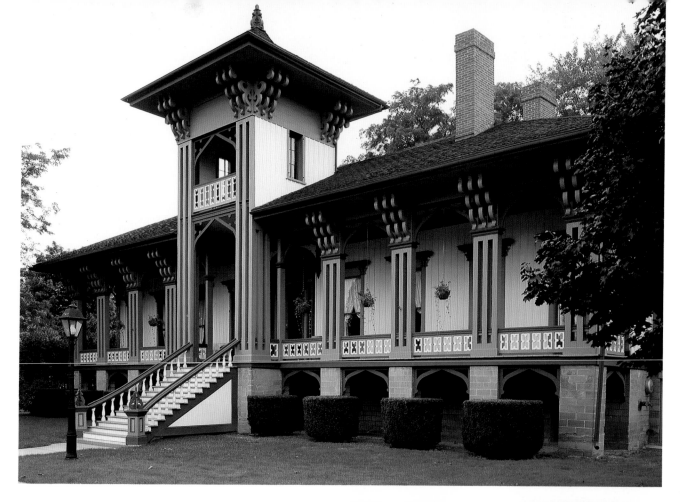

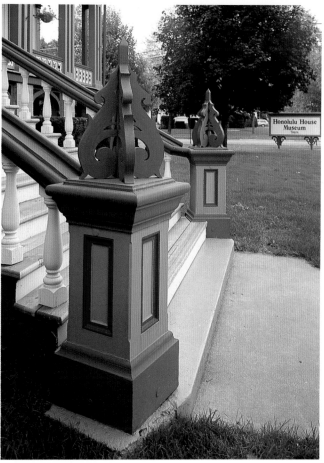

SALEM

(Opposite). 505 North Main Street. Queen Anne. 1898. Legend has it that one of Mattie Gladden's amours, P. T. Barnum, helped finance this house, which was opened as a "house of the evening" and then shut by public pressure. The owner, Chris Bundy, who teaches theater and has a background in set design, used five authentic colors to bring this statuesque beauty to life. The house was white until the owner got a copy of *Painted Ladies* as a Christmas present. When three painters refused even to offer bids, he painted the place himself—including the 350 three-color spindles. Neighbors have responded so positively that he has created sixteen other color designs in Salem because he enjoys doing it.

MICHIGAN

MARSHALL

(Above and right). Honolulu House Museum. Fountain Circle, 107 Kalamazoo Avenue. Eclectic. 1860. This astonishing National Historic Landmark was built by Abner Pratt, who wanted to remember his palmy days in Honolulu as consul to the Sandwich Islands. Tropical and Victorian elements such as the wide, graceful verandah with ornamental railing, decorative pineapple finials and the distinctive pagoda-shaped tower have been combined harmoniously. The interior has been carefully restored.

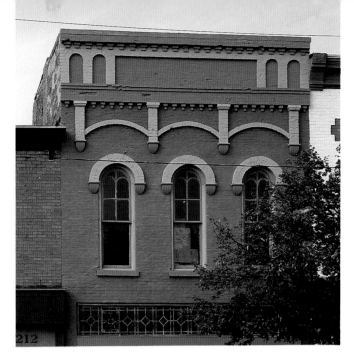

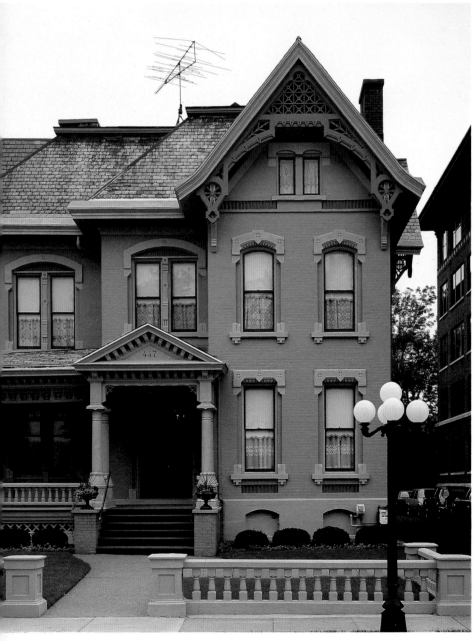

MARSHALL

(Left, above). 210 West Michigan. Italianate. 1864. You can't miss this vivid combination of teal and clay pinks on the main street. Marshall is a railroad town with the same population it had after the Civil War. It was supposed to become the state capital, and wealthy businessmen from New York moved in and built mansions. But when Lansing was named the capital instead, the businessmen left their mansions to their fates until the 1980s spirit of restoration prevailed.

KALAMAZOO

(Left, below). Kalamazoo House. 447 West South Street. Queen Anne. 1878. Preservationists Lou and Annette Conte restored this impressive home built for cigarmaker David Lilienfield and until recently a funeral home, and have given it a new life as a luxurious hotel.

Annette chose Florentine colors to accent this building with its Italianate influences and Lou used authentic sand paint for texture on the painted brick stucco which was originally meant to look like stone. The lilac bargeboards crown the building like a diadem.

The interior is glamorously authentic and colorful. And if a Victorian bathroom ever had a hot tub, we're sure it would look just like the one in the Kalamazoo House.

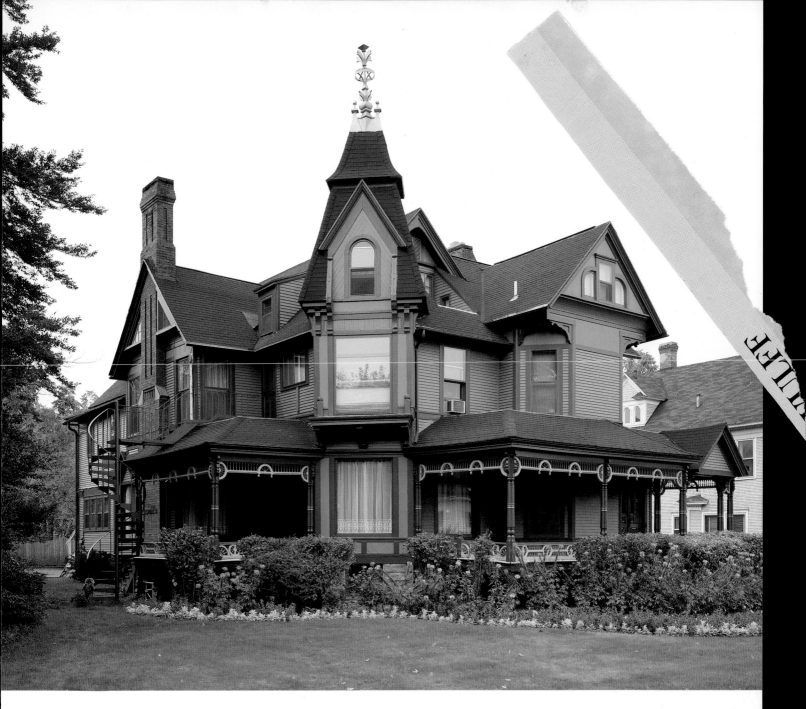

KALAMAZOO
(Above and right). 229 Stuart Street. Queen Anne. 1886. Built by
Edgar Bartlett, this classic Queen Anne has been named The
Bartlett-Henry-Upjohn house. In 1986, when Andrea Casteel
decided to do away with seventy years' worth of white paint, she
used three teals and a dark red to capture the original colors. The
gold-tipped cast-iron finial is also original.

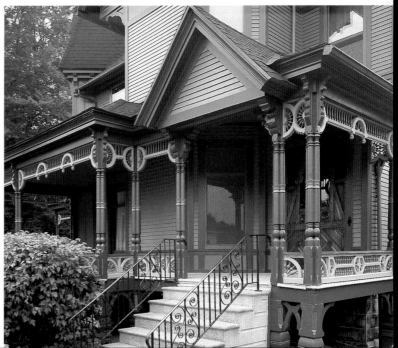

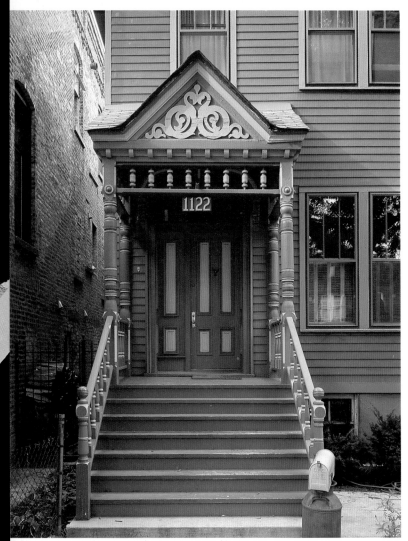

ILLINOIS

CHICAGO

(Left). 1122 West Webster Street. Stick/Eastlake. 1886. In 1982, architect Richard Monastra was inspired by an exhibition of glass by Louis Comfort Tiffany and chose a striking palette for this colorful home. The contrast of the barn red trimmed in green, brown, red, blue, gold, and peach, reminiscent of San Francisco's Hippie House in *Painted Ladies*, sharpens on a bright day.

While Doug Keister was taking this photograph, a man walked up with a young child and said "My daughter has a present for you." The little girl handed him a drawing of daisies.

CHICAGO

(Below, left and right). 921 Wrightwood. Stick/Eastlake. 1883. Asbestos shingles had hidden the three sunbursts and remarkable balusters until the owner went to San Francisco, saw the Painted Ladies, and said "I want one." Story-book colors now brighten this tree-shaded house in the windy city.

OAK PARK

(Opposite). 344 North Kenilworth. Queen Anne/Stick. 1885. The Rudolph Johns House was built according to a formula often repeated in Oak Park in the 1880s: entrance to one side with an octagonal tower behind, a combination of gable and hipped roofs, and a wide front porch. The owner chose a strong, vivid palette to create this authentic-looking home.

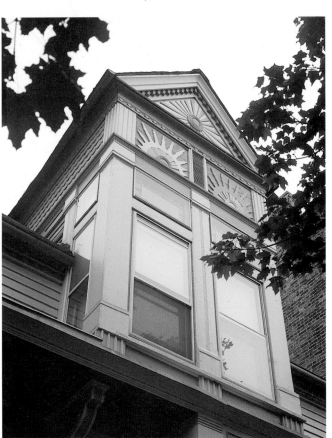

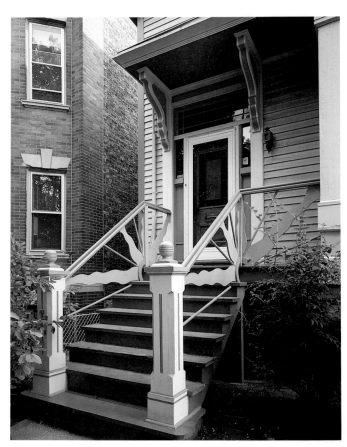

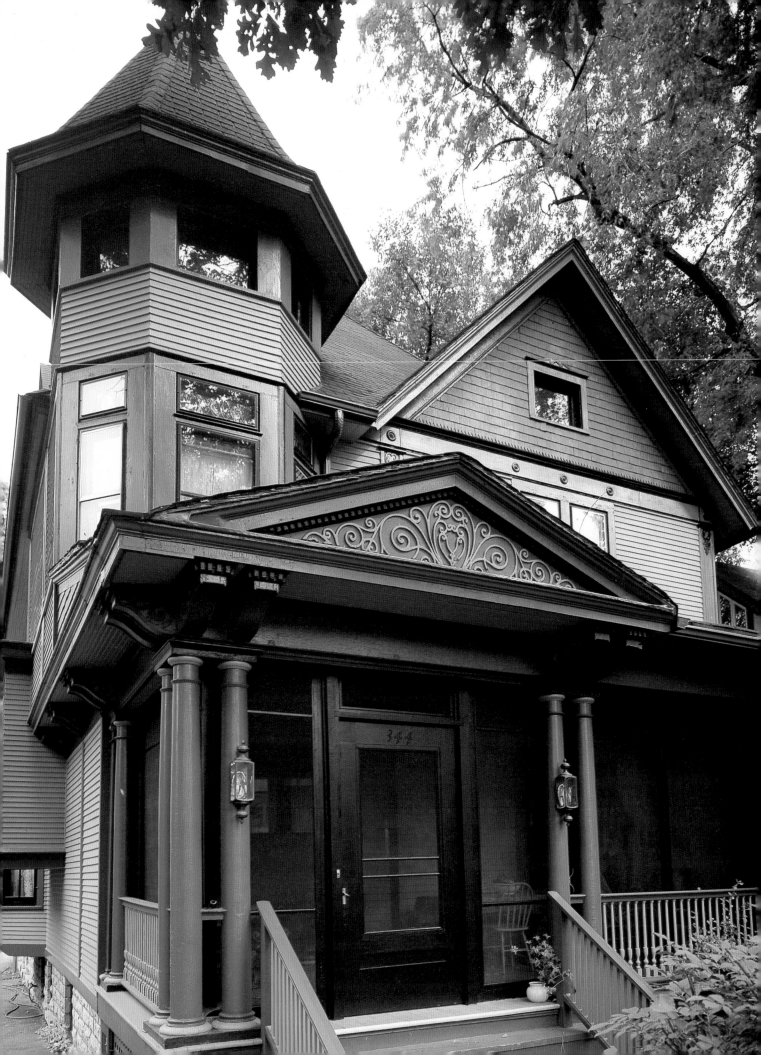

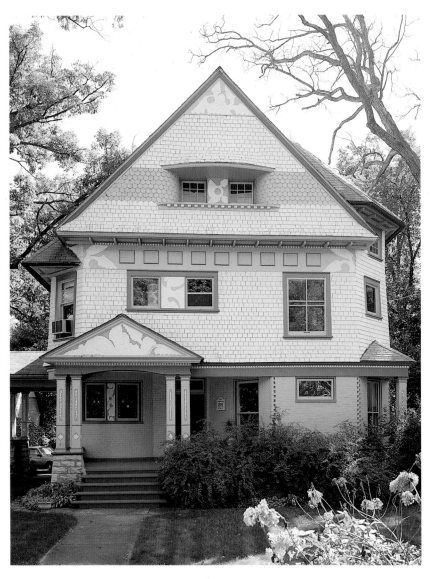

GLEN ELLYN

(Left and below left and right). 679 Main Street. Queen Anne/Shingle. 1891. Philo K. Stacy built this house but lived across the street. In 1985, James Jereb, inspired by the stained-glass windows, designed and painted what had been a boring red and yellow using seven colors—grays, mauve, and burgundy.

The fascinating floral carvings on the pillars, sides, and front of the house are unique. Each of the columns has a different flower—daffodils, irises, sunflowers—carved and highlighted with paint. The owners hadn't noticed them before they were painted.

Jereb explains, "I'm an artist whose medium is Victorian homes. I conceptualize my houses as blank canvases—white with primer like a gesso canvas. The house or facade is my canvas. My brushes are larger, the cans of paint bigger, but the conceptual approach is the same as any artist. These details and ornaments were meant to be seen. A craftsman didn't spend hours carving an oak column just so it could be painted white." Like other artists, Jereb signs his creations, the only color designer in the country to do so.

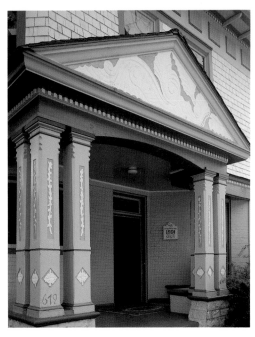

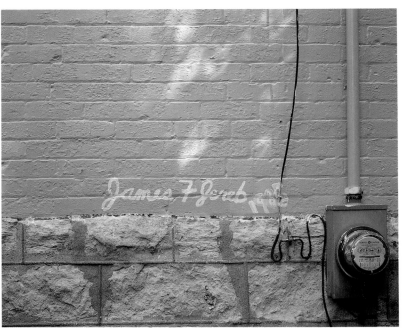

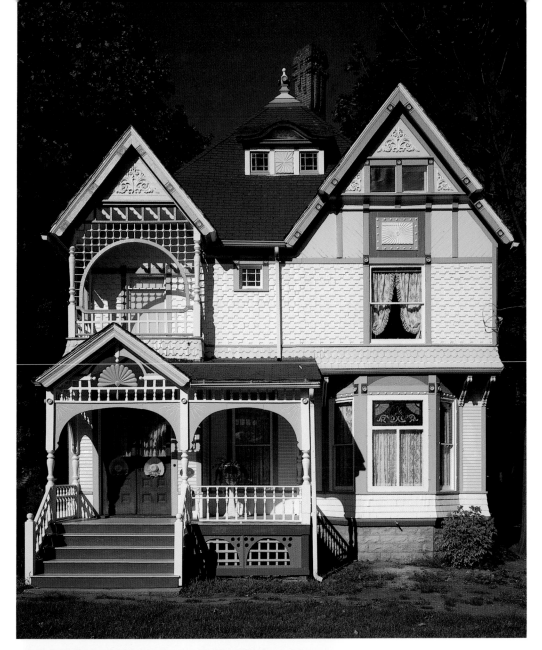

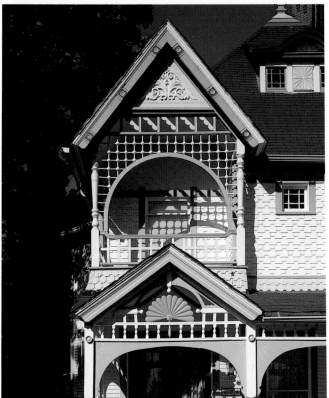

WHEATON

(Above and left). 404 Main Street. Queen Anne/Eastlake. 1890. This spacious, stunning house, which is now on the National Register of Historic Places, boasts a wealth of gingerbread, cedar shingles, scallops, fish scales, and gables. The dominant motifs of the Victorian period, the sunburst and the sunflower, are in evidence in both the exterior and interior of the house, and the fan which gives the house its name, The Fan House, is repeated inside on a staircase carving and in the jeweled windows. Because the color scheme reminded Jereb of a Savannah gentleman's shirt, he chose peach-apricot, kelly green, sage, grays, and white. The nine colors include purple-lilac for the carved fans.

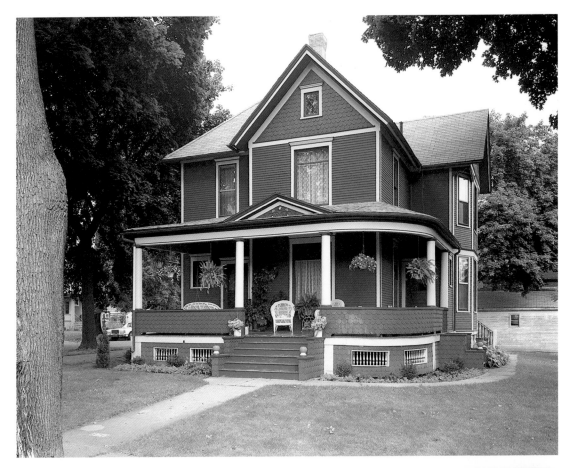

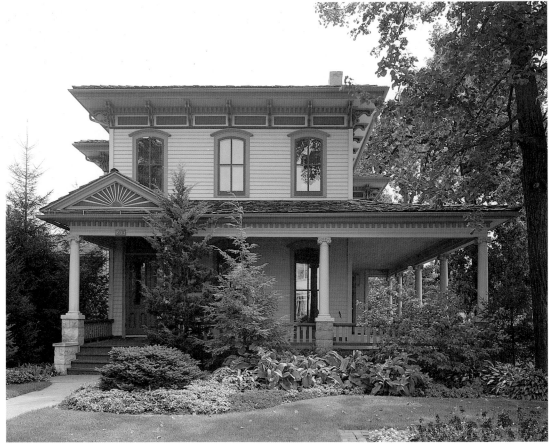

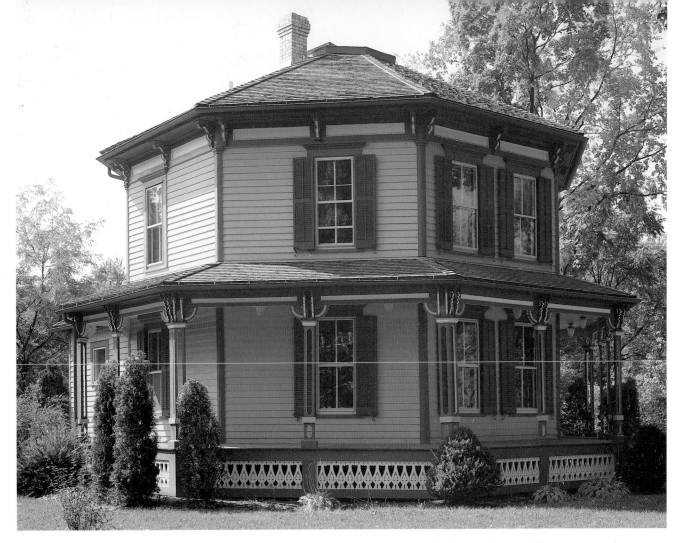

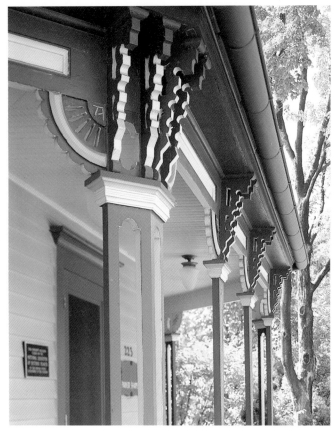

ELGIN

(Opposite, above). 870 Mill Street. Colonial Revival/Queen Anne. 1900. Maurey Garvey even painted the fireplug in front to match this corner house. The cream trim is like thread tying together the burgundy and dark green sections of this simple, comfortable home.

Elgin, an agricultural center, once set the nationwide price of butter. Today it is a thriving, self-reliant town concerned about preservation.

ROCKFORD

(Opposite, below). 803 North Church Street. Italianate. 1870s. Gold, orange, brick red, and brown highlight the cornice brackets and dentils in this handsome renovated office building.

Rockford is the home of the celebrated Tinker Cottage, a Swiss chalet that is filled with Victorian treasures and preserved exactly as it was, complete with greenhouse, when businessman and inventor Robert Tinker lived there.

BARRINGTON

(Above and right). 223 West Main Street. Octagon. 1878. This meticulously painted eight-faceted gem is highlighted by the flutings and bracket crests on the columns. This carefully restored building is listed on the National Register.

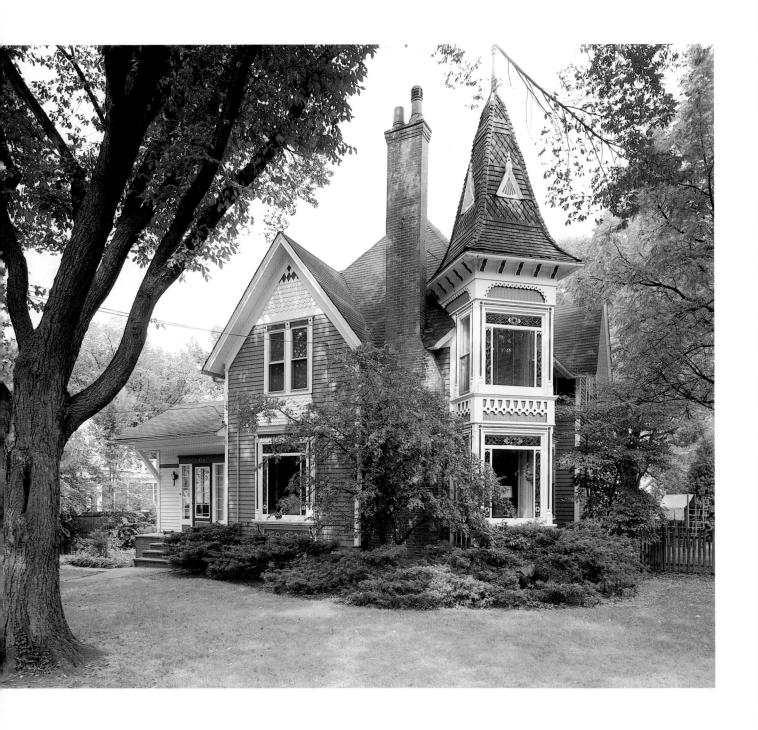

WISCONSIN

MILWAUKEE

(Opposite). 2623 Wahl. Queen Anne/German Victorian. 1904. The delicious gingerbread on the porch and "consumption porch" of this blue and red brick building were given a lacy peach, cream, and blue luster by Landmark Painting. Although Milwaukee was called "the cream city" because of its cream-colored building bricks, this is a splendid example of the homes constructed at the turn of the century. Consumption porches were built so tubercular family members could remain at home but spend most of their time in the invigorating fresh air.

BARRINGTON

(Above). 216 West Street. Queen Anne. 1891. The owners of this red, white, and blue home, painted during the Bicentennial, were looking for new ideas when we met. The three Queen Annes on this street were all built by a Mr. Halvey for his daughters. The house next door, seen through the trees, once pea green, red, and gold, had recently been painted a soft dainty yellow, trimmed in white and blue—and the neighbors were aghast.

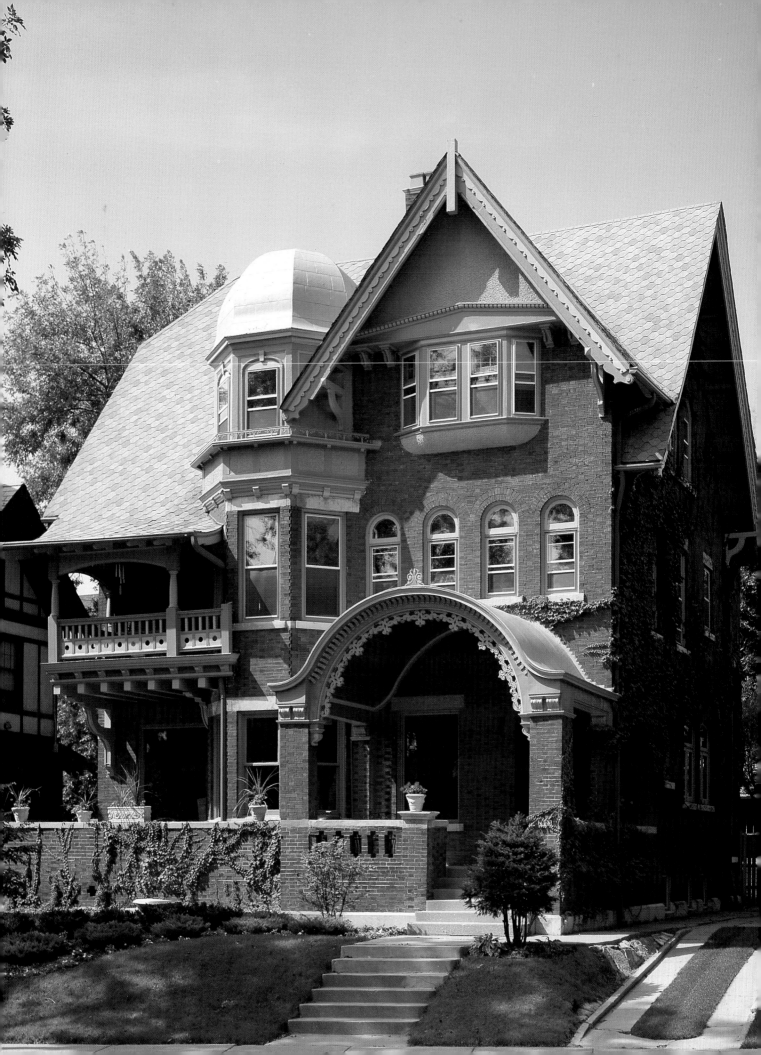

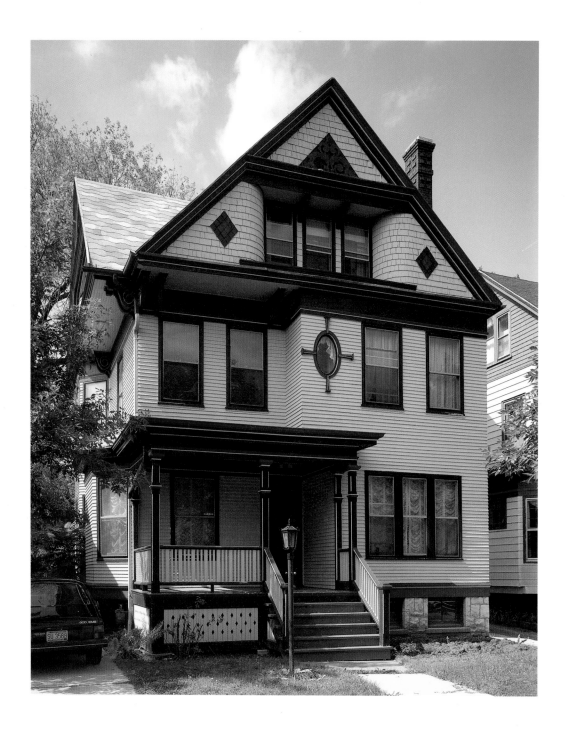

MILWAUKEE

(Above). 2909 North Hackett. Stick/Colonial Revival. 1900. John Lough of Heritage Painting revitalized this house in three greens and a burgundy. He used luminescent paint for his "signature" pin-stripes on the gable.

To encourage homeowners, Lough sometimes adds a third color at no charge. Another Milwaukeean chose a pink and rose combination because "It looks like one of those San Francisco houses. It's a welcoming sight in winter."

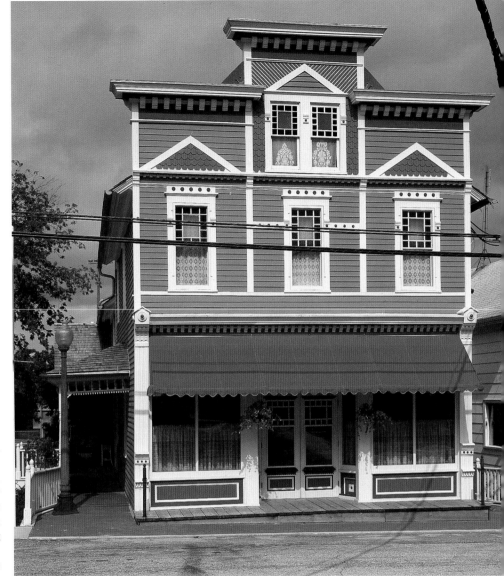

NEWBURG

(Right, above). The Painted Lady. 518 Main Street. Italianate/Stick/Queen Anne cottage. 1875. Charles Mayhew III, whose ancestor sold the island of Nantucket for thirty pieces of silver and two beaver hats, saved Max Weinhard's Saloon from the wrecking ball after he tried in vain to save the house across the street from being burned down for fire practice.

Lauded as one of the best unspoiled examples of its kind in Wisconsin, the building has always been a tavern. Now it's a successful restaurant, enhanced by the restoration of the etched and stained glass in the windows, the shiny bar, and the unusual interior molding.

Mayhew, who has worked with the Conservancy of Natural Resources, practices preservation with "adaptive reuse," of which The Painted Lady is a stellar example. He admits that like most Newburg oldtimers, he was not aware of the building's beauty, which was shrouded under paint that masked its lively facade.

BARABOO

(Right, below). The House of Seven Gables. 215 6th Street. Carpenter Gothic. 1860. A. J. Downing would be very pleased to see that the owners of this immaculately restored home (with two B & B rooms complete with Gothic Revival furnishings) have followed his recommendations. The peach, salmon, and burgundy paint light up the tasty gingerbread in a romantic way.

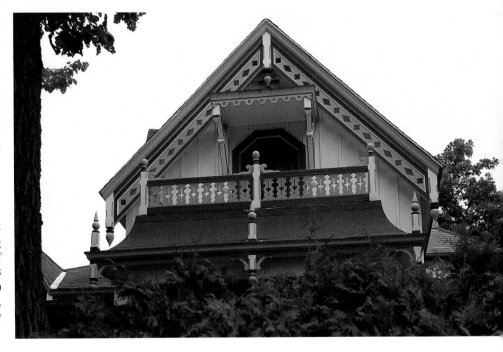

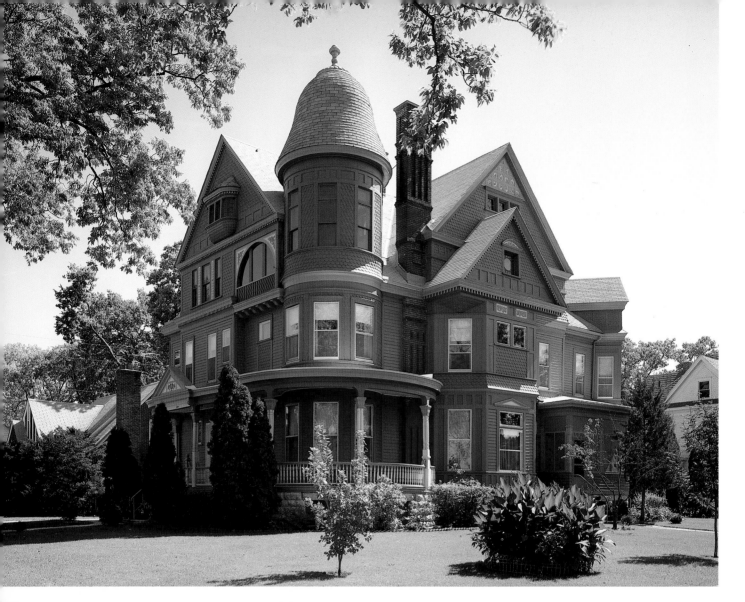

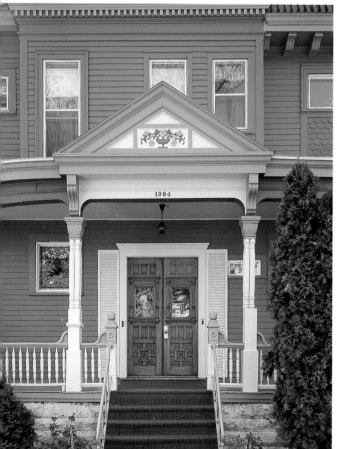

LA CROSSE

(Above and left). 1304 Main Street. Queen Anne. 1886. The owner of this superb beauty, who also owns a bridal shop, chose Victorian wedding colors to celebrate the house's one hundredth anniversary and her own fiftieth wedding anniversary.

Blessed with the scenic grandeur of the Mississippi River on the west and towering bluffs to the east, La Crosse has preserved much of its rich river history.

LA CROSSE

(Opposite above and below). 1803 Charles. Queen Anne. 1890. Loreen Henry Carter, granddaughter of Patrick Henry, wanted a doll house and got it from her new husband, A. C. Carter, a patent-medicine man. Days of Grandeur, a husband and wife restoration team from Madison, who saved the building from razing, were still at work when we found this Southern belle, painted in its original colors. New gingerbread to match that found in an old photograph of the house was being made to order. Last on the agenda was the replacement of the entrance-porch columns, which had been modernized in 1903, to match those on the second story. This faithful restoration was one of the most delightful surprises on our journey.

76

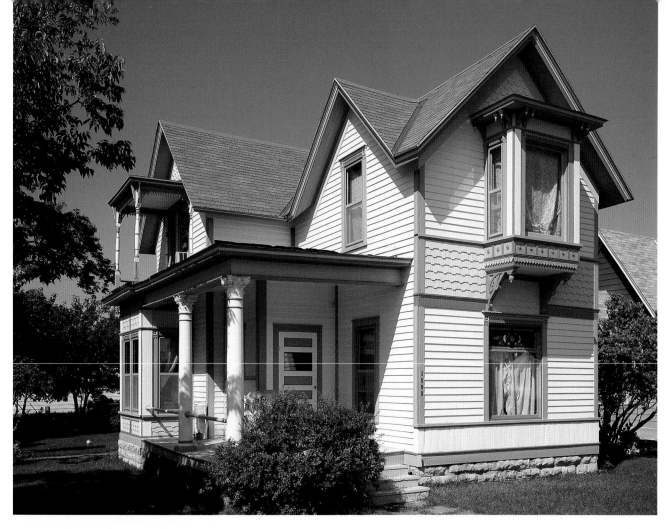

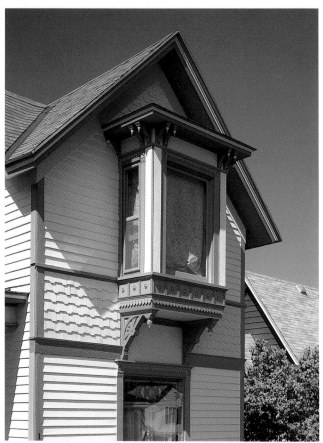

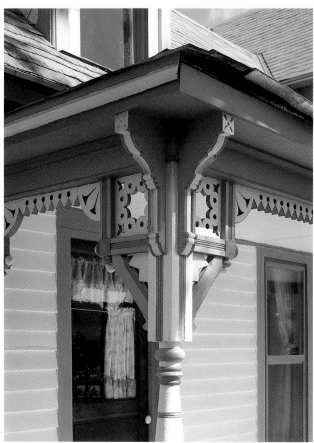

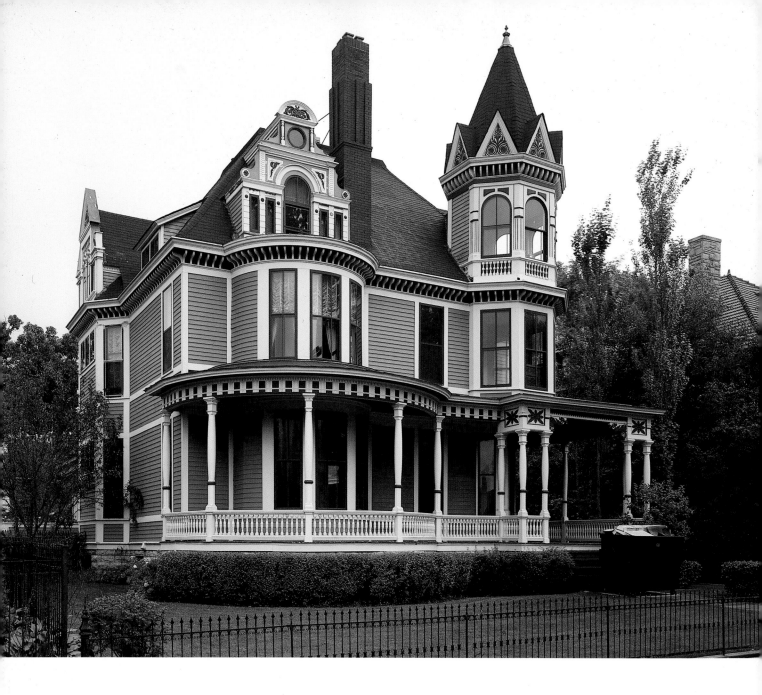

MINNEAPOLIS

(Opposite). 2001 Kenwood Parkway. Queen Anne. 1880s. Neil Hiedeman's painting of The Ridge House reflects the owner's desire for dignified anonymity, although it's on the same block as the Mary Tyler Moore house seen on the popular Mary Tyler Moore TV series. Painted in six different shades and sheens of burgundy, with gold-leaf accents, it gleams in the winter snow. And in any weather, the house looks like a marvelous *grande dame* in her rustling taffetas.

Hiedeman respected the owner's wishes and did not include his patterned shingle "signature." Dubbed by the media the fairy godfather to St. Paul's Cinderella houses, Hiedeman replaces asbestos with spindlework. He feels "It's neat to take something that somebody else wanted to just throw away and make something of it."

MINNESOTA

ST. PAUL

(Above). 507 Summit. Queen Anne. 1890. Empty when we found it, this imposing building is in a transition period, as are the Twin Cities.

The Mississippi River starts here. St. Paul is on the east side, Minneapolis is on the west. Over the years, Minneapolis has been the progressive twin, tearing down the old for the new. St. Paul was not as commercial, so more of its Victorians have survived.

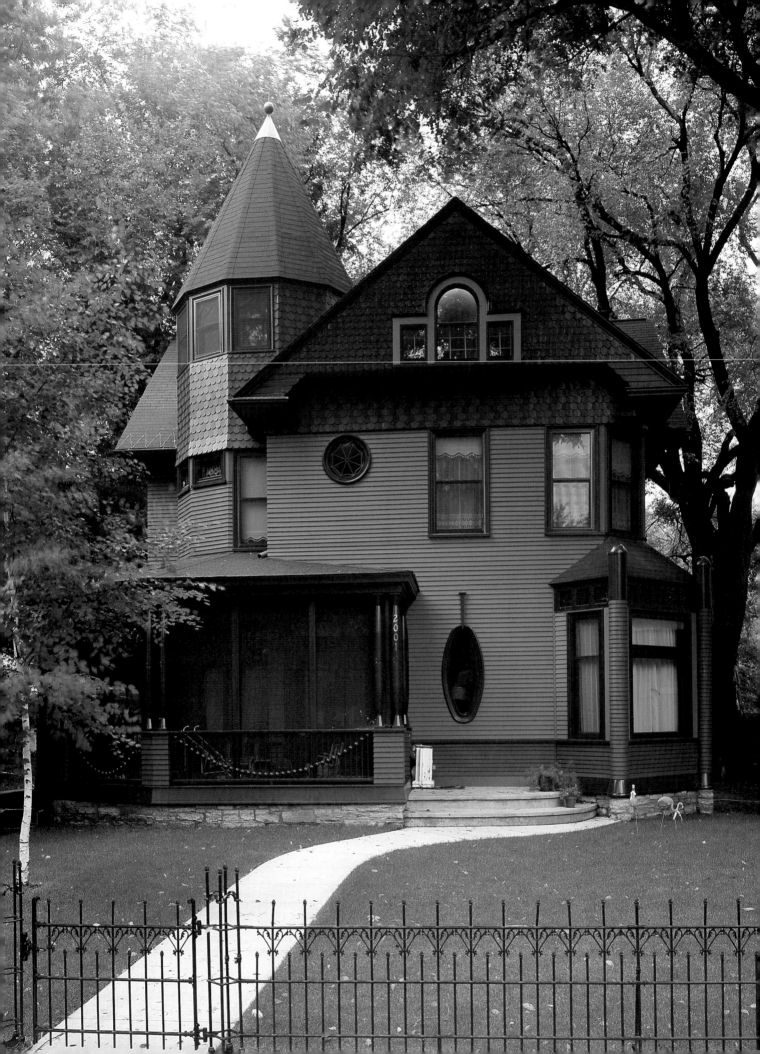

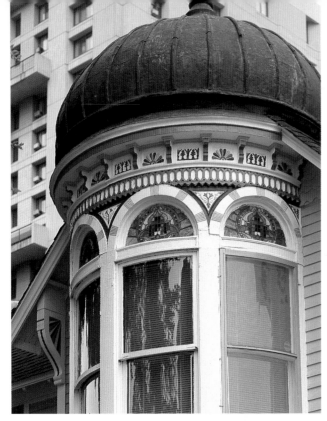

MINNEAPOLIS

(Left). 2500 Portland. Queen Anne. 1882. After this was moved from a block being redeveloped, Classic Painters used the pink, raspberry, grape, and white in the stained-glass windows to embellish the fantasy in the Turkish turrets.

MINNEAPOLIS

(Below). 2616 Colfax. Queen Anne. 1888. The owners tried a test strip two feet wide up the back of the house before painting in three grays, burgundy, and gold leaf with bronze powder. They also stenciled the screen door for another period touch.

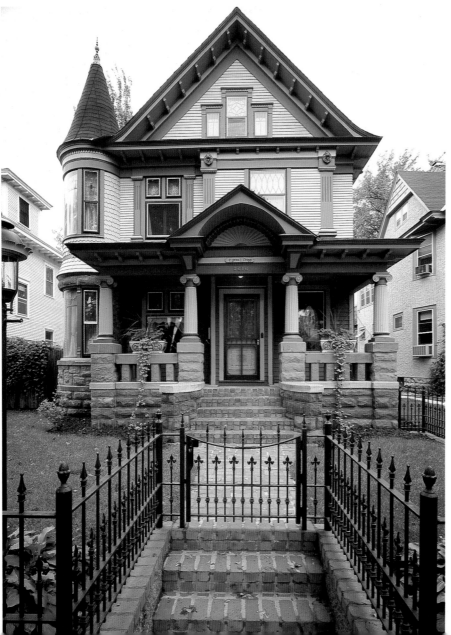

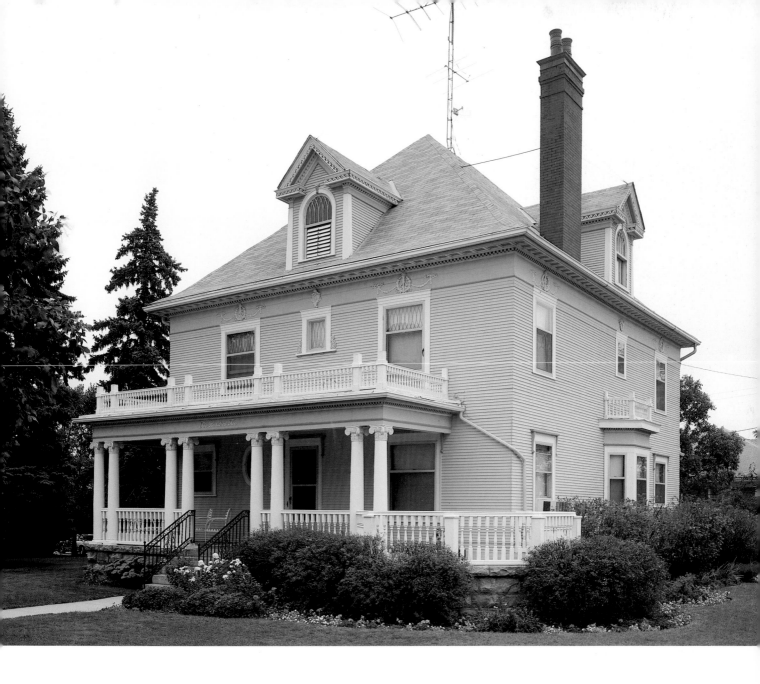

SOUTH DAKOTA
SIOUX FALLS

(Above). 202 North Duluth. Neo-French Colonial. 1904. Built by Will Hollister, President of the State Banking & Trust Co., this house was a sad gray and black when Bill Novetzke decided to rehabilitate it in 1982. He felt that the South Dakota winters were long and depressingly gray and wanted to "dress up this corner," so he handed Jim Cambronne a copy of *Painted Ladies* as a guide with which to develop a new color scheme. Bright yellow, blue, cream, and peach "stood the town on its ear," but proved to be a definite boon on a dull day and a bright delight in sunlight, and the neighbors grew to love it. The antiques-filled house is now on the National Register.

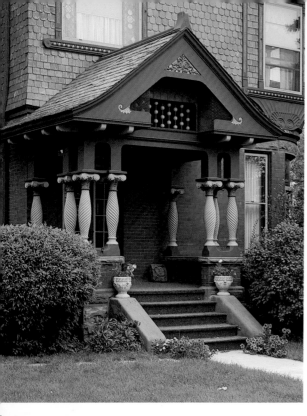

SIOUX FALLS

(Left). 103 South Duluth. 1888. Queen Anne. The C. C. Carpenter home was built by Artemas Gale according to plans drawn by architect W. L. Dow. Charles Carpenter, treasurer of the Sioux Falls Stockyards, died while in New York buying furniture. His widow, Frances, lived here until her death in 1925. Although the use of color was limited because of the slate siding, the swirled columns and portico are stylishly highlighted in red, green, cream, and chocolate.

IOWA

RED OAK

(Below). 711 Coolbaugh. Queen Anne. 1893. A man who worked for the Chicago, Burlington, and Quincy Railroad built this house and painted it to match the CB&Q depots. The original yellow-gold with olive trim, burgundy accents, and teal-painted roof shingles had faded, but were brilliantly repainted in 1985.

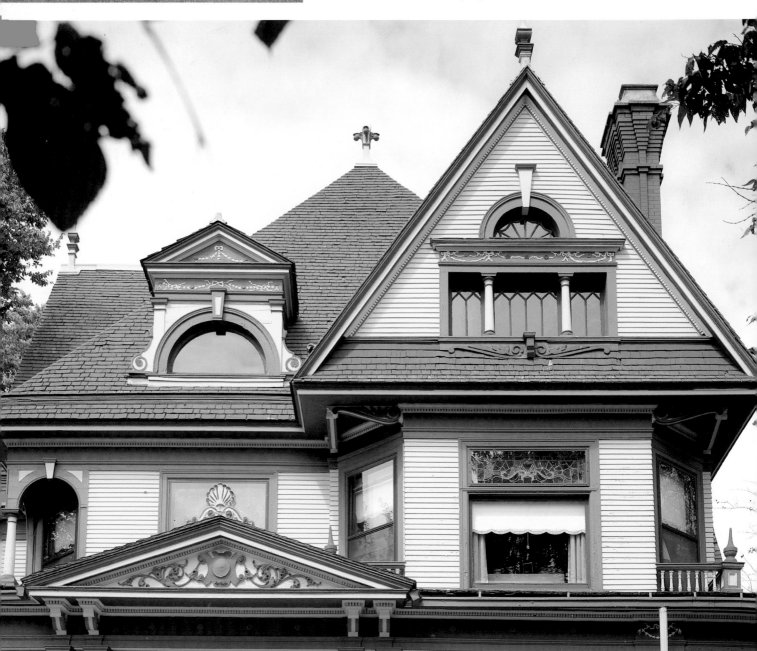

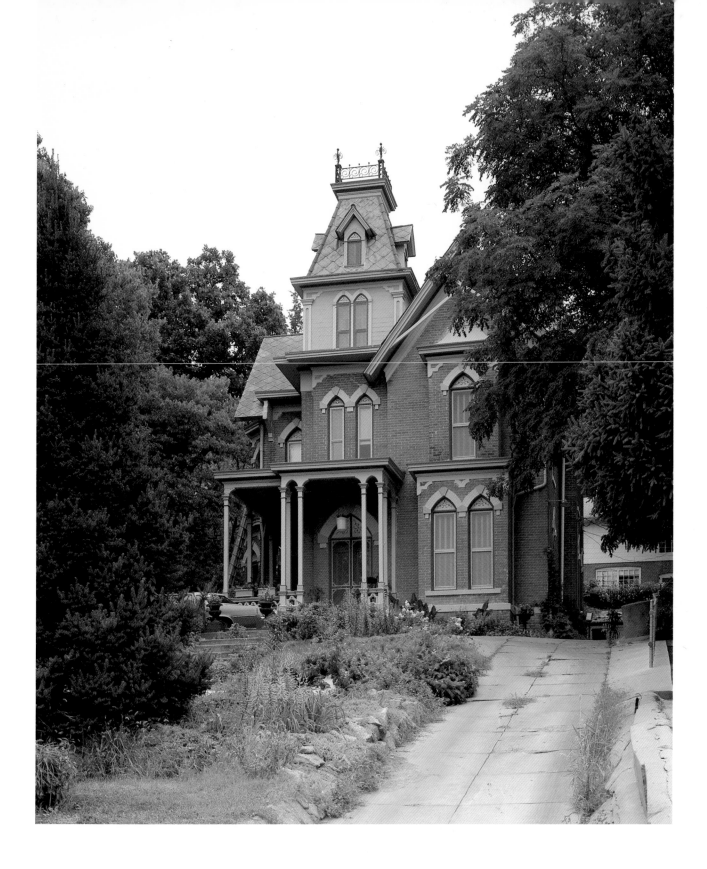

COUNCIL BLUFFS

(Above). 125 Park. Second Empire. 1877. Matching the light and dark areas in a photograph of the original home, owner Bob Pashek chose three colors that are more compatible to the slate roof than the original yellow and brown. This stately stone and brick princess, built for Civil War Colonel Lysander Tulleys, seduces the eye with its sedate blend of rose-beige, pink, and wine.

Council Bluffs, where Lewis and Clark and the Indians had their powwow, or council, is Omaha's "twin"—the city across the river that did not go commercial and so retains more of its fine architectural heritage. However, tasteful restoration is bringing new life to Omaha's riverside warehouse district.

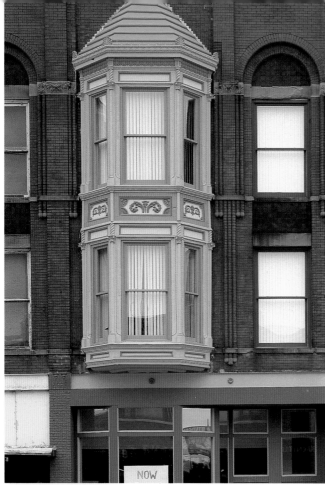

NEBRASKA
SOUTH OMAHA
(Left). 4831 South 24th Street. Italianate with Romanesque arches. 1880s. This brightly colored bay in gold, two shades of peach, turquoise, and magenta, lights up the block. It also satisfies historians because the colors are authentic.

LINCOLN
(Below). 700 North 16th Street. French Second Empire cottage. 1878. Built for Reverend M. Elisha Lewis, the Lewis Syford House, now part of the State Historic Society and listed on the National Register, is beautifully proportioned and sweetly painted in three greens, yellow, and two roses. The cast-iron cresting is authentic.

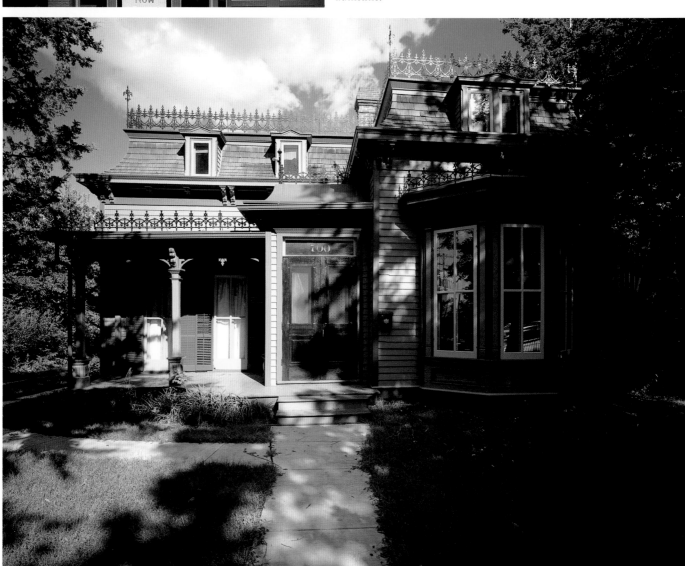

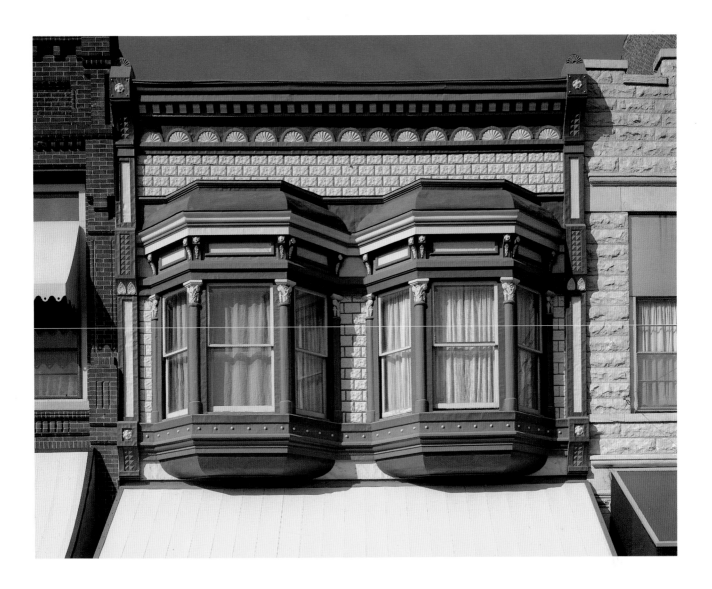

KANSAS

FORT SCOTT

(Above). 118 South Main. Italianate. 1884. Fort Scott, the "crack post of the Frontier," maintained the peace from the 1840s, when Osages and settlers lived peaceably within their own boundaries, to the 1870s, when railroads cut through the land.

Architect/builders David and Janet Irvin were inspired by San Francisco's Painted Ladies to add fresh cosmetics to the many buildings they were restoring in this historic town. This was originally a cooperative hardware store in what was called the Union Block.

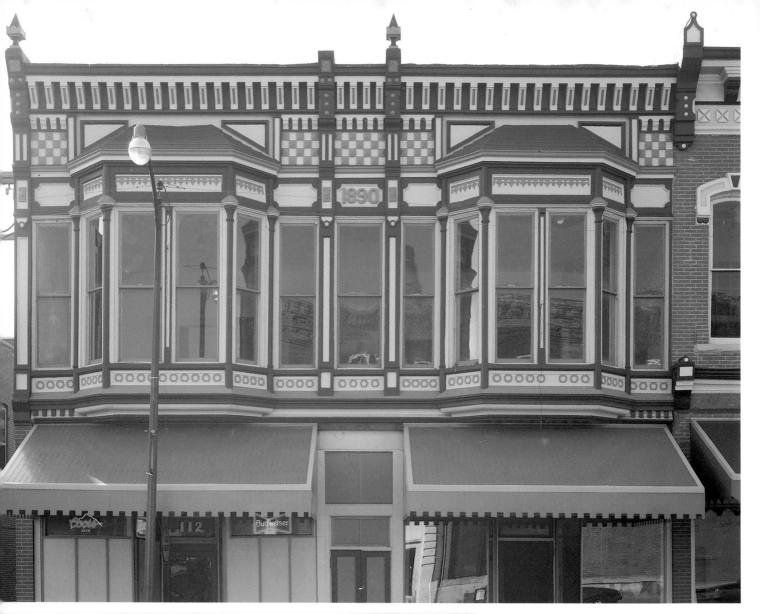

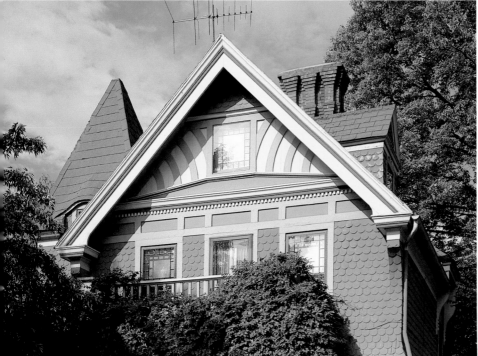

FORT SCOTT

(Above). 112 East Wall. Stick/Eastlake. Earth tones are used with dramatic impact in the checkerboard-pattern band of this 1890 restaurant, designed by David Irvin.

TOPEKA

(Left). 429 Greenwood. Queen Anne. 1886. Albrecht Marburg used a local contractor to build his home, notable for the stair tower and fluted chimney stacks. The proud owners used six colors to highlight the varied ornamentation.

THE SOUTHWEST

The Westerners we met were open to new ideas and new approaches. In Colorado, the colors on houses are sometimes brighter than anywhere in America, including San Francisco. Here colors are inspired by the individualists who thrive on the spectacular scenery and brilliant blue sky rather than by a Victorian palette. As many of the houses are vacation or second homes, the owners feel freer to experiment than they do at home.

Aspen has some of the brightest Painted Ladies in the country, following San Francisco's lead faster than any other town. In fact, the colors are now being toned down, rather than brightened up as elsewhere. The weekend we were there for the Aspen Writer's Conference, the mayor was marrying the owner of a local bookstore. A vivid rainbow had graced the gable of the bookstore until the week before—when it was painted a proper mayoral white. Paint has been important to Aspen ever since Walter and Elizabeth Paepke helped revive what was almost a ghost town in 1945, when they offered people free paint with which to renovate if the Paepkes could choose the colors. Now it's a bustling ski center, with a core population of 15,000 that balloons to 55,000 in winter.

Colorado's Victorians offer two regional small-scale variations on the Stick style: Miner's Stick and Mountain Stick.

It was encouraging to see Texans, especially those in Galveston, revitalizing their towns by preserving the past. Ghost-mining towns in Arizona and New Mexico are also coming to life through restoration.

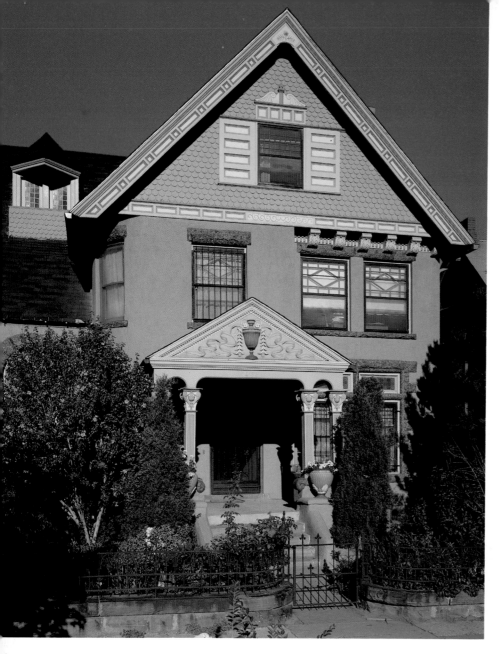

COLORADO

DENVER

(Left). 2105 Lafayette Street. Queen Anne/
Eclectic. 1890. William Lang, Denver's finest
eclectic architect, built this elegant mansion for
LaNeve Foster, one of Denver's few millionaires
to diversify before the Sherman Silver Act caused
the panic of 1893. Unfortunately, Lang's fortunes
fell with Denver's, although many of his creations
still stand. James Martin of The Color People
provided the five-color design and the owners also
asked the Denver Center Theater Company to
highlight Lang's signature—the gargoyles and
flower urns—and the porch ornamentation. The
colors and design of the gable over the entrance
make this a lovely work of art.

LEADVILLE

(Left, below). 131 West 5th. Miner's Stick. 1904.
Designer Dick Smith's color scheme for this
"tunnel house" accentuates the shingle pattern in
the gable. Some Coloradans call this a shotgun
house, because you can stand at the front door
and shoot a shotgun blast out the back door.
There's not a lot of ornamentation on this house,
but what there is, to quote Tracy about Hepburn,
is "cherce."

Leadville, the home of gold millionaire
Horace Tabor before he met the celebrated opera
heroine Baby Doe, is the highest city in the
United States at more than 10,000 feet. It has its
own style of architecture, miner's cottages that
go straight back, like "railroad flats," filling the
lot. The steel chimneys are also a unique feature of
Leadville's tunnel houses.

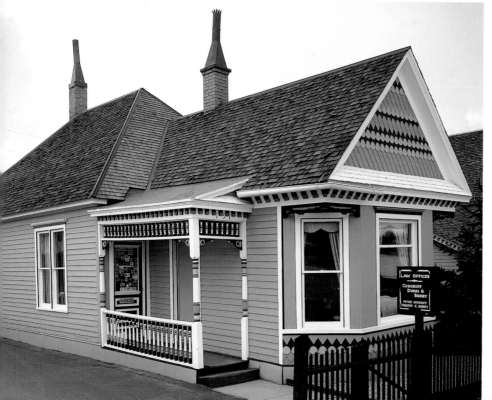

ASPEN

(Opposite). 450 South Riverside Drive. Mountain
Stick. 1883. This cheery breath of mountain air
welcomes you to Aspen when you come in over
Independence Pass. The brilliantly colored patterned gable is a Colorado hallmark. Jim Weber,
local color designer, took off from the owner's
color suggestions and used twenty-five colors—
fourteen blues of the sky and oranges from the
sunset—in this small-scale extravaganza of a
gable. Except for a bay window, the rest of the
house, which, like many mountain homes, has
been modernized, is in earth colors.

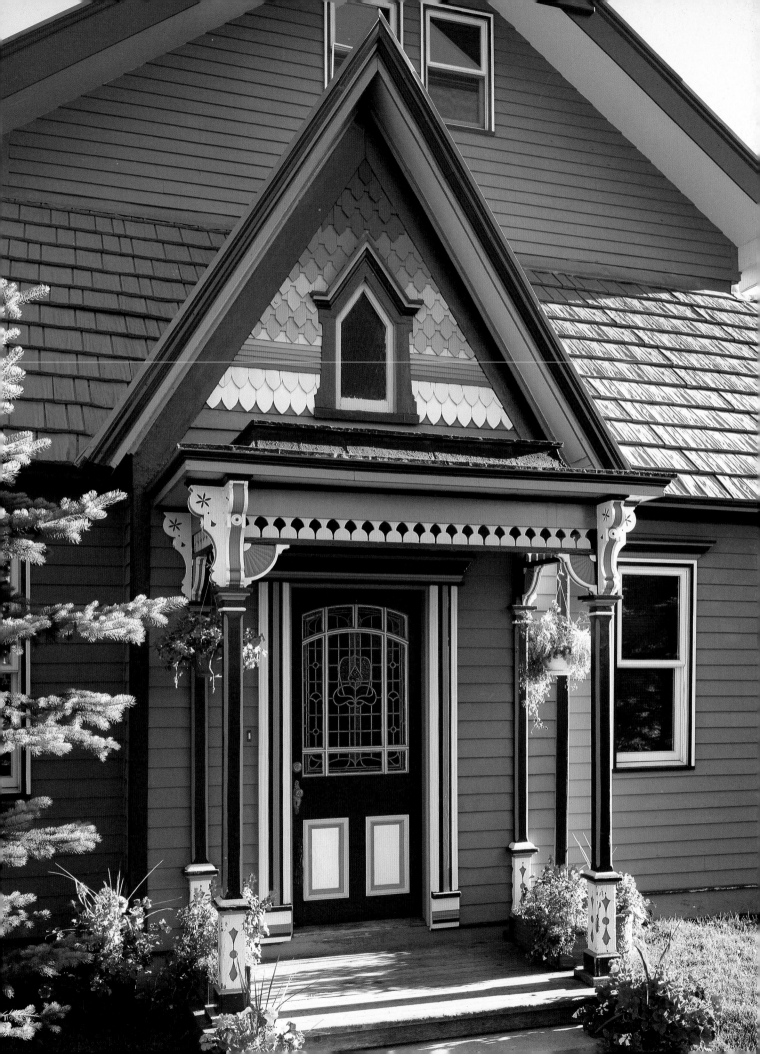

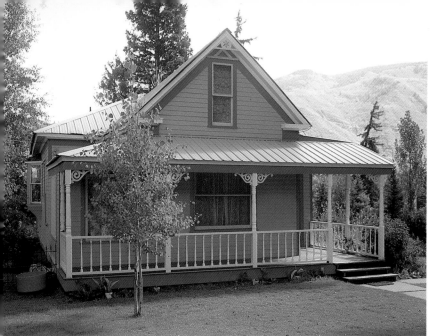

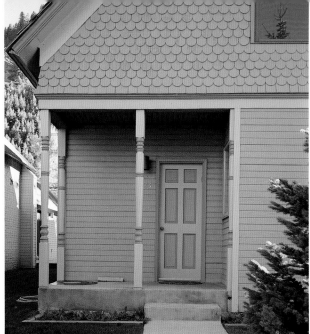

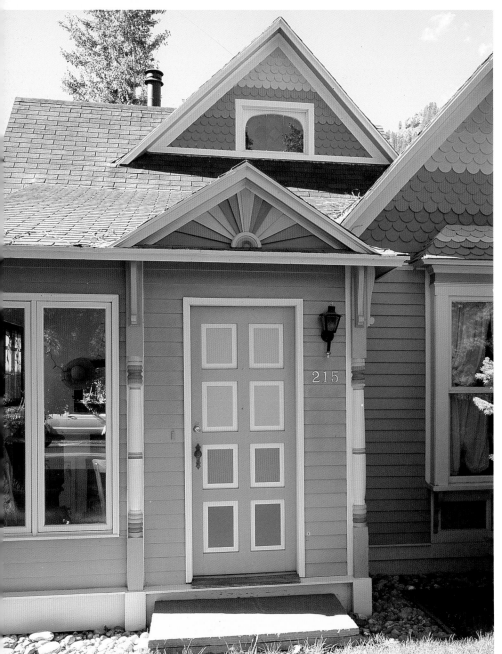

ASPEN

(Above, left). 210 Lake Avenue. Mountain Stick. 1894. The owner chose bright yellow, periwinkle, and purple because they reflect the transformation she felt in her life. For her (and us), they resonate with harmony.

ASPEN

(Above, right). 633 West Main Street. Mountain Stick. 1894. Once the home of Judge and Mrs. Shaw, this cottage is bedecked in colors that glow in summer, and are iridescent against the snow, vying with the mountain scenery.

ASPEN

(Left). 215 West Bleecker Street. Mountain Stick. 1880. Although the living-room porch has been modernized to take advantage of the view, the rainbows on the three gables have always adorned this little house. We especially like the detailing on the columns. The owner is from Santa Fe and wanted to use New Mexico colors. A Kachina doll provided this palette.

Seven hundred three-room cottages like this were ordered by a catalogue and shipped to Aspen by train during its heyday as a mining town. A family would live in two rooms and rent out the third.

90

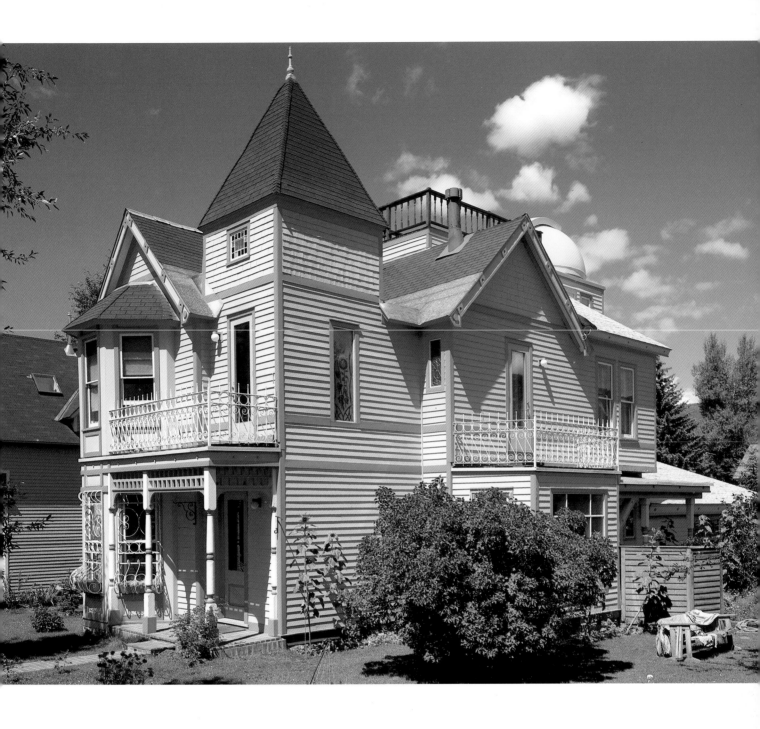

ASPEN

(Above). 214 East Hopkins Avenue. Queen Anne. 1888. The purples and saffron used here glow against the summer sky. The owner installed an observatory for her son who was interested in astronomy. A catalogue house, this is the most photographed home in Aspen.

A note on etiquette: The besieged owner now has to keep her door locked because one day, a tourist couple just walked in on her. When she saw them, she said "Excuse me, I live here…" "That's O.K.," they replied, "we don't mind." The moral: some people are more open to visitors than others, but if you can't write first, at least telephone or knock!

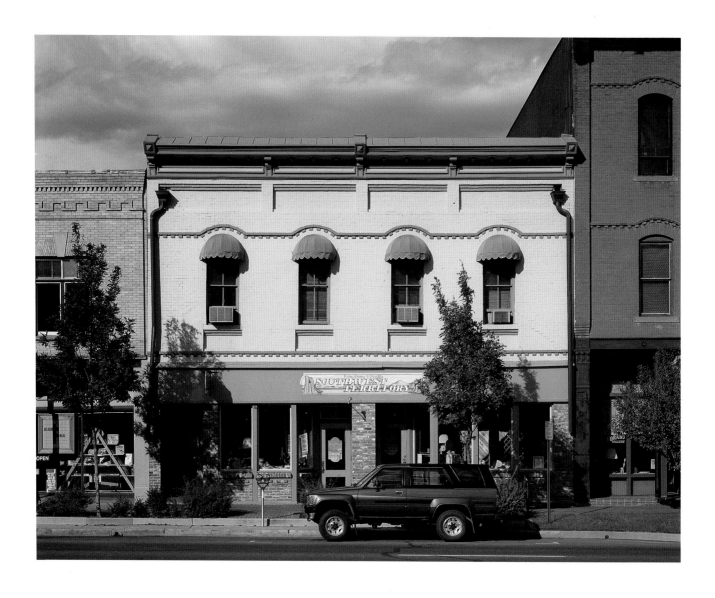

OLD COLORADO CITY
(Above). 2506 West Colorado Avenue. Italianate. 1888. Southwest Territories used color—peach, teal, and tan—to evoke the spirit of the Southwest. The owner of this American crafts store discovered a tunnel under her building that had been used for delivering bootleg whiskey during prohibition.

Old Colorado City, just across an invisible border from Colorado City, was built for the miners and workers who kept "society's" Colorado Springs humming. Liquor was against the law in Colorado Springs, so saloons flourished in Colorado City. The state capital was supposed to be here, but a big shootout made the politicians think the place was just too rowdy, so Denver was chosen as the capital. The ninety-eight buildings in seven square blocks of Old Colorado City form a National Historic District.

Colorado Springs was founded in 1871 by thirty-five-year-old General William Palmer, who led the Pennsylvania brigade in the Civil War. He bought a 3,000-acre tract for $1 an acre, as a utopia for the rich who came for the clean air and the waters. The streets were laid out wide enough for Palmer's regiment to walk abreast. Even the trees were planted by Palmer, who also brought gallons of brown paint for the sanitariums. Palmer built two railroads to bring visitors to town. Today many of the houses in the original part of Colorado Springs are striking polychromes.

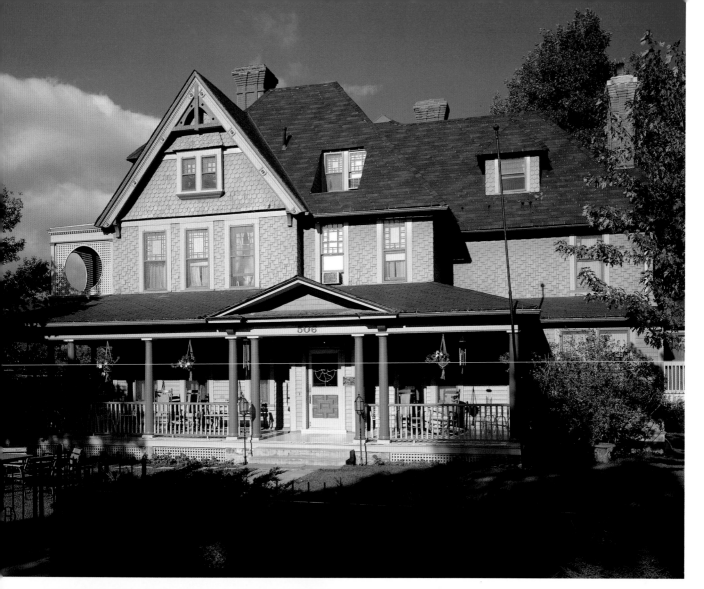

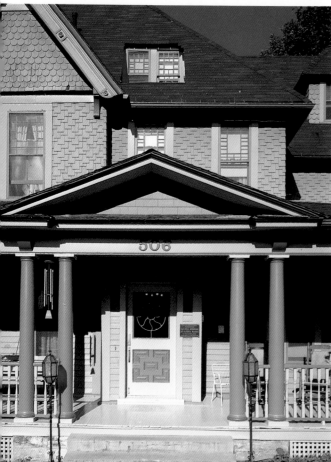

COLORADO SPRINGS

(Above and left). Hearthstone Inn. 506–515 North Cascade. Queen Anne and Colonial Revival. 1885 and 1900. A carriage house behind the first handsome building was brought forward to join it with the house next door to create this expansive, congenial Bed & Breakfast inn.

Dot Williams and Ruth Williams restored the empty, vandalized victims with their friends' help. They hung 792 rolls of paper and Dot's mother made curtains for 146 windows. William Odum of Dallas created a color scheme to suit the owners' taste for something bright and Victorian. The main house is in seven colors, and the detail shows what a felicitous choice of colors they are.

The other "half" uses the same pink, lilac, and gray, plus two colors. The colors merge and blend in the carriage house. The State Historic Site committee turned down the Hearthstone's initial request to be on the National Register because of the paint choices, but when the owners proved that the colors were authentic, the decision was reversed.

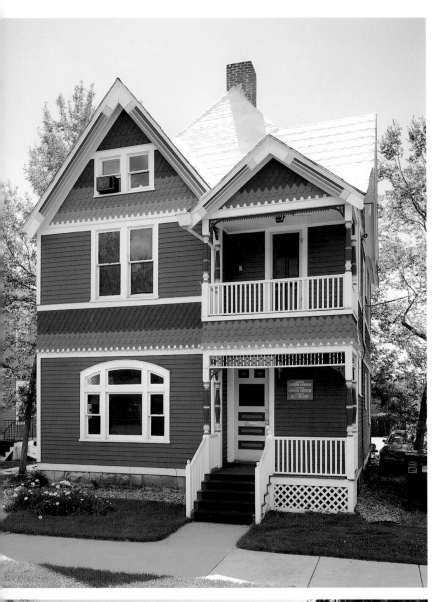

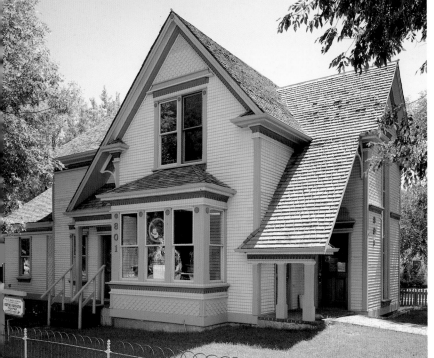

COLORADO SPRINGS

(Left, above). 219 St. Vrain. Queen Anne. 1880s. Thoughtful detailing has made the most of the gingerbread and shingling on this carefully restored home. Although this house first appears on the city map in 1890–1892, the former owners, who did the color design, believe that the house was of an earlier vintage.

COLORADO SPRINGS

(Left, below). 801 South Tejon. Queen Anne. 1885. Its vivid colors earned this building the title of The Wonderbread House. The house was condemned before builder Chuck Murphy spurred the town's preservation committee to save it.

Murphy feels that restoring is like "shaking hands with the past." He also explained that most wooden buildings live as long as humans do, about 100 years, and restoration recycles buildings and gives them another 100 years. Murphy admits "We really care about the city and wanted to give something back to the city that has given so much to us." Chuck Murphy Jr.'s Pikes Peak Tours shares the city's past with its Victorian house tours.

TEXAS

GALVESTON

(Opposite). 210 Kempner Avenue. Neo-Renaissance High Victorian. 1882. The Trueheart-Adrian Co. Building, now on the National Register, was designed in five contrasting colors of brick by architect Nicholas C. Clayton for H. M. Trueheart, proving that all Painted Ladies don't have to be wood. The blue shutters and sashes, and the panel detailing on the first floor enchance the facade.

Galveston, once "The Queen City of the Gulf," is undergoing an exciting downtown rehabilitation. The Junior League of Galveston restored this outstanding building as part of the city program.

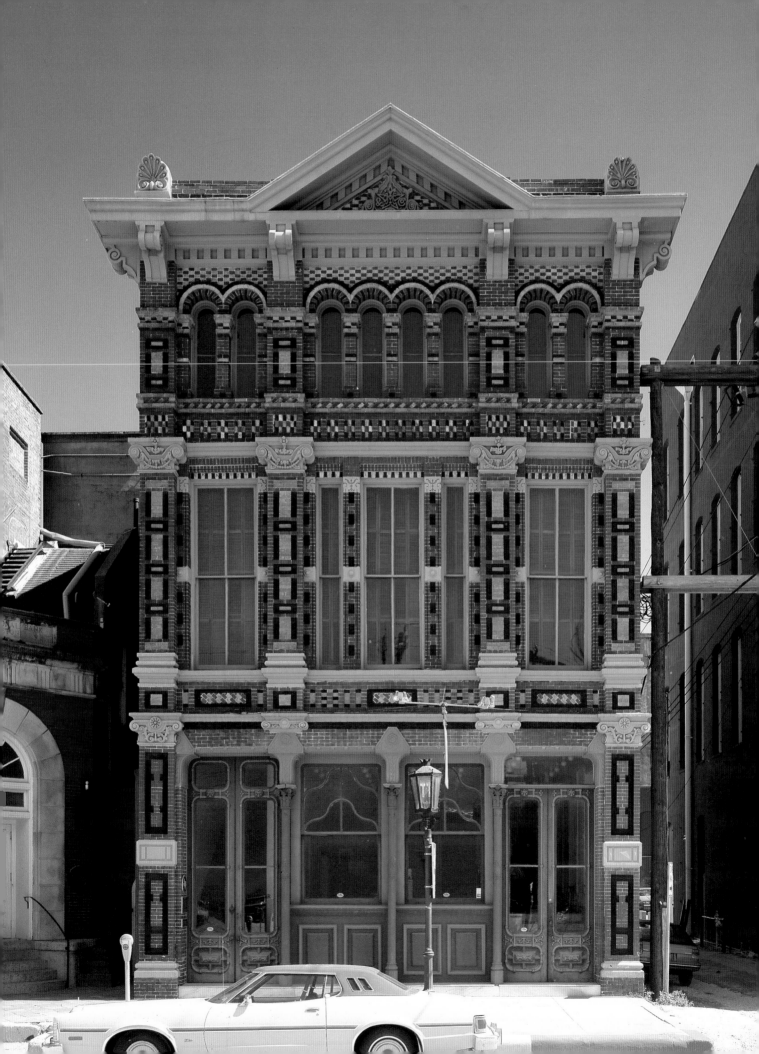

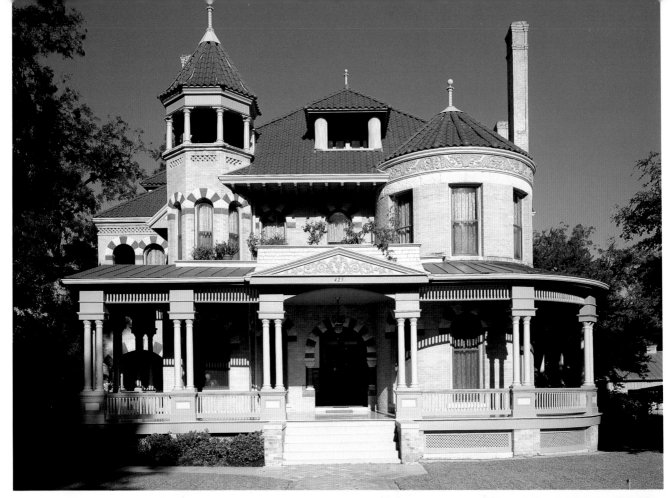

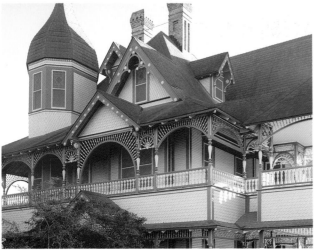

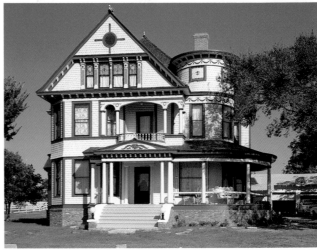

SAN ANTONIO

(Top of page). 425 King William Street. Romanesque Queen Anne. 1892. Designed by James Riely Gordon, the most celebrated of all nineteenth-century Texas architects, the Kalteryer house again wears the polychrome arches that adorned it in 1893. Two greens, yellow, red, blue, and gray gleam under the sunny Texas sky.

ORANGE

(Above, left). The W. H. Stark House. Queen Anne/Eastlake. 1894. Industrialist W. H. Stark and his bride, Miriam Lutcher, built this massive home of longleaf yellow pine and exotic woods

in homage to the Newport mansions of Mrs. Stark's youth. The Stark House is now a completely restored state landmark open to the public by reservation.

COLLEYVILLE

(Above, right). 5317 Bluebonnet. Queen Anne. 1895. The two women who fell in love with this house moved it in four pieces from one Dallas suburb to another. The original owner, Dr. Robert Kincaid, had moved the house from Tennessee to Texas and painted it red and white. The new owners did all of the priming and two coats of flat and gloss themselves and are now so proud of their dream come true that they open it to the public on weekends.

THE NORTHWEST

The hardy lumber, mining, and seafaring folk that settled the Northwest liked to flaunt their success by building grandiose Victorians. Closeness to California has influenced today's color choices, but a Northwestern sense of identity has produced stately, dignified homes, such as the Flavel Mansion in Astoria.

Doug Keister's off-the-beaten track discoveries in Idaho and Montana were surprises. And the sprightly town of Port Townsend, with its history and dozens of grand homes preserved with paint and enterprise, is the Cape May of the West.

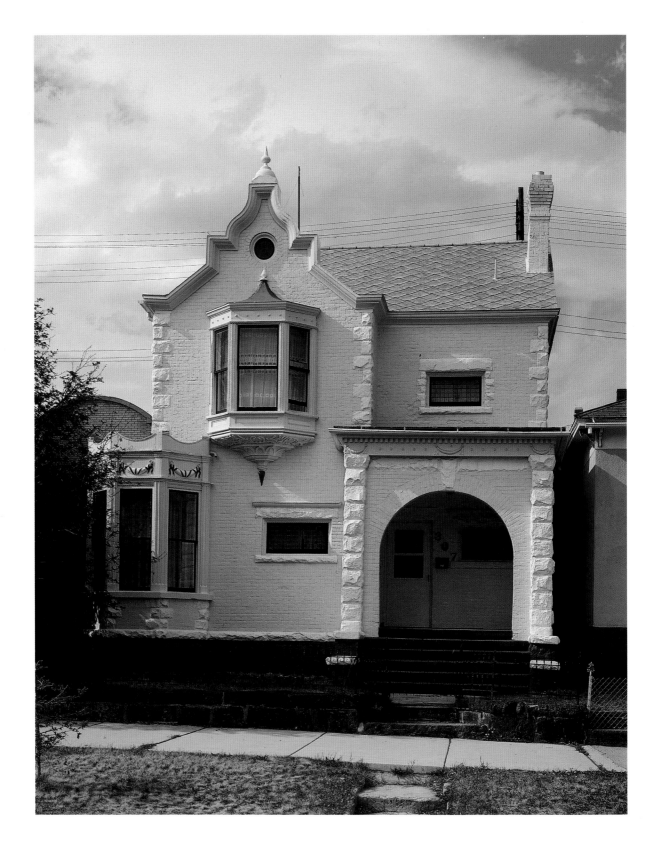

MONTANA
BUTTE

(Above). 307 West Broadway. Eclectic. 1896. This unusual stucco home, originally owned by Dr. Donald Campbell, with its Italianate outlines, bay window, small side bay and a romantic gable, is brought to life with an offbeat pastel palette. Irene McCarthy worked on the design with two painters and came up with white, black, dark red, mint, and yellow.

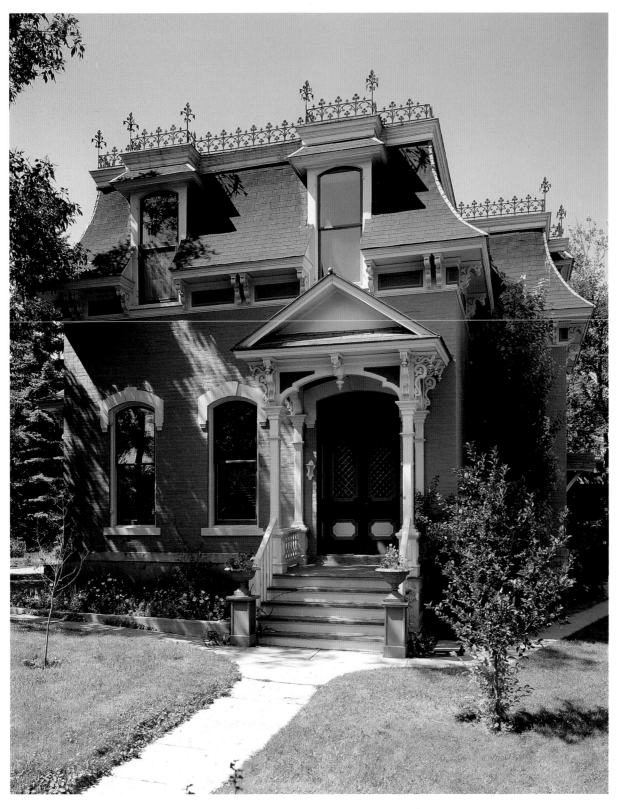

(Above). 404 Benton. Second Empire Mansard. 1879. The Christmas Gift Evans house, named for its owner who was born on Christmas Day, looks as if it is trying its best to be a small, stylish mansion.

Mansard roofs were popular in France, because at one time, homeowners were taxed by the number of stories in their house. The dormers in the mansard allowed people to live comfortably on the top floor, while giving the appearance of being just a tall roof instead of another full story.

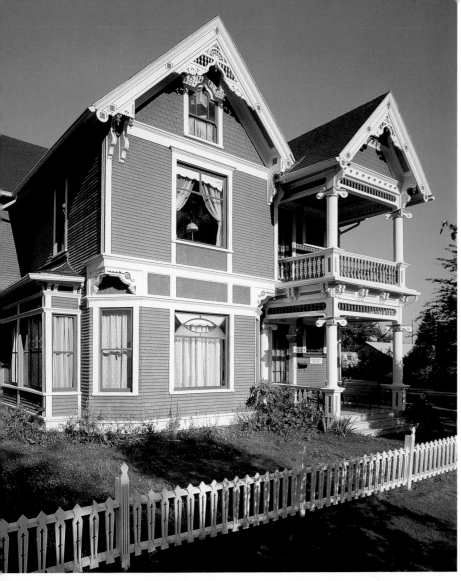

WASHINGTON

BELLINGHAM

(Left). 2215 Utter Ave. Stick/Eastlake. 1895. Classic Restoration repaired the porch and restored the delicious gingerbread on this handsome polychrome home, and sunshine adds the finishing touch.

BELLINGHAM

(Below). The Castle. 1103 15th Street. Queen Anne. 1890. Jim Wardner was a smooth-talking miner, investor, and promoter who wandered the globe making and losing fortunes. Both Wardner, Idaho, and Wardner, British Columbia, were named for him. Wardner's hillside Castle overlooking the Pacific is now a gracious B&B painted in the owner's favorite sunset colors.

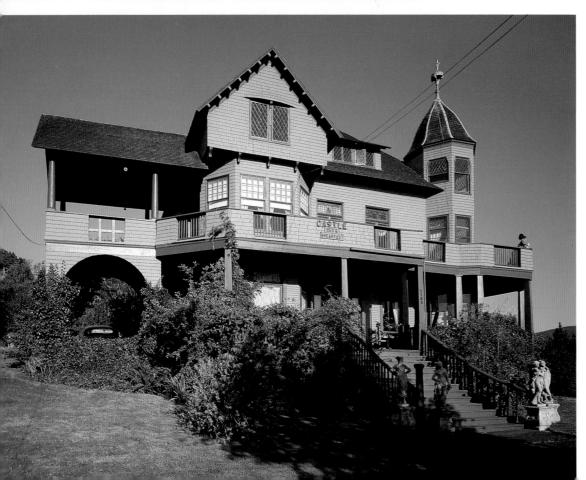

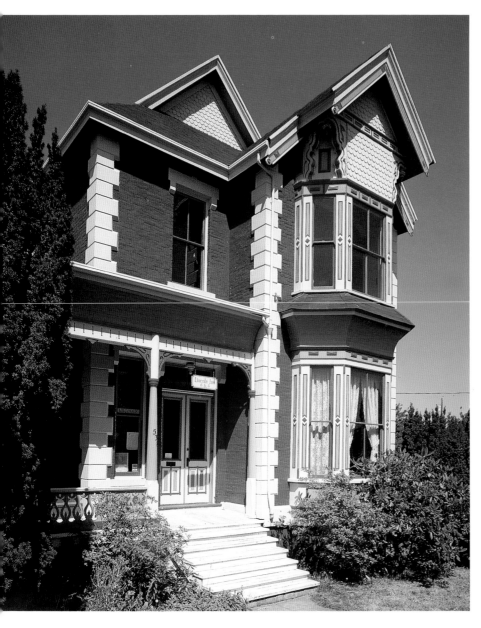

PORT TOWNSEND

A National Historic District, this charming seaport calls itself an anachronism. It beckons visitors with a comfort, hospitality, and human scale cheerfully reminiscent of yesteryear.

(Above). The Lincoln Inn. 538 Lincoln. Eastlake. 1888. Built as a showplace for Elias DeVoie and the DeVoie masonry business, this B & B in red, white, and two blues is one of many Victorians in town saved from neglect by "adaptive reuse."

ELLENSBURG

(Right). The Davidson Building. 4th and Pearl Streets. Queen Anne. 1889–1890. This red-brick business building has been given a facelift and her flowers are blooming once again in a blue, green, tan, brown, and terra-cotta color design by Gil Braida. Saved from becoming a parking lot, the Davidson Building is now the jewel in the crown of Ellensburg's National Historic District.

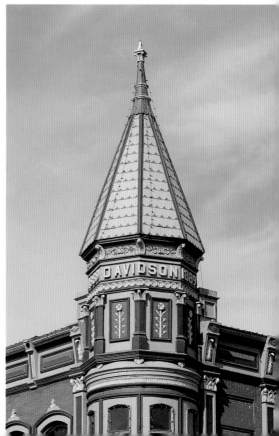

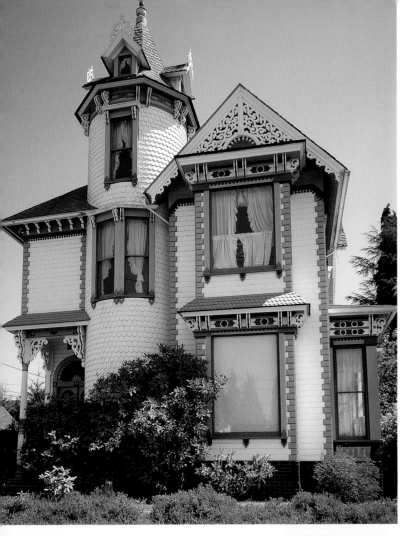

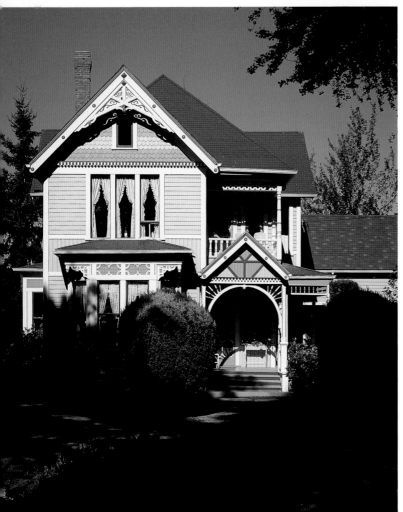

SNOHOMISH

(Left, above). 223 Avenue A. Queen Anne. 1887. The acroteria on the peaks of the tower, flowery bargeboards, and fine detailing in the cornices make this house an unexpected pleasure in this small town above Seattle. After a trip to San Francisco, the owners removed the old shingles, designed and made the ornamentation, and mixed their own paint colors.

LaCONNER

(Left, below). 1624 LaConner-Whitney Road. Queen Anne. 1892. The owner of this adorable cottage set back from the road really believes in changing coats of paint with her change of taste. By the time you see this book, the warm creams and toasts will be replaced with rosy pinks to reflect a new interior.

COUPEVILLE

(Opposite). 702 North Main. Italianate. 1887. Built as a retirement home, this was called The Blue Glass House because of the Evening in Paris cologne bottles lining the windows. Then new owners moved in and, inspired by the book, wanted a Painted Lady of their own and chose a rose, blue, and cream color scheme. At first, as townspeople pulled out of the post office across the street, they shouted complaints, but now, the owner says, "You'd think it was their idea to do it this way. And people think we did lots of restoration of brackets and gingerbread, but we didn't. It was all here but you couldn't see it because it was all white." This classy confection is on the National Historic Register.

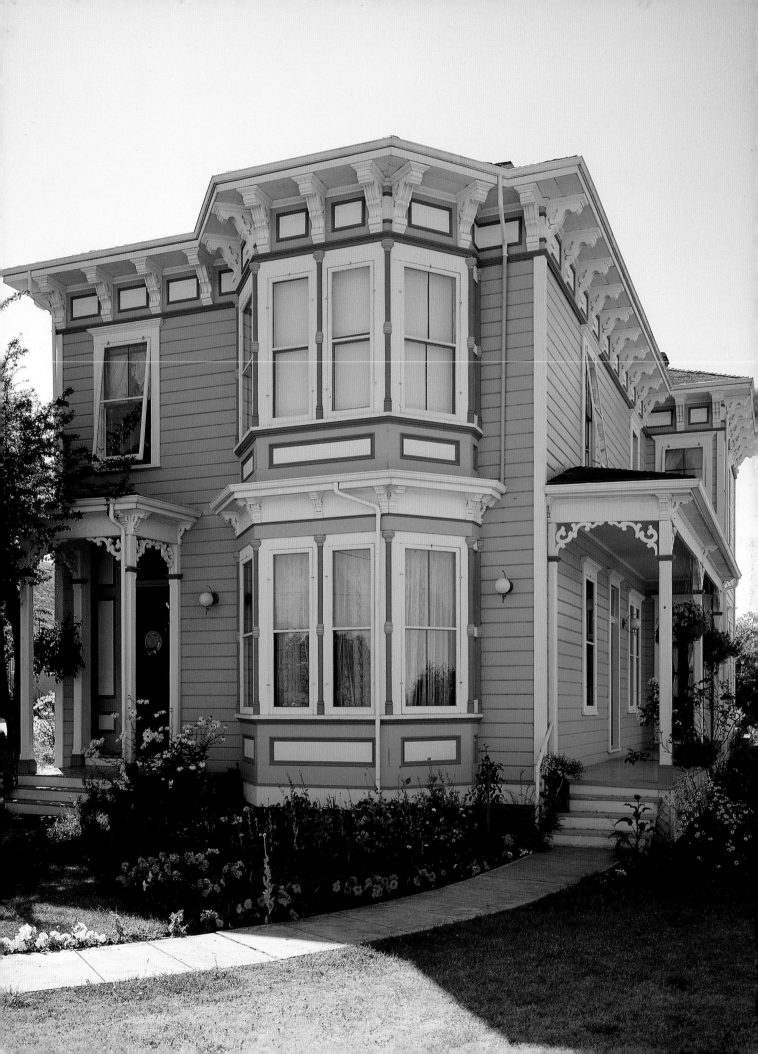

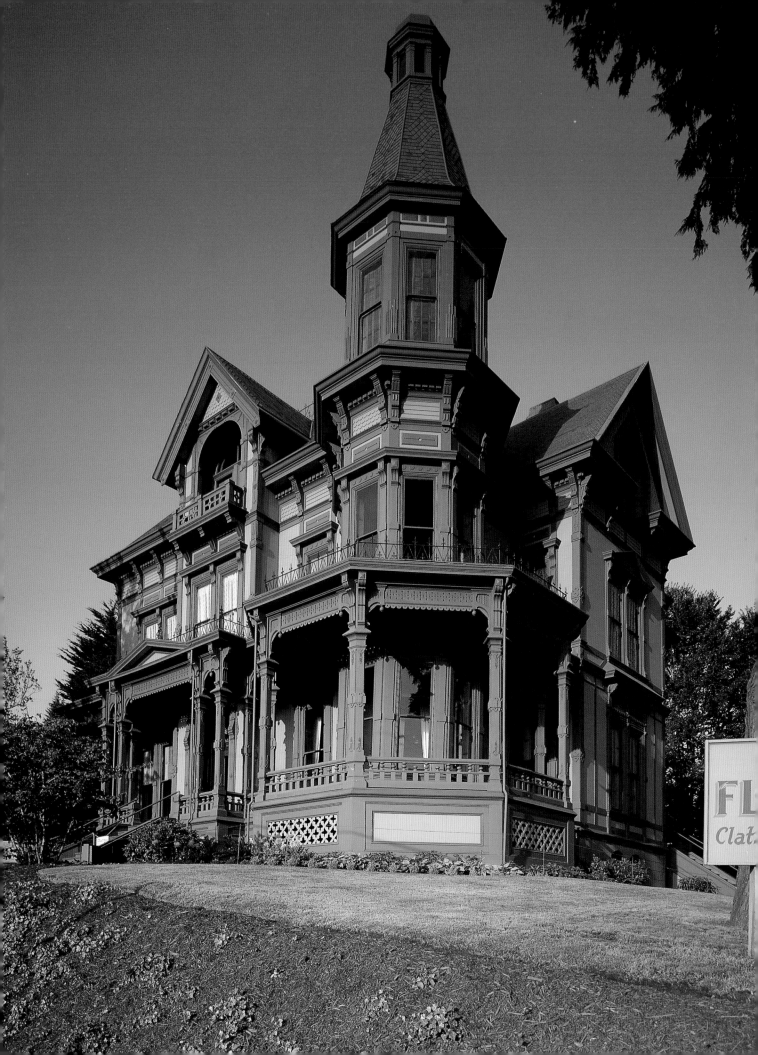

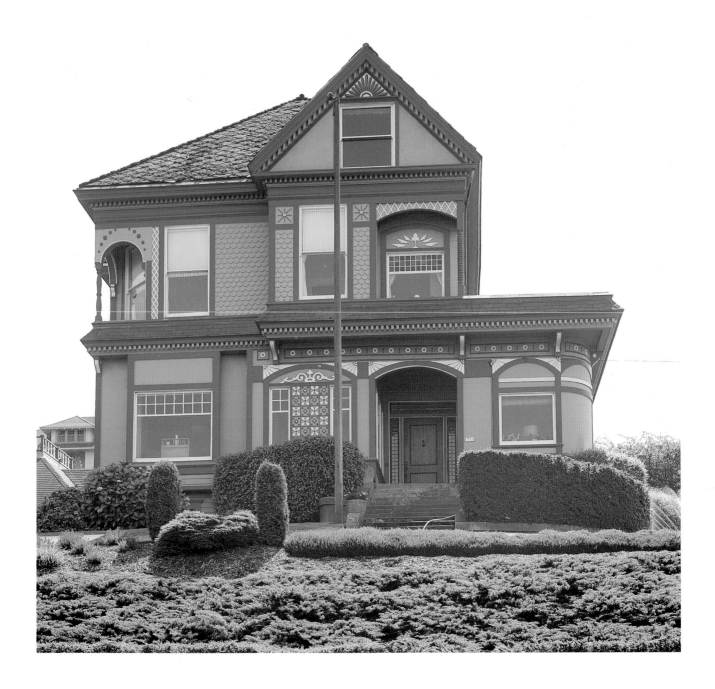

OREGON

ASTORIA

(Opposite). Flavel House. 441 8th Street. Queen Anne/Italianate. 1883–1885. Sea Captain George Flavel built this imposing home for his wife, Mary Christina. He installed a gazebo in his office so he could see his ships sailing into the harbor at the mouth of the Columbia River near the Washington border. Now a museum, the home was given to the county by Patricia Flavel and has recently been meticulously redecorated with period furnishings.

ASTORIA

(Above). 1711 Grand Street. Queen Anne. 1889. George W. Sanborn, an early salmon packer, built his home overlooking the bay. An innovator with the American Can Co., Sanborn was the first in the salmon industry to install sanitary can-packing machinery. The owners have used a handsome combination of dark and light cream, French blue, and a touch of red to show off the fine architectural detailing.

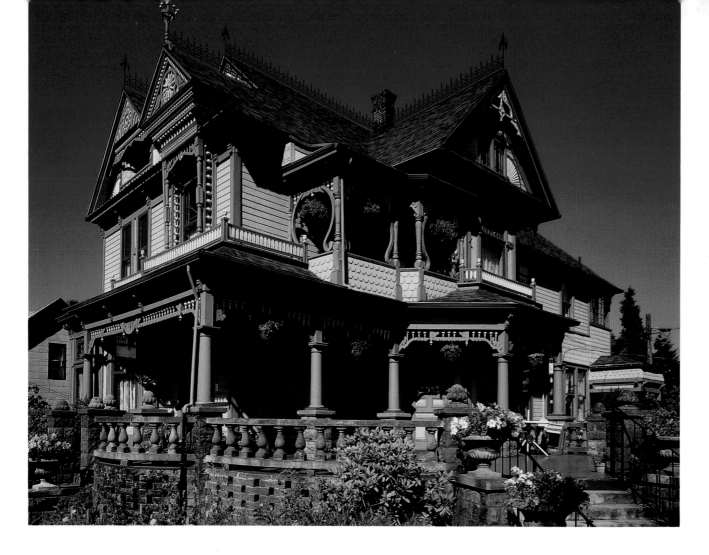

PORTLAND

The Palmer House. 4314 North Mississippi. Queen Anne. 1890.
In 1968, Dick and Mary Sauter paid $10,000 to buy a decaying
dream house in Portland's unsavory Albina district. John Palmer
built the house as a showplace for his contracting business. The
Birdsall family took over the house in 1896, followed by Lotta and
Charles Oskar Hoch, who operated the Multnomah Conservatory
of Music here from 1907 until 1968.

It took eighteen years for Dick and Mary to restore the house
by hand, with the help of friends and family. Each of the five gables
is different, and the elaborate spool and spindle work, roof
cresting, and rails had to be restored. Now the house is an elegant
yet comfortable B&B and the whole neighborhood is primping
and polishing.

We thought you might enjoy peeking inside a Painted Lady,
and fortunately, The Palmer House is a Painted Lady both
inside and out. A few years ago, Mary remarked, "They
seem to have hung everything outside, the interior was so
comparatively simple—no fireplaces, no parquetry floors.
However, stained-glass windows do impart a rich color to
the rooms." The following pictures will show you how the
Sauters have made "authentic" better than "original."

Victorians approached the decoration and adornment
of their homes with an almost evangelistic fervor. Home
was a retreat, something to be proud of and be comfortable in. Their homey clutter was not chaos, but a love of
flamboyant details, patterns, and prints. Rooms were not
gloomy, but shadowy and romantic, lit by chandeliers,
lamps, and girandoles—the candelabra-style table lamps
that dripped with excess. This is what the Sauters aimed for.

When the Sauters had finally fixed the house up
enough to begin wallpapering, they knew that they wanted
something special—Victorian yet affordable. At the same
time, Bruce Bradbury of Bradbury & Bradbury Fine Art
Wallpapers in Benicia, California, near San Francisco, was
just getting started and having a hard time persuading
people to use more than one pattern of wallpaper in the
same room as the Victorians did.

The Sauters wanted the works: wainscoting, dados,
ceiling fans, borders, friezes—everything Bradbury had to
offer. Dados are wide panels or borders on the lower part of
a wall. Paper for the main part of a wall is called filling.
Friezes are eighteen-inch borders above the picture rails.
Ceiling borders are nine inches wide or less. Crown-decora-
tion ornaments and enrichments or accent pieces in deeper
colors on the ceiling finish the room. Bradbury gave them
a break on the wallpaper and the Sauters gave him five
rooms in which to experiment, to see how everything came
together. Thirty-seven fabulous wallpapers illuminate The
Palmer House, each radiant, gorgeous, and silkscreened
by hand.

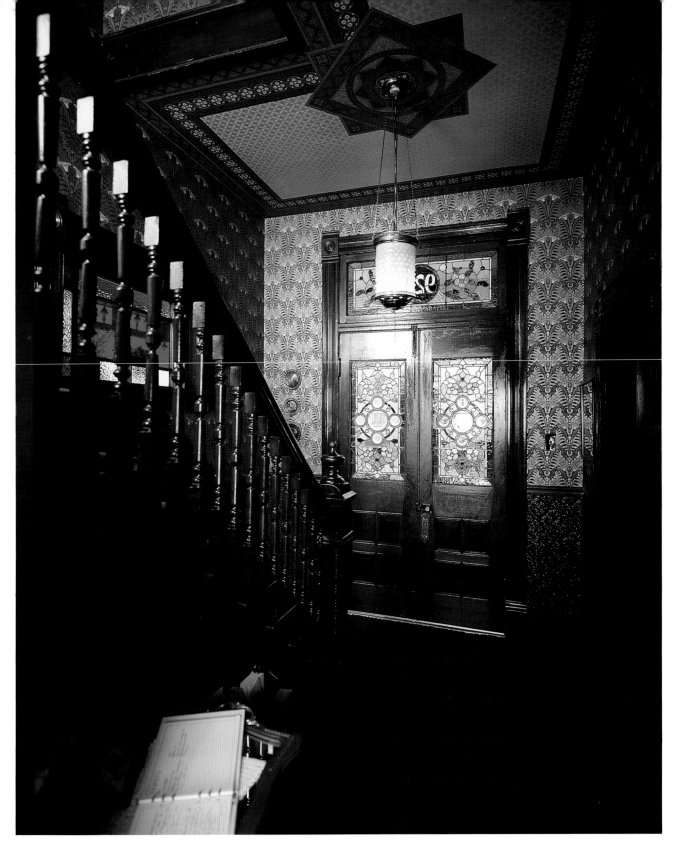

(Above). Palmer House hallway. This hallway is papered in a relatively dark wine-brown patterned with gold. But an underlayer picks up the light so that the paper looks completely different depending on whether it is seen in lamplight or sunlight. This ability to shine and shimmer in varying lights is called "bloom." Victorians used gold, bronze, and silver powder in their fine wallpapers to achieve that magical quality.

When you see old Victorian paper that's dark and dead-looking, remember that it probably once had a sheen to it that made it glow. According to Bradbury, the darkness is "only a ghost of what was there." Flocks and embossments also intensified the surface textures of Victorian wallpaper.

Note the leaded-glass window in the stairwell, which also casts appealing rosy tones on the wall in the afternoon, and the stained-glass panels in the entrance doors. The Sauters picked up its colors when painting the exterior.

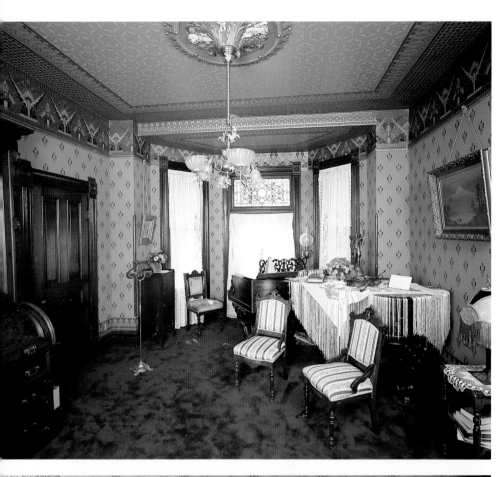

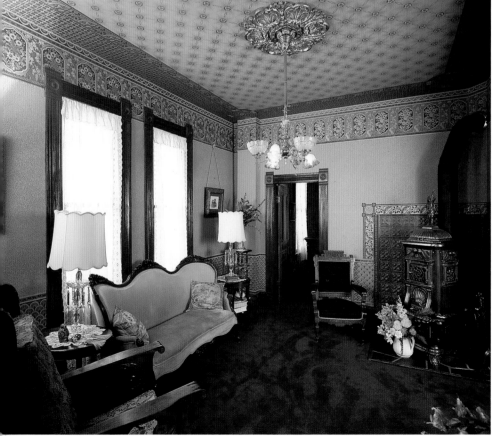

(Left, above). Palmer House front parlor. The benign ghost of Lotta Hoch sometimes sits at the 1860 Gaveau piano in the front room, when the Sauters, who are opera buffs, aren't there. Mary stood on a ladder to paint the leaves and flowers of the lovely crown ornament with colors that complement the radiant blue papers.

(Left, below). Palmer House back parlor. The pale green "Anglo-Japanese" wallpapers in this room reflect the influence of the Aesthetic Movement, with its sunflower emblem. The stove is more elaborate than the original coal burner, but it is still of the period.

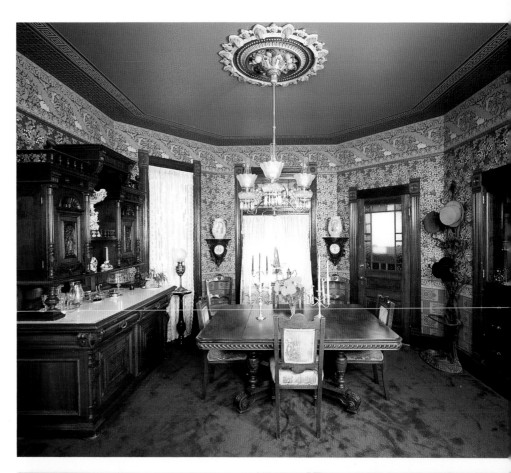

(Right, above). Palmer House dining room. Believe it or not, this dining room is sparsely furnished, compared to how it probably looked a century ago. At that time there would have been more chairs and the sideboard and side tables would have been covered with memorabilia. There were lots of chairs in Victorian rooms because a gentleman would always stand up when a lady entered the room; yet as he wouldn't think of allowing her to sit in his warmed chair, there always had to be a cool one at the ready.

The filling, or basic wallpaper here, is called Raspberry Bramble. Another decorative crown ornament painted by Mary Sauter anchors the chandelier. Note how the dark woods serve as a foil for the artfully orchestrated chorus of color and pattern.

(Right, below). Palmer House bedroom suite. Starfish on the ceiling and shells on the walls glow in both rooms of this suite, which boasts its own hand organ, a "fainting couch" for women in tight corsets, and a "consumption porch" where family tuberculosis patients were expected to thrive in the fresh air both summer and winter. If you look at the wall of the sitting room, you can see how different lights affect the colors and sheen of the paper.

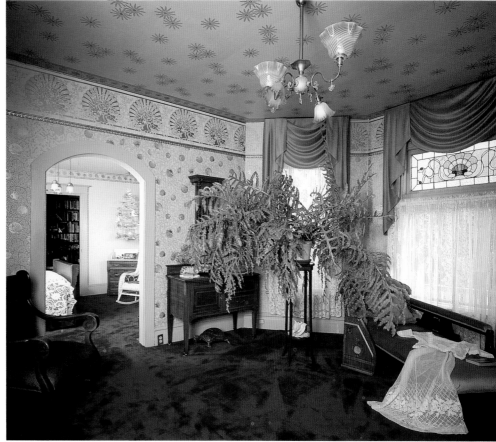

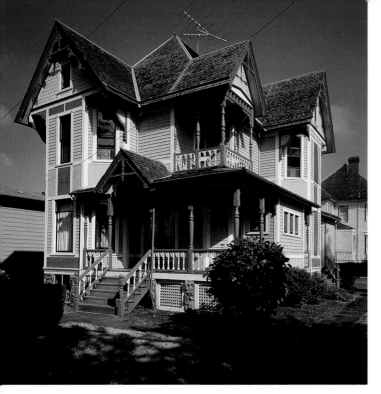

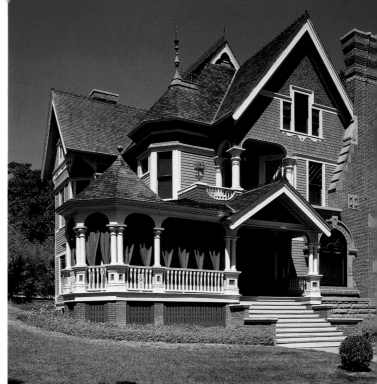

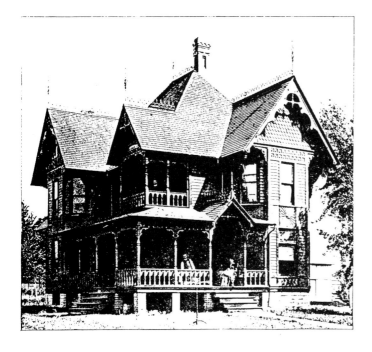

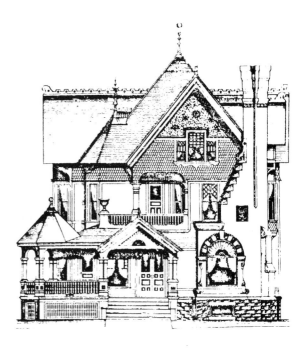

JACKSONVILLE

(Right, top and above). Jeremiah L. Nunan House. 635 North Oregon Street. Queen Anne. 1892. Jeremiah Nunan, a successful merchant, miner, and rancher, bought a Christmas present for his wife, Delia, and celebrated his good fortune in this thriving gold-rush town by ordering Design No. 43 in the *George Barber Cottage Souvenir Book.*

This catalogue house and its carriage house cost Nunan $7,800, including freight, materials, and labor. Barber even sent along a foreman to supervise assembly of the kit. This illustration shows the catalogue page Nunan ordered from. Barber advertised the Nunan House as an example of his best work. The red brick, pressed stone, and striking polychrome paint scheme are all authentic.

ALBANY

(Left, top and above). 237 6th Street. Stick/Eastlake. 1888. George Hochstedler, co-owner of the Hochstedler & Sears Planing Mill, spent $6,000 on this Barber catalogue house. George F. Barber sold pattern books containing floor plans and pictures with detailed descriptions of interiors and exteriors. Interested buyers purchased the plans, specifications, and full working drawings for $12.50. Or they had the house delivered "prefabricated," usually for a four-figure sum. Hochstedler chose to put his porch on the right side, instead of on the left, as it was illustrated in the catalogue. Now an apartment house, the color scheme is the original beige, rust-orange, pink-orange, white, and wine.

CALIFORNIA

Proximity to San Francisco has stimulated contemporary and traditional paint schemes in both Northern and Southern California. Other towns besides San Francisco made use of the nearby and inexpensive redwood which was handsawed and jigsawed into swooping, swirling gingerbread. Towns time passed by also provided fewer excuses for knocking down old buildings to build new ones, so many fine examples have survived.

To the north, the lumber towns of Eureka and Ferndale discovered that freshly renovated stores and housefronts can be tourist attractions. And towns that had little or no industry are now coming to life with paint. Ferndale's prosperous dairy farmers built ornately decorated homes dubbed "Butterfat Palaces," which are popular B&B's today. Eureka's picturesque Old Town has also sprung back to life.

To the south, Victorians are blooming again in Heritage Squares in Los Angeles and San Diego, which also boasts a newly revitalized "Gaslamp" district. Small towns such as Monrovia, Ventura, and Oxnard are also finding a future in their past.

San Francisco has itself produced a splendid new crop of painted beauties which we're saving for a sequel to *Painted Ladies*.

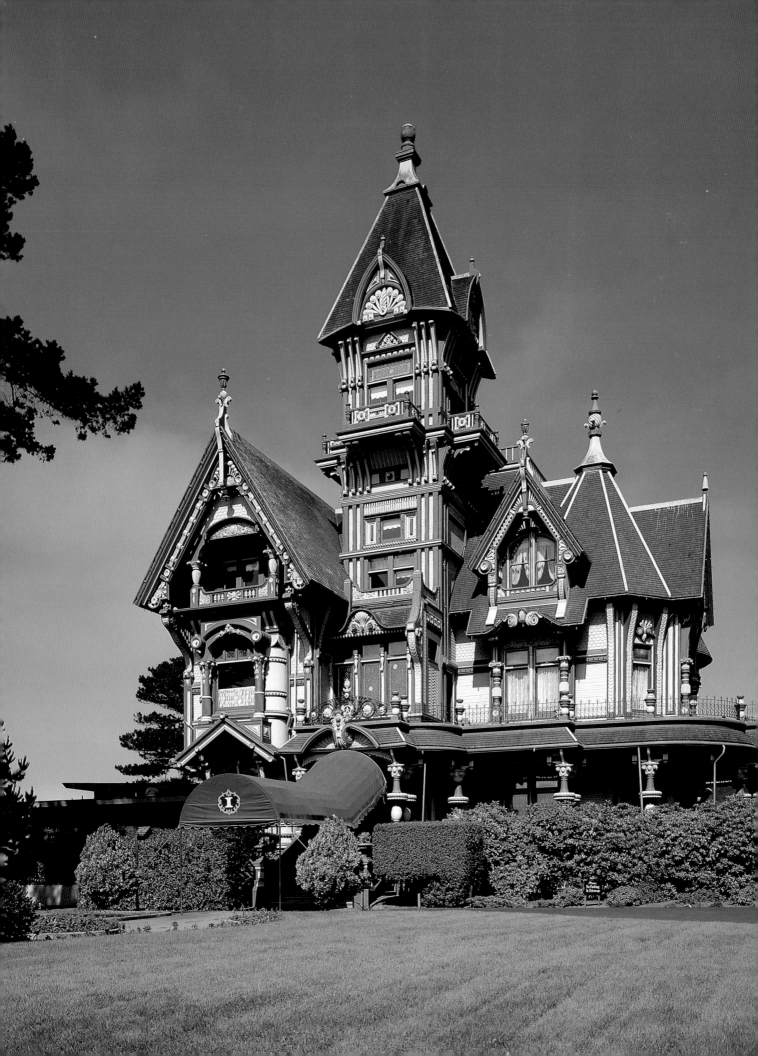

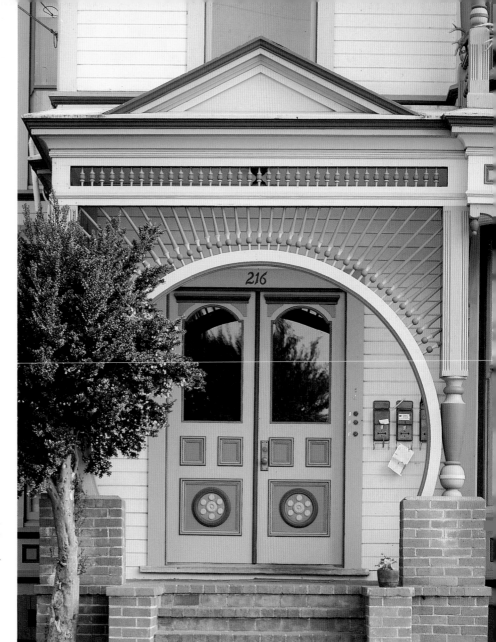

EUREKA

(Opposite). The Carson Mansion. Second and M Streets. Queen Anne. 1884–1886. Lumber baron William Carson built this truly astonishing edifice to keep his workers busy during the off season and to be used as a showcase for the different kinds of wood he sold. William and Sarah Carson's children had already fled the nest by then, so there are only three bedrooms in this mighty pile. Designed by the Newsom Brothers of San Francisco, and now a men's club, this landmark building incorporates almost every possible embellishment: gables with balconies and porches, intricate moldings, pillars, spindle work, festooned bargeboards, and a flurry of finials. It is a temple of the woodcarver's art, a one-stop museum of "drop-dead" Victorian decoration.

EUREKA

(Right, above). 216 Hillsdale. Queen Anne. 1886. Also designed by the Newsom Brothers, the harmonious rainbow effect on the spindlework of this curved porch is a marvel to behold.

EUREKA

(Right, below). 1228 C Street. Eastlake/Queen Anne. 1885. The carved garland over the porch had disappeared from sight until the new owners, who are stained-glass artists, gave it this floral headband.

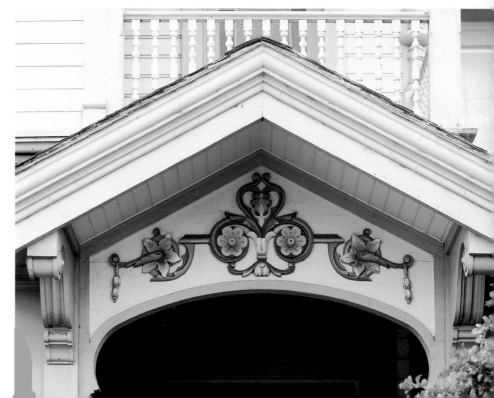

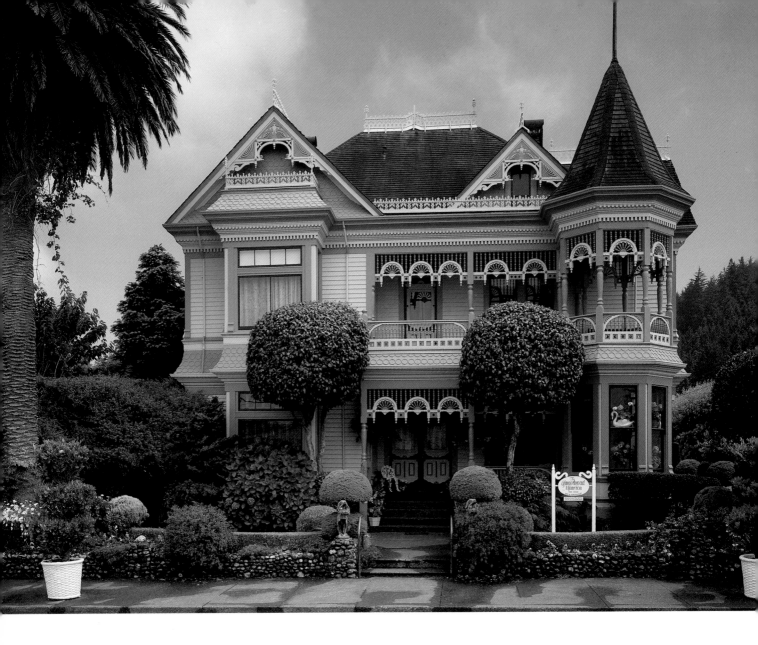

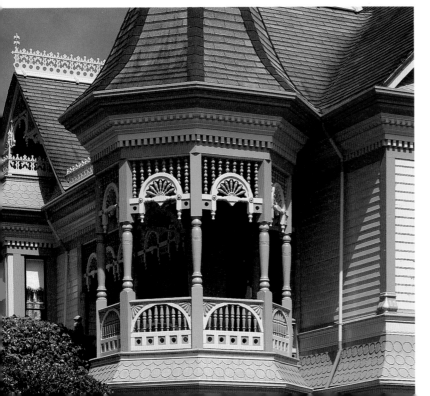

FERNDALE

(Above and left). The Gingerbread Mansion. 400 Berding Street. Queen Anne. 1889. Dr. Hogan J. Ring and his wife, Orcelia Lowe Ring, built this scrumptious house and later enlarged it to include a small hospital in back.

The hospital rooms have now become elegant guest rooms in this lovingly restored Bed & Breakfast inn, and guests are welcome in the picture-postcard gardens surrounding the place. The balcony needs only a moonlit night to become a perfect setting for a love scene. The polychrome paint scheme attracts tourists from around the world to The Gingerbread Mansion.

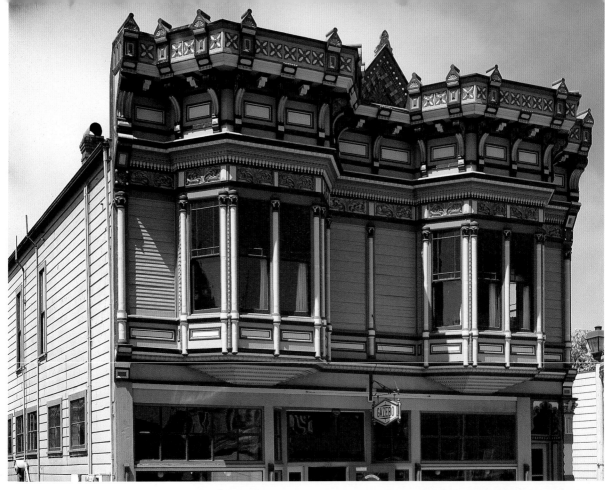

FERNDALE

(Above). 475 Main Street. Eastlake. 1898. Built by G. W. Willis and W. T. Kraus, the building later became Lee Taubman's Red Star Clothing Store. This storefront exemplifies the vividly restored Main Street of a town now called "The Victorian Village."

PETALUMA

(Right). McNear Building. One 4th Street. Eastlake. 1886. Yankee trader John A. McNear started a mercantile dynasty in 1856 with an empire of real estate, grain, shipping, banking, and railroads. His son built a feed-mill empire serving the emerging egg industry (Petaluma has been called the chicken capital of the world), and his family gave the town its first electric lights. The Stroke & Kote Paint Company used three colors to highlight the designs on the capitals of this outstanding commercial building.

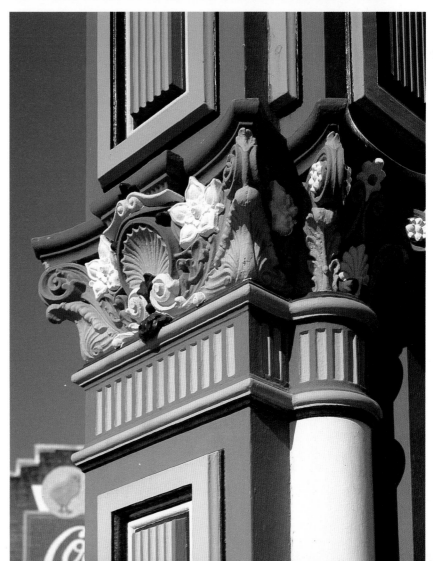

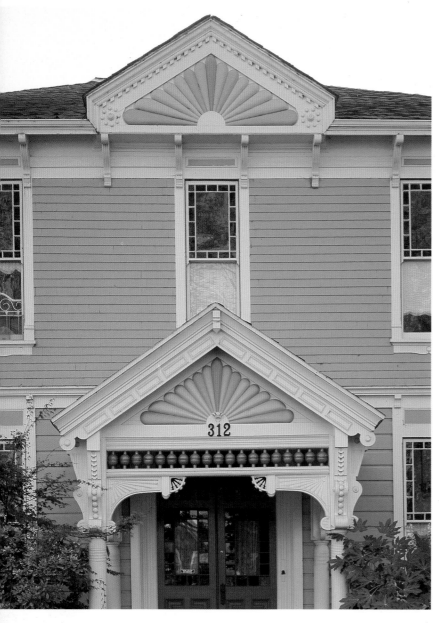

PETALUMA

(Left, above). 312 6th Street. Stick/Eastlake. 1882. Built as a wedding present for Senator A. P. Whitney's oldest son, Arthur Leslie, this charming house is called "The Rainbow House." The colors may not be historically correct, but rainbows certainly make us happy whenever we see them.

BENICIA

(Left, below). 121 East J Street. Stick. 1880s. The antiques dealers who own this charming cottage were inspired by the cover of *Painted Ladies* to create their own version. The neighbors love it.

The first state capital of California, with a handsome capitol building to prove it, Benicia is a small bay town known as an antiques center.

VALLEJO

(Right, below). 627 York. Queen Anne cottage. 1894. Who could resist the detail of this welcoming doorway?

A strong Vallejo Architectural Heritage Foundation has helped to revitalize a neglected town with fresh paint and volunteer effort. One of the foundation's success stories is Heritage House, an Eastlake cottage scheduled to be demolished, which was moved to a city lot rented for one dollar a year, and totally renovated and restored. It now serves the community as a meeting hall.

ALAMEDA

(Opposite). 2070 San Jose at Willow. Queen Anne. 1888. Pattern number 27 in Barber's *The Cottage Souvenir, Revised & Enlarged*, was priced at $2,600 to build, but you can be sure that Mr. D. Brehaut spent much more than that. Intersecting, multifaceted forms with inset porches and projecting bays replete with keyhole windows and spooled columns helped Mr. Brehaut make the house his very own. San Francisco color designer Bob Buckter used a palette of three greens, cream, and white, caught here in the morning light, to do justice to this stellar example of Victorian architecture. The city was so proud of the result that they put it on the cover of the telephone book.

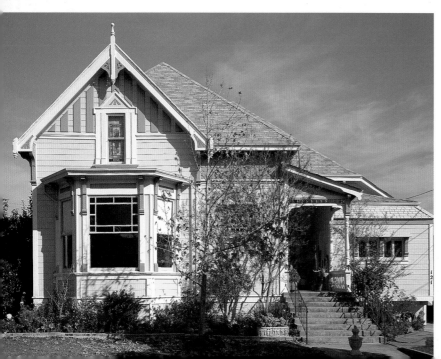

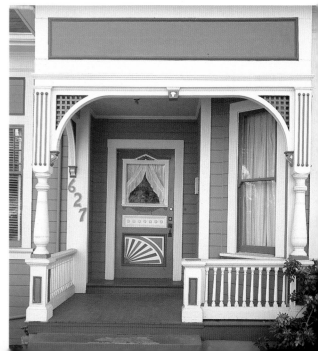

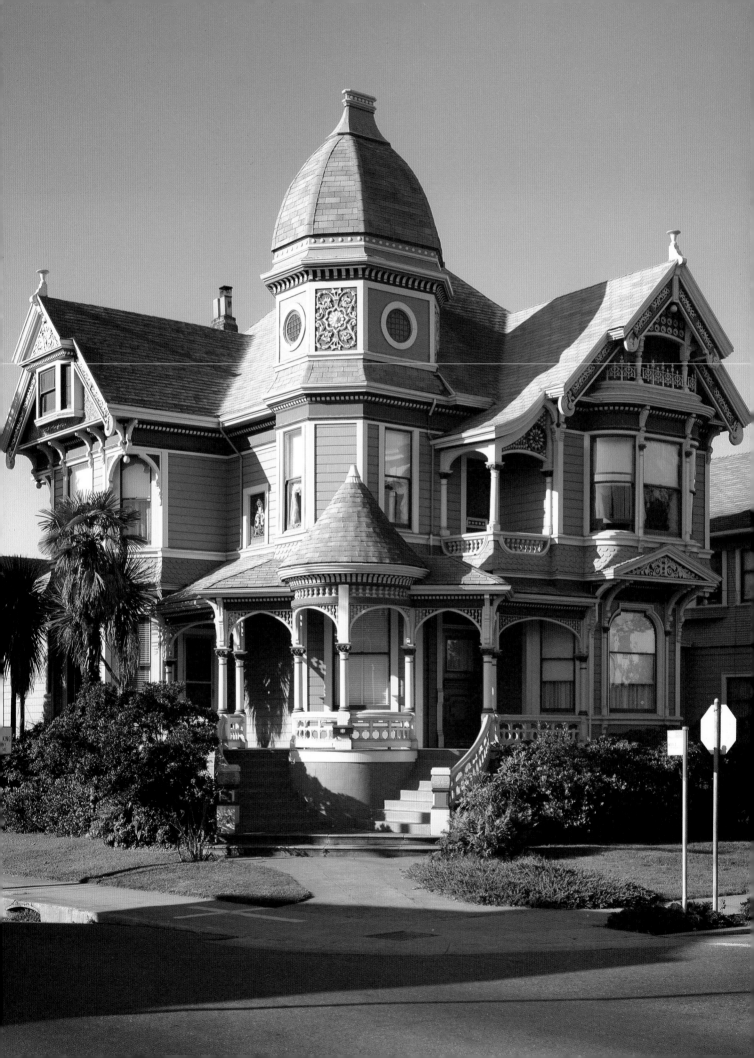

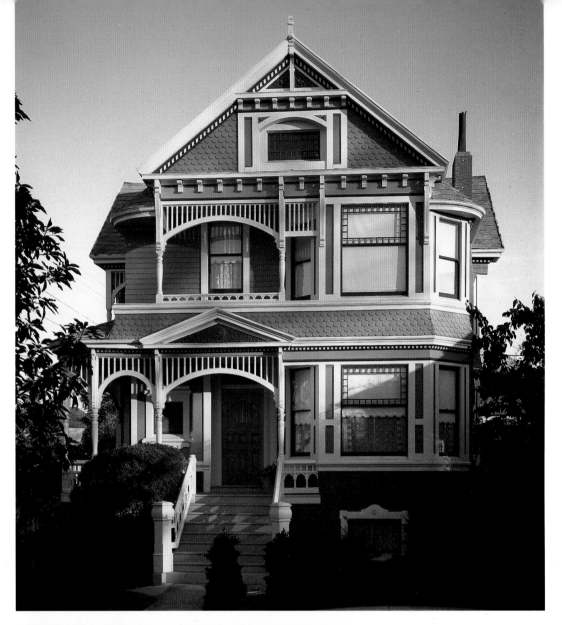

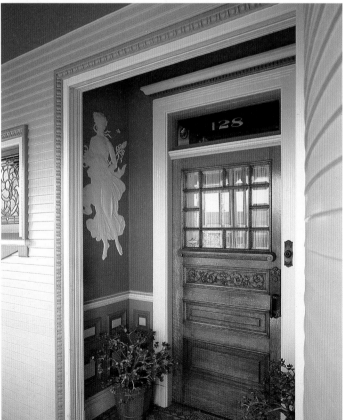

ALAMEDA

(Above). 1024 Union. Queen Anne. 1890. Built by J. A. Leonard, the eyes in the gables were a big surprise to the neighbors, who discovered them after the owners painted their house in dark blue, dark aqua, raspberry, wine, and cream with the help of artist Lisa Baker. This house is a beguiling, mutually enhancing blend of color and architecture.

Alameda, an island in San Francisco Bay, is a treasure trove of Victorian homes now being lovingly restored by families moving into the revitalized town.

WATSONVILLE

(Left). 128 East Beach. Queen Anne. 1894. When the new owners moved into the Judge Lee house in 1966, it was both empty and stripped. They learned how to make stained glass to replace the windows and worked with colorist Doni Tunheim to capture the house in seven shades of gold, peach, and orange. The bas-reliefs of dancing ladies that flank the front door welcome visitors to this award-winning home.

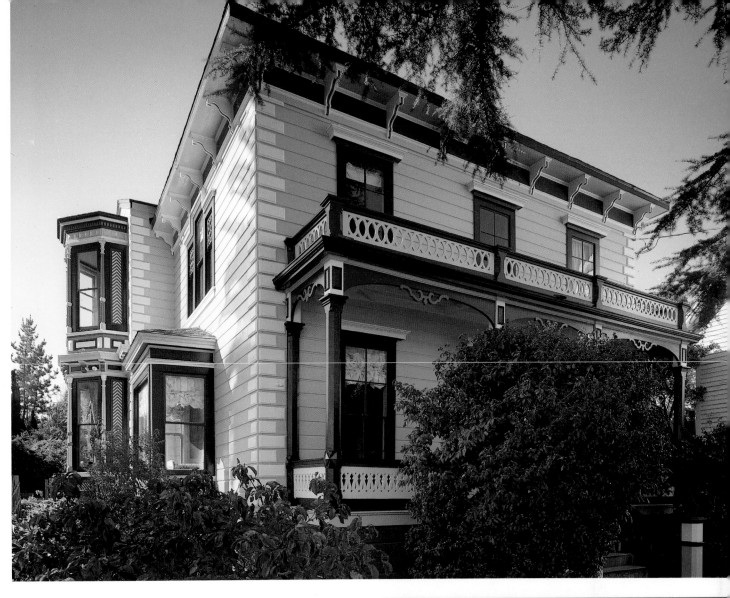

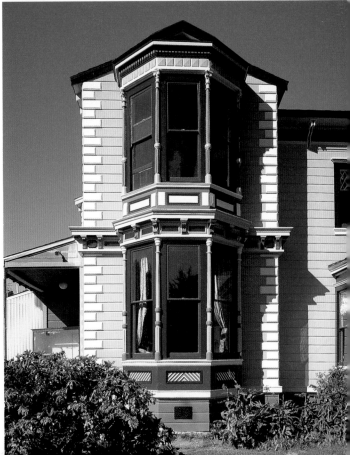

SANTA CRUZ

(Above and right). 123 Green Street. Eastlake. 1864. Built as a Methodist Episcopal Church in 1850, the V. W. Reynolds House was modernized in 1864. For her own home Doni Tunheim chose a palette of Chinese red, dark oily green, bright creamy yellow, white, and gray. The only embellishment this brilliant yellow beacon needs is sunlight.

119

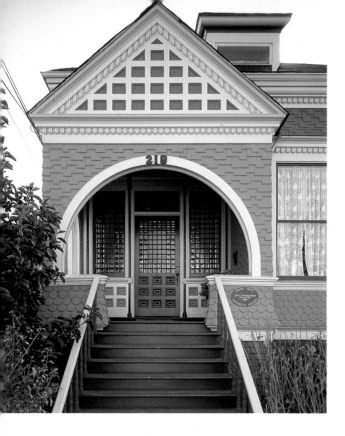

SANTA CRUZ

(Left). 219 Walnut Street. Queen Anne. 1895. Doni Tunheim used white, yellow-ochre, black, and three shades of Mexicali rose to dress up the Carl E. Lindsay House, a Santa Cruz landmark. The blue plaque was put up by the Santa Cruz Historical Society.

SALINAS

(Below). 402 Cayuga Street. Queen Anne. 1898. Built for $2500, and originally painted chartreuse and red, this small wonder is awash with encrusted gables and porches. Shaped shingles, fretwork, and incised ornament are highlighted by the delicate paint design created by owner Linda Piini and color consultant Tony Caneletich.

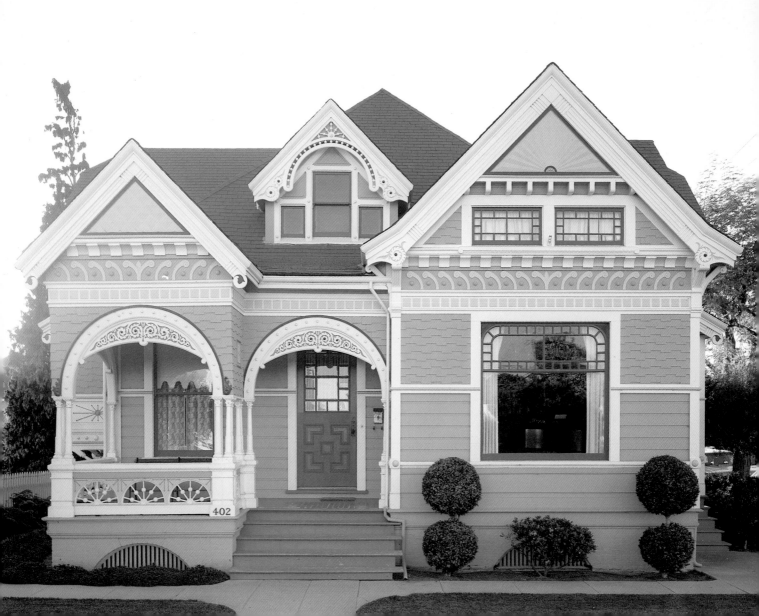

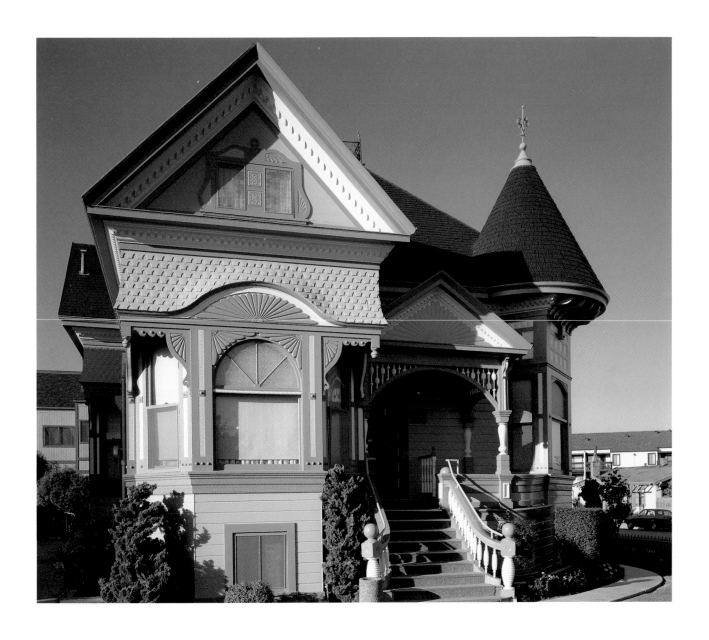

SALINAS

(Above). The Steinbeck House. 132 Central. Queen Anne. 1897. John Steinbeck was born in this storybook cottage and wrote his first two books here. Historians claim that he immortalized the house, remembered from his youth, in *East of Eden*: "It was an immaculate and friendly house, grand enough but not pretentious, and it sat inside its white fence surrounded by its clipped lawns and roses and cotoneasters lapped against its walls."

Since 1973, The Valley Guild has funded the preservation of The Steinbeck House with a homey lunchroom. San Francisco color consultant Butch Kardum did the color design that captures the sun-baked flavor of The Big Valley.

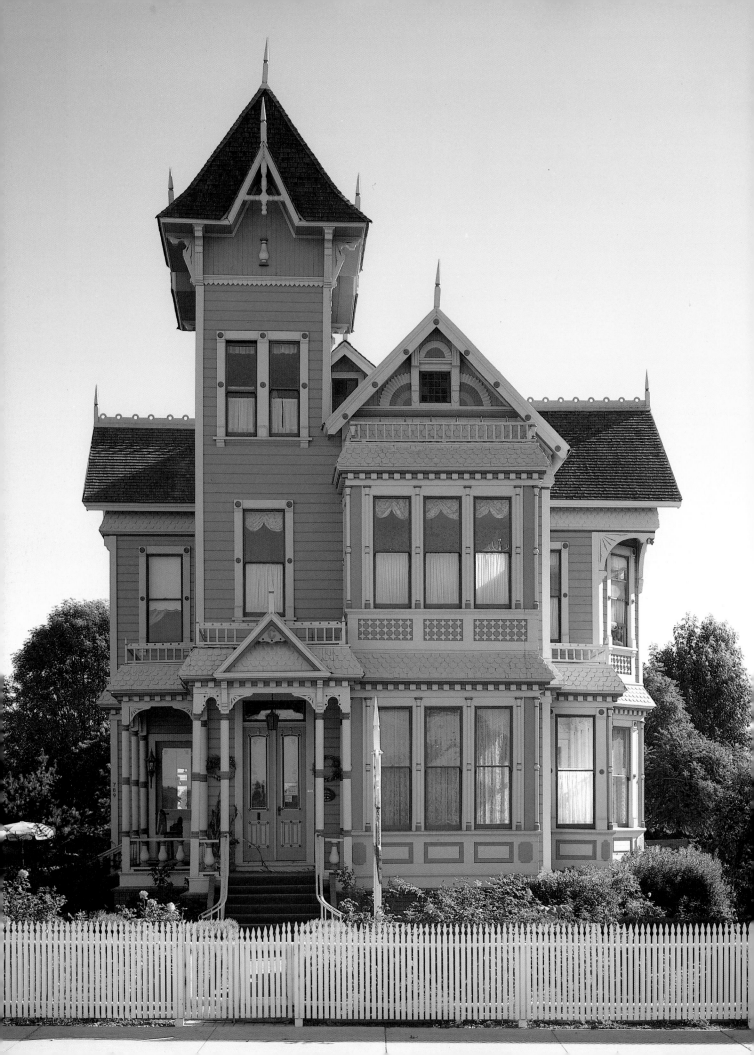

ARROYO GRANDE

(Opposite). The Rose Victorian Inn. 789 Valley Road. Stick/Eastlake. 1885. Charles and Henrietta Pitkin built this extraordinary mansion in the middle of farmland. The haunted tower overlooks the Pacific. Now painted in four shades of rose, with touches of green and white, the inn is surrounded by a rose garden.

Each room is named after a specific rose, a bud of which usually graces the dresser, and provides the theme for the room. For example, Sterling is all silvery and Tropicana is bright oranges. The Rose Victorian inspired its distant cousin, on page 28, another bouquet of roses, in Malden, Massachusetts.

MONROVIA

Monrovia, a town outside of Los Angeles, celebrated its 100th anniversary in 1986, and The Monrovia Old House Preservation Group has revived the town. The program director of the group, Mary Ann Otero, who rents her Queen Anne to film companies, explained that when she had her imposing home enlivened by Bob and Don Buckter, with inspiration from *Painted Ladies*, it turned the Monrovians on to paint and polish. In her words, "*Painted Ladies* saved the town!"

MONROVIA

(Right, above). 444 Concord Street. Gothic. 1880s. Hansel and Gretel would have been very happy in this charming little peach and green cottage. When it was built for the Knudsen Milk family, the house had a solar heating system of copper pipes on the roof. When gas became less expensive, the system fell into disuse and was not discovered until the new owner, a cabinetmaker who made his own fanciful gingerbread, repaired the roof.

REDLANDS

(Right, below). The Edwards Mansion. 2064 Orange Tree Lane. Queen Anne. 1890. Bought for one dollar and moved in halves, the Edwards Mansion has been born again as a restaurant. Bob and Don Buckter designed the rosy-gold color scheme to glow in the sunset. Gold leaf helps to highlight the house's profuse ornamentation.

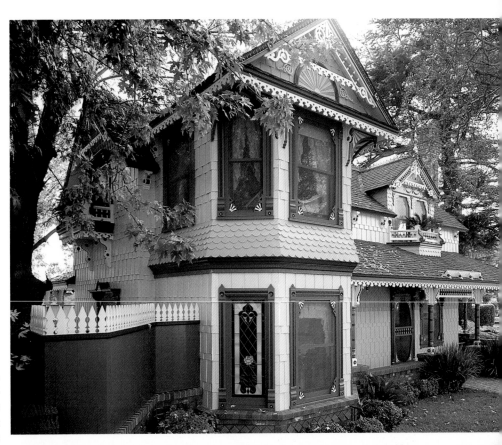

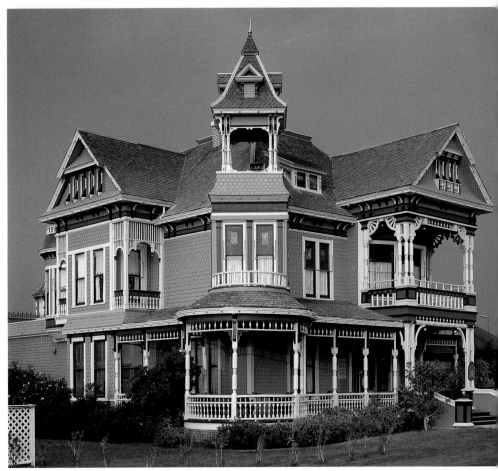

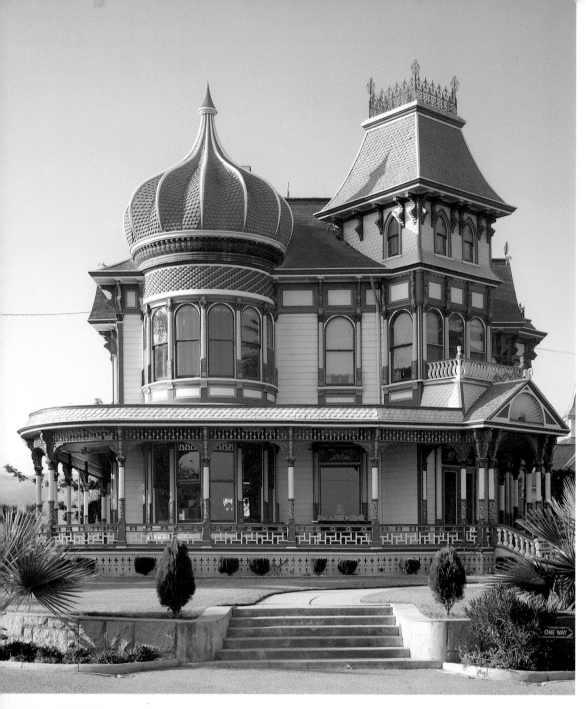

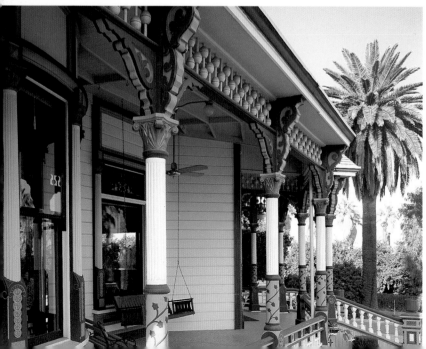

REDLANDS

(Above, left, and opposite). The Morey Mansion. 190 Terracina Blvd. Queen Anne. 1890. San Francisco ship-builder David Morey spent $20,000 building his dream retirement home in an orange grove. Morey himself turned the stair-balustrade spindles and carved the orange blossoms around the doors and windows. Orange blossoms and ship's wheels decorate the woodwork and inlaid bronze hardware indoors and out.

In 1957, John Maass included a picture of the Morey Mansion, then a ghostly white derelict, in his book *The Gingerbread Age*. The ensuing deluge of letters inspired Maass to call it "America's favorite Victorian house." New owners have turned it into a beautifully restored, luxurious B&B popular with honeymooners. The two yellows, three greens, blue, two reds, two grays, beige, black, white, gold, and gold leaf are the original fifteen colors chosen by the Moreys.

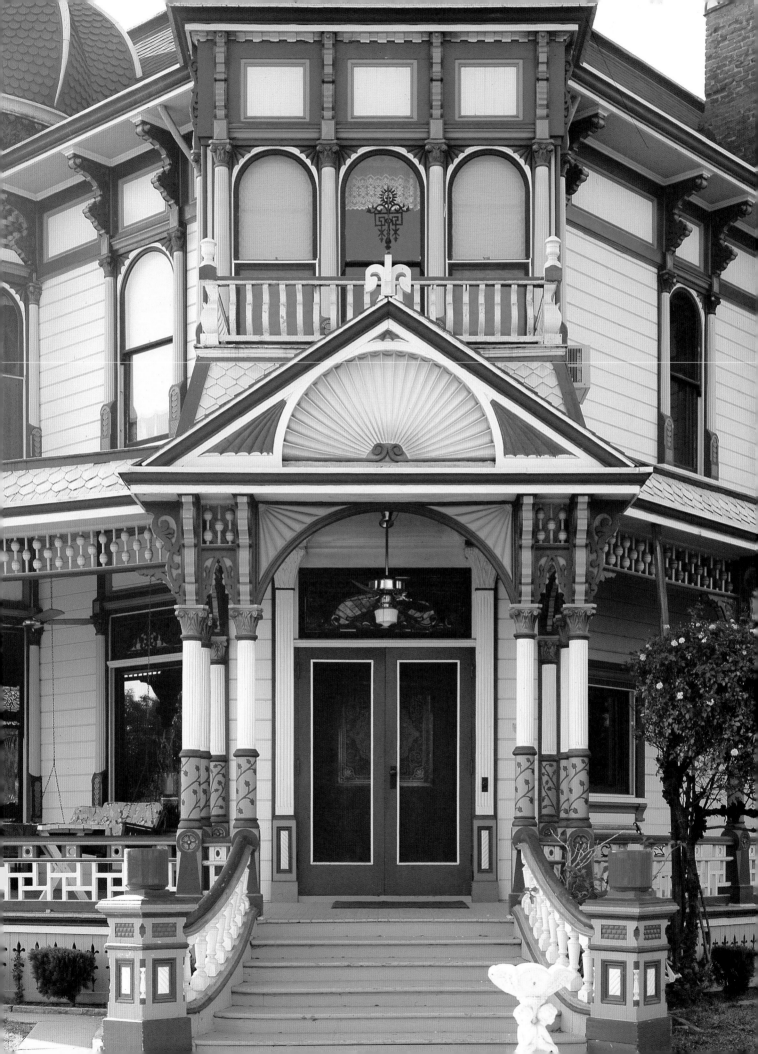

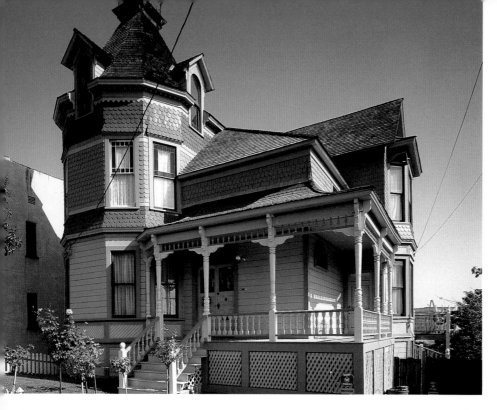

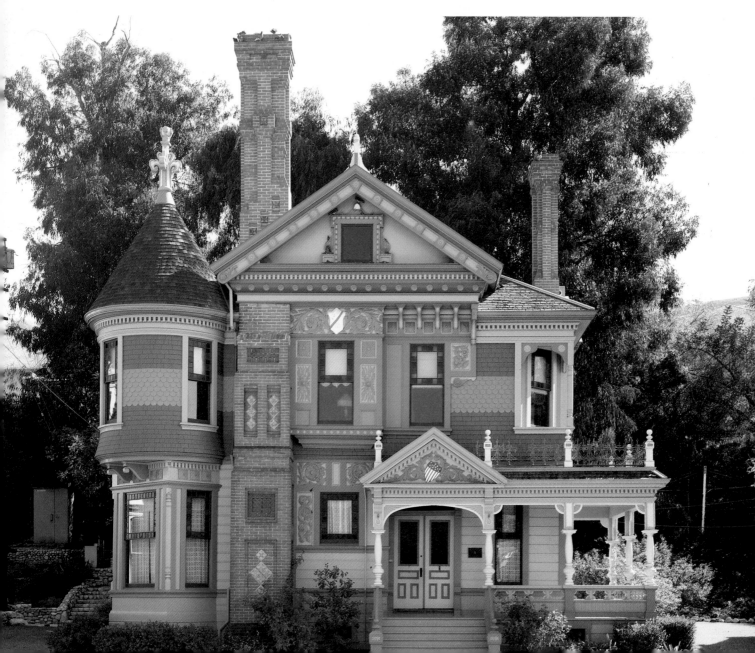

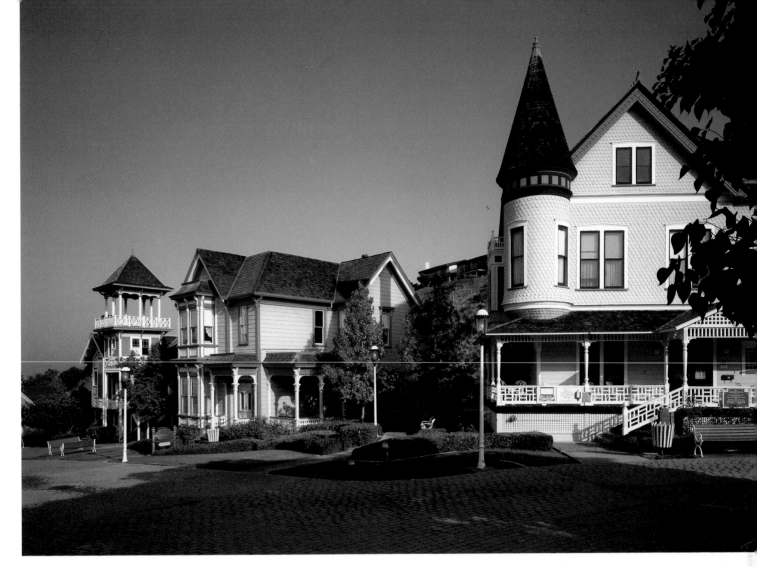

LOS ANGELES

(Opposite, above). 724 East Edgeware. Queen Anne. 1886. Located at the entrance to Carroll Avenue, this proud home was painted by the owners in authentic colors and striped design, from the dark roof to the clay-pink shingles and lime-green first story.

Carroll Avenue shelters one of the West Coast's most remarkable groups of Victorian homes. Once a questionable neighborhood, Carroll Avenue now hosts House Tours. The owners have restored their houses inside and out. Plenaria Price, one of the owners, has been instrumental in moving Victorians doomed to demolition to Carroll Avenue, restoring and painting them, and using her collection of Victorian wallpaper as inspiration for the color schemes.

LOS ANGELES

(Opposite, below). Hale House, Heritage Square. 3800 Homer Street. Queen Anne/Eastlake. 1887. James and Bessie Hale moved into this home, then at Avenue 45 and Figueroa, in 1900. It was rumored to have been designed by the Newsom Brothers, known for Eureka's Carson Mansion. Bessie lived there until 1967. In 1970, Hale House was moved to Heritage Square, a sanctuary for threatened Victorians created by the Cultural Heritage Foundation of Southern California. The Foundation is a volunteer organization that lovingly restores, refurbishes, and shares the rescued buildings with the public.

Now listed on the National Register, Hale House is used by the State of California Parks and Recreation Department as a guide to be followed by other historic preservation projects throughout the state.

In 1978, a local paint company painted the house in thirty-nine "nonclashing" colors, but the extraordinary result caused so many accidents on the nearby Pasadena Freeway that the Foundation decided to repaint the house in its original paint scheme, which accentuates the fine architectural details of the California redwood and the towering red brick chimneys. The result is irresistible.

SAN DIEGO

(Above). Heritage Park Bed & Breakfast Inn. 2470 Heritage Park Row. Queen Anne. 1889. Built for Harfield and Myrtle Christian, the simple mansion on the right was featured in *The Golden Era Magazine* in 1890 and called "an outstandingly beautiful home of Southern California." It is one of seven Victorian buildings, each a different style, which were saved and moved to this park dedicated to the preservation of San Diego's Victorian heritage.

The other buildings are offices and gift shops, but, alas, the Park officials have limited the color palette.

Elsewhere in the city, San Diego's Main Street efforts in "Gaslamp" San Diego have succeeded in restoring brick, stone, and wooden Victorians and changing a slum into a popular shopping and business center.

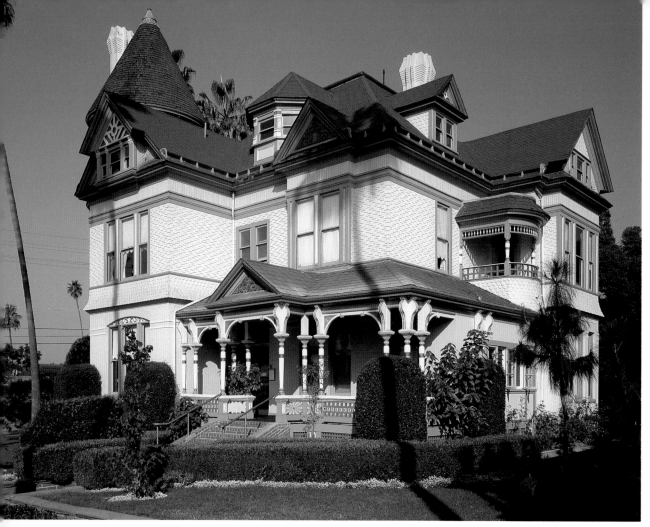

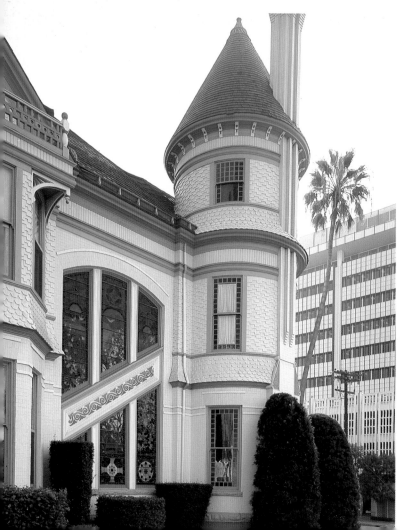

SAN DIEGO

(Above, left, and opposite). The Britt House. 406 Maple Street.
Queen Anne. 1887. The sunny California seaside colors designed
by the innkeeper with white, golds, and blues, echoes the colors in
the huge stained-glass window that lights the stairwell.

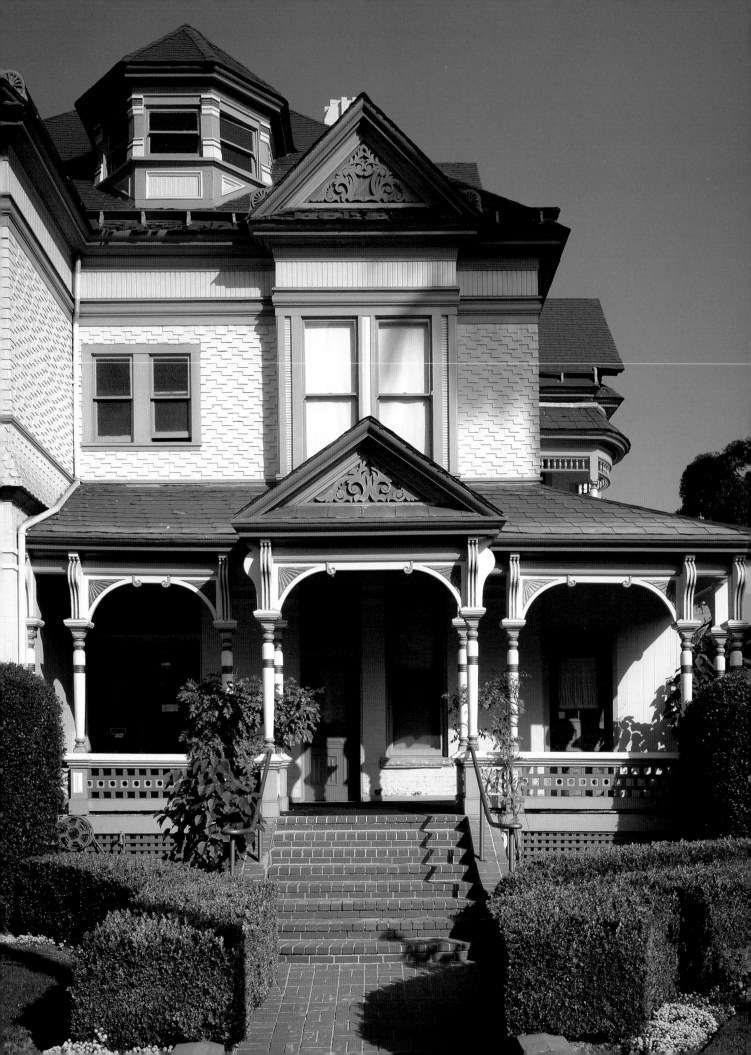

Epilogue

In Search of Painted Cousins

We envision the contemporary use of color joyfully spreading to other kinds of architecture and other countries. Painted Ladies are being spotted around the globe. Our Canadian cousins are beginning to rescue their Victorian white elephants and bring them to vivid life. Eighteenth-century Queen Annes bedecked with sunflowers still bloom in England. In Germany, the Berlin motif of dark reds, greens, and yellows still lives on Queen Anne structures. We haven't decided whether or not the edelweiss-trimmed blue, red, and white Swiss chalets are part of the family. In the Caribbean, pastel pastiches light up tropic towns. Thai temples are roofed with shattered patterned china and crushed colored glass. Mirrored glass and gold leaf are used more lavishly as exterior decoration in Thailand than anywhere on the planet.

And in Australia, Painted Ladies are beginning to line the sidewalks. Here is one of them:

Strelitz Buildings. 30 Mouat Street, Fremantle, Perth, Western Australia. Built in 1890 for German merchant brothers Paul and Richard Strelitz, this house was later sold to George Evans, who established the first paint manufacturing business in Western Australia. A young American mining engineer and future President named Herbert Hoover was an early tenant.

In 1981, a young restauranteur moved into the top floor and opened a restaurant on the ground floor. He found San Francisco color consultant Bob Buckter through *Painted Ladies* and commissioned this magical color design, a first for Western Australia.

Some day, we hope to do a book (which we promise *not* to call *Distant Cousins of Painted Ladies*!) about vividly colored traditional architecture to be found throughout the world. If you should discover any likely candidates, please tell us about them or send a slide or photograph.

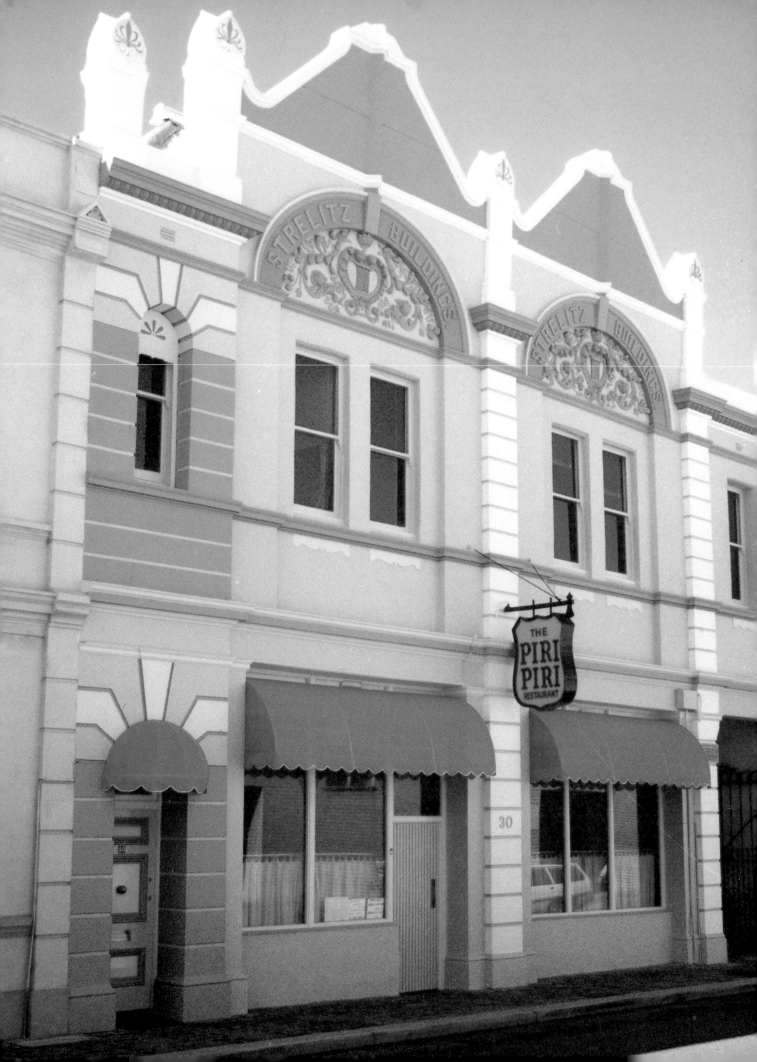

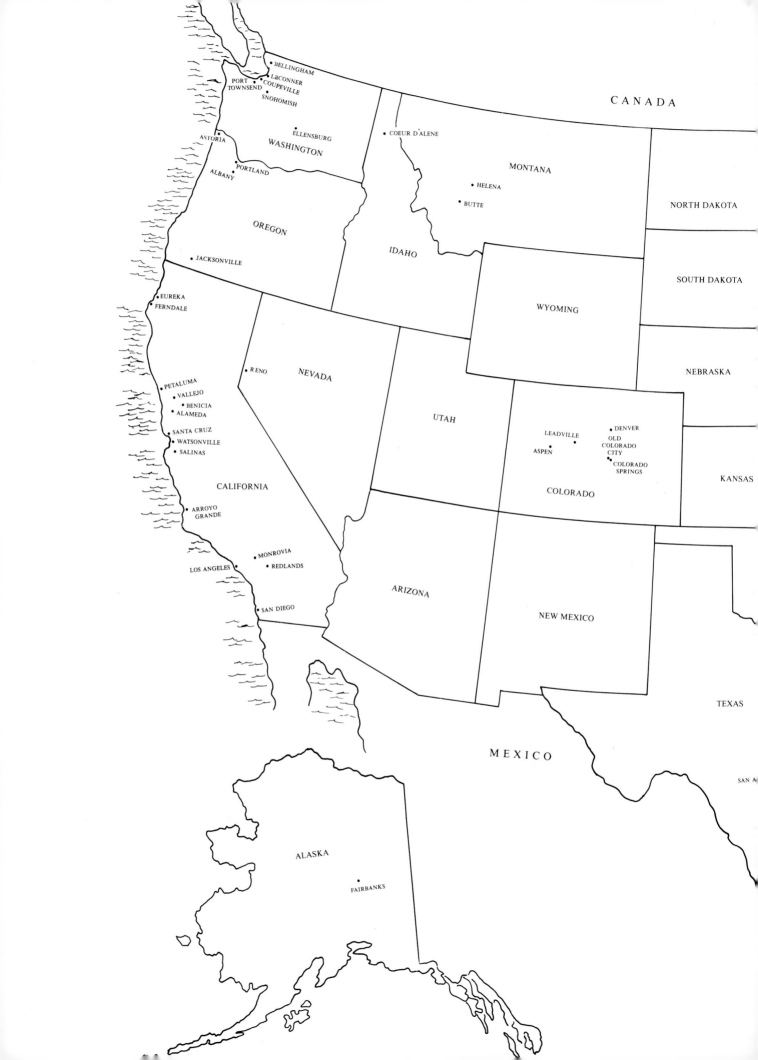

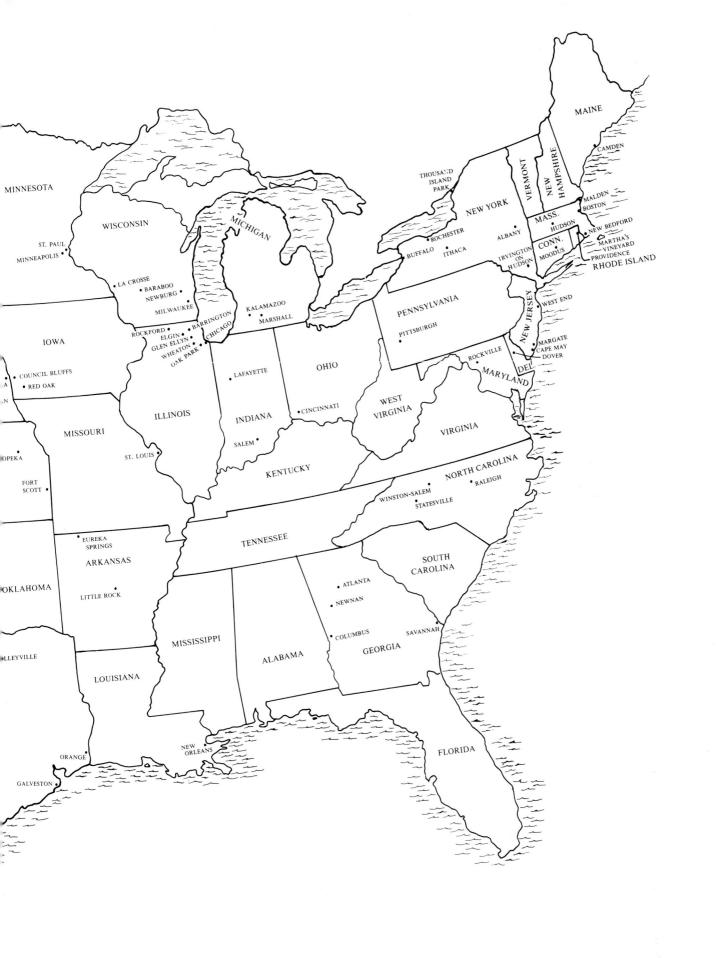

Daughters of Painted Ladies Deserving Honorable Mention

Houses appearing in this list are arranged in the same geographical order as those illustrated in the book.

Northeast: 158 Danforth Street, Portland, Maine; 438 State Street, Portsmouth, New Hampshire; Wallingford Inn, Wallingford, Vermont; 36 Stimson, Providence, Rhode Island; *140 W. Broad Street, Pawcatuck, Connecticut; *507 Whitney, New Haven, Connecticut; Mark Twain House, Hartford, Connecticut; 122 Broad Street, Guilford, Connecticut; 405 County Street, New Bedford, Massachusetts; 398 County Street, New Bedford, Massachusetts; 152 Cottage Street, New Bedford, Massachusetts; 99 Hickory Street, Rochester, New York; 412 S. Albany Street, Ithaca, New York; 290 United States, Thousand Island Park, New York; Coast Avenue West, Thousand Island Park, New York; 164–168 Jay Street, Albany, New York; 165 Lancaster, Albany, New York; 211 Union Street, Saratoga Springs, New York; Mansard House, Amenia, New York; 531 W. 8th Street, Plainfield, New Jersey; 13 Ocean Pathway, Ocean Grove, New Jersey; 117 Passaic, Spring Lake, New Jersey; 102 Columbia Queen Victoria, Cape May, New Jersey; Merry Widow, Carpenter and Jackson Streets, Cape May, New Jersey; 264 E. Broad Street, Bethlehem, Pennsylvania; 1203 North Street, Pittsburgh, Pennsylvania; 1319 Sheffield Street, Pittsburgh, Pennsylvania; 1128 Sheffield Street, Pittsburgh, Pennsylvania; 1130 North, Pittsburgh, Pennsylvania; 1319–1329 Liverpool Street, Pittsburgh, Pennsylvania; Library, 3rd Street, New Castle, Delaware; The Castle, 112 W. 6th Street, New Castle, Delaware.

South: 533 High Street, Petersburg, Virginia; 1053 Main Street, Richmond, Virginia; 308 S. Third, Wilmington, North Carolina; 39A and 39B Smith Street, Charleston, South Carolina; 200 Macon at Abecorn, Savannah, Georgia; 423 Mabry, Selma, Alabama; 509 Tremont, Selma, Alabama; 2809 Esplanade, New Orleans, Louisiana; Crescent Inn, 211 Spring Street, Eureka Springs, Arkansas.

Midwest: 701 E. High, Boonville, Missouri; 1104 18th, St. Louis, Missouri; 1901 Hickory Street, St. Louis, Missouri; 2342 Widdimore, St. Louis, Missouri; 523 E. Vermont, Indianapolis, Indiana; 309 W. Michigan, Marshall, Michigan; 213 Elm, Kalamazoo, Michigan; 219 E. 3rd Street, Hinsdale, Illinois; 679 Main, Glen Ellyn, Illinois; 600 E. Chicago, Elgin, Illinois; Tinker Cottage, Rockford, Illinois; St. Moritz, 327 Wrigley, Lake Geneva, Wisconsin; 920 Main Street, Lake Geneva, Wisconsin; 326 3rd Avenue, Baraboo, Wisconsin; 1532 Madison, La Crosse, Wisconsin;

528 Dayton, St. Paul, Minnesota; 704 19th Street, Des Moines, Iowa; 410 Iowa Avenue, Iowa City, Iowa; 126 Park, Council Bluffs, Iowa; 1130 Plum, Lincoln, Nebraska; 711 N. Catalba, Pittsburg, Kansas; 270–24 N. Main, Fort Scott, Kansas; 120 Cody, Fort Scott, Kansas; 104 Greenwood, Topeka, Kansas; 313 Greenwood, Topeka, Kansas; 305 Greenwood, Topeka, Kansas.

Southwest: Gay Nineties, 719 Third, Aspen, Colorado; 201 N. First, Aspen, Colorado; 627 N. Main, Aspen, Colorado; 201 Smuggler, Aspen, Colorado; Cog Railway, Manitou Springs, Colorado; Barker House, Manitou Springs, Colorado; The Painted Lady, Colorado Springs, Colorado; Hallmark House, Colorado Springs, Colorado; 2402 Avenue L, Galveston, Texas; *1102 Heights Boulevard, Houston, Texas; 919 6th Street, Las Vegas, New Mexico; The Castle, Virginia City, Nevada.

Northwest: 201 S. Washington, Butte, Montana; 45–55 W. Granite, Butte, Montana; 1301 N. 16th, Boise, Idaho; Stark House, 514 Clay, Port Townsend, Washington; Terry and Main, Coupeville, Washington; Marshall House, Evergreen Boulevard, Vancouver, Washington; 1661 Grand, Astoria, Oregon; 208 7th, Albany, Oregon; 632 Washington, Albany, Oregon; 829 Washington, Albany, Oregon; 532 Ferry, Albany, Oregon.

California: 1249 Rose, Ferndale; Annie's B & B, Grass Valley; 131 Townsend, Grass Valley; 111 Liberty, Petaluma; 728 Capital Street, Vallejo; The Wedding Chapel, 896 E. Main, Ventura; 150 N. Myrtle, Monrovia; Idlewild House, 255 N. Mayflower Avenue, Monrovia; 1316–1330 Carroll Avenue, Los Angeles; 1330 Carroll Avenue, Los Angeles; The Los Angeles Architectural Preservation Center, 1308 W. 25th Street and 1314 W. 25th Street, Los Angeles.

Copies of the photographs taken of these houses, and those in the book, with the exception of those identified by asterisks, can be obtained directly from Michael Larsen/Elizabeth Pomada, 1029 Jones Street, San Francisco, CA 94109.

Despite all the wonderful help we received, we have undoubtedly missed some gems. If you should locate one, please let us know about it. We'd like to see photographs or slides of likely candidates for the next volume of *Daughters of Painted Ladies*. And, of course, we always like to feature new beauties in our slide shows.

Creating Your Own Painted Lady

Painting only the facade in polychrome, as you can on San Francisco row houses, is not possible elsewhere, for most houses are freestanding. Because painting in more than two colors takes more time and attention, polychrome does cost more than sprayed-on monochrome.

Other factors that must be answered in figuring costs are:

What prepwork is needed?

Will the surface take another coat of paint or does it have to be stripped?

How much work will it take to correct moisture problems, remove peeling and chalking paint, to clean before you prime?

What's the best primer and finishing coat combination?

Time costs money. But good prepwork will make a paint job last longer, so you will be saving money in the long run.

Follow these six steps in painting your house:

1. Pick your colors.
2. Choose the desired sheens and finishes.
3. Select your tools and other materials.
4. Prepare the surface.
5. Apply the paint.
6. Clean up.

What Is Paint?

A little background on color and paint will help you make your house say what you want it to say. Paint is simply coloring pigments mixed with oil or water. It is a barrier, a sacrificial, renewable film that protects a house. Paint is also a cosmetic, a way to bring out the best in the architecture of a building.

Until the Industrial Revolution, colors were mixed on site by the painter. Oil paint was usually linseed oil-based, perhaps with white lead as a color base. Water-based paint was cheap, sometimes just slaked lime and water. Milk and chalky calcimine were also used as water-soluble bases. Colored with blood, milk paint was exceptionally long-lasting.

The color red came from clay, from trees, such as brazilwood; carmine, from dried insect bodies. Blue was from cobalt ore. The rare, expensive Prussian blue came from prussic acid; ultramarine from lapis lazuli. Copper ore produced green; acetic acid yielded verdigris green. Burnt sienna—a favorite Crayola color today—came from heated iron and manganese. Saffron and buckthorn berries produced two shades of yellow; three more came from sulphur, mercury, and arsenic. Burnt peach pits made a deep blue-black; wine lees made Frankfort black.

A hundred years ago, in *Colour in Decoration,* an artist wrote "to master colour is to exercise in secret...an almost despotic power over human thoughts and feelings." Today's color designers know how to make your house a happy house, a somber one, or one that's quietly dignified.

Every arrangement of color demands the presence of the three primary colors: red, yellow, and blue. The green, violet, and orange that border these colors on the color wheel are called complementary colors to the primaries. In 1877, *The Painter's Magazine* dictated, "Blue is cold; orange is warm or fiery; yellow is bright and advancing; violet is retiring; red is hot and glaring; green is quiet and cool. This is the basis of the whole theory of the laws of contrast in coloring." This is still true.

Tertiary colors are each primary color mixed with those next to it on a color wheel. The intensity or saturation of a color or hue is called chroma. Shades are colors darkened with black. Value is the light to dark scale. When choosing colors, choose a color palette in which there is a relationship of both hue and value running through all the colors.

In practical terms, this can translate into actually mixing in a little of each color with the one next to it when painting highly contrasting colors on a house. This little bit of mixing in creates harmony between colors. Transition colors can also buffer high-contrast areas. The Hale House in Los Angeles was painted in thirty-nine contrasting colors, which harmonized because of the color placement.

When Is Original Original?

Researching and determining original paint colors is still a matter best left to experts with microscopes. Matthew J. Mosca, the scientist who documented and recreated the correct warm interior colors at Mount Vernon, has explained that what you see when you scrape away layers is usually not the colors that were originally applied, for paint fades in sunlight and darkens with age. Linseed oil yellows and darkens with time. So does white lead paint. Exposure to ultraviolet light can counteract the yellowing, but it can't always lighten the color enough to be true.

Some pigments are stable. Blues and greens are not, so they sometimes disappear, leaving a brown. Verdigris turns black. "Spanish brown," frequently identified as an original color, is often the brown primer, not the paint itself.

One color myth is that Victorians did not paint their houses blue. Prussian blue paint and wallpaper were actually status symbols, for they were very difficult to make and very expensive.

Even photographs can mislead. We found a sweet Victorian in Cortland, New York, and we couldn't figure out why they had painted the metal roof turquoise. It seems that the owner had copied a hand-colored photo-postcard of the original house. It had a blue-green roof that turned out to be oxidized copper.

Authentic color is also very different today than it was, because today's paint manufacturers are not allowed to use the poisonous white leads, arsenics, and chromium yellows that made paints glisten. True yellows and real whites are hard to create because manufacturers have to conform to new health laws. Saturated colors are hard to find. And the natural linseed, nut, or poppy oils that created the deep, delicious, dark oily greens no longer exist.

Modern paint has three elements: pigment, a binder such as linseed oil or acrylic or latex resin, and a thinner such as mineral spirits, turpentine, or water. Pigment is what gives the paint color. The binder, the most expensive part of the paint, is the key to good paint. Cheap paint will not last as long as good paint, so choosing paint on price alone will be a false economy.

The primer provides a uniform surface for the topcoat or finish coat. It seals old surfaces and promotes adhesion between old and new paint. A primer also lengthens the life of the pigment in the topcoat.

Topcoats can be oil/alkyd or water/latex. The traditional oil-base paints brush on well and have good penetrating properties. Some are self-cleaning. Oil-base paints have greater hiding power than latex, which can reflect what's underneath more easily. And because of the oil, they're naturally glossier than water-base paints.

Latex-acrylic topcoats are just as durable as oil-base paints. Latex is quicker drying. Latex color fades less, and since latex usually has a flat or matte finish, touch-ups are easier. Because they are water-soluble, clean-ups are also easier.

Remember, however, that when you put paint on top of old paint, it must stick, and oil paint sticks better to old oil paint than latex will.

Experts recommend mixing small amounts of paint first. Keep in mind that the color of wet paint is different after it dries, and that there are disparities in types of paint, brands, and finishes, so you should probably wait until the sample dries to make sure that the color is satisfactory. Latex dries in about an hour; some alkyds need twenty-four hours; some oil-base paints take two weeks to dry and set. When it's time to make a big batch, pour the desired amounts of each paint into a mixing vessel and stir thoroughly. Then you can use and store small portions that are all identical.

Select colors that won't fade quickly. For deep tones, start with the factory-colored base closest to your chosen color and then mix with lighter, standard, factory-ground colors. Don't use an ultra-deep base that is "shot" by formula into a white base; it will fall apart and fade faster than it should. For paler tones that would ordinarily demand two or three coats of paint, choose colors that at least have a minute amount of raw umber, raw sienna, or lamp black in them. They will last much longer.

Weather is an important factor in the life of your paint and the colors you choose. Talk to professionals in your area to see what works best. In California, for example, houses that face north weather better than those that face south. Dampness, cold, and heat are also factors.

Variations in sheen add dimension and visual texture to a paint job. There are four types of sheen: satin, flat, semi-gloss, and gloss. Satin works well on the major trim as does semi-gloss on small, well-balanced accent areas. Glossy oil-base paints lose their sheen in one to three years, depending on weather and the house's exposure to it. Semi-gloss acrylic enamels can keep their sheen for up to seven years.

To estimate how much paint you will need, multiply the height and the width of the house to obtain the area in square feet, and then deduct ten percent for the windows and doors.

Quality brushes also save time and money in the long run. Brushes should have sturdy, easy-to-use handles and hefty bristles. Professionals use two sets of brushes. One set is used for oil paint, varnish, and polyurethane, and the other for acrylic paint. Four of each usually suffice: a 4-inch brush, a 2½-inch brush, a 3-inch tapered brush for window sashes, and 1½- or 1-inch brushes for accents. Brushes soften with age, leaving fewer brush marks. China or sable bristles work well for non-water soluble finishes; 100 percent polyester brushes can be used for any finish.

The key to a durable paint job is preparation, which may mean four to eight hours of prep work for every hour of painting. Strip old paint with heat, sand-blasting if the house is stone, or chemicals. Strip over "alligators," cracks and splits in old paint. Mildew spots, blisters, dirt, chalking, anything that interrupts the smooth flow of paint—including neighbors who assure you with absolute confidence that your house has always been white—must be removed. Glossy surfaces should be sanded so the new paint will adhere to the surface. Aim for thin coats of oil paint or thick coats of acrylic paint on dry, well-seasoned lumber.

If you are removing asbestos shingles, the "skin disease" of misguided modernization, don't burn them—they'll pop like bursting glass bombs.

Joe Adamo, St. Louis's premier color artist, does most of his work on stone buildings. His painters first chemically remove the old paint and power wash the surface, then they apply an epoxy masonry sealer. Masons replace lost pieces. Carpenters spruce up the doors, gables, and woodwork. Fences and steps are restored. Then a pigmented bonding primer is applied, followed by an acrylic finish. Adamo has found that acrylics have the elasticity to survive St. Louis's freezing winters and blistering summers.

A painter in Delaware explained that no exterior painting can take place once the mercury dips below 42 degrees because the paint will not adhere. In New York, a homeowner was told she couldn't paint her house until spring "when there are no bugs in the air." Paint is best applied in shadow, not in direct sunlight. Be wary of electric wires, stripping chemicals, unsteady ladders, and wasp nests.

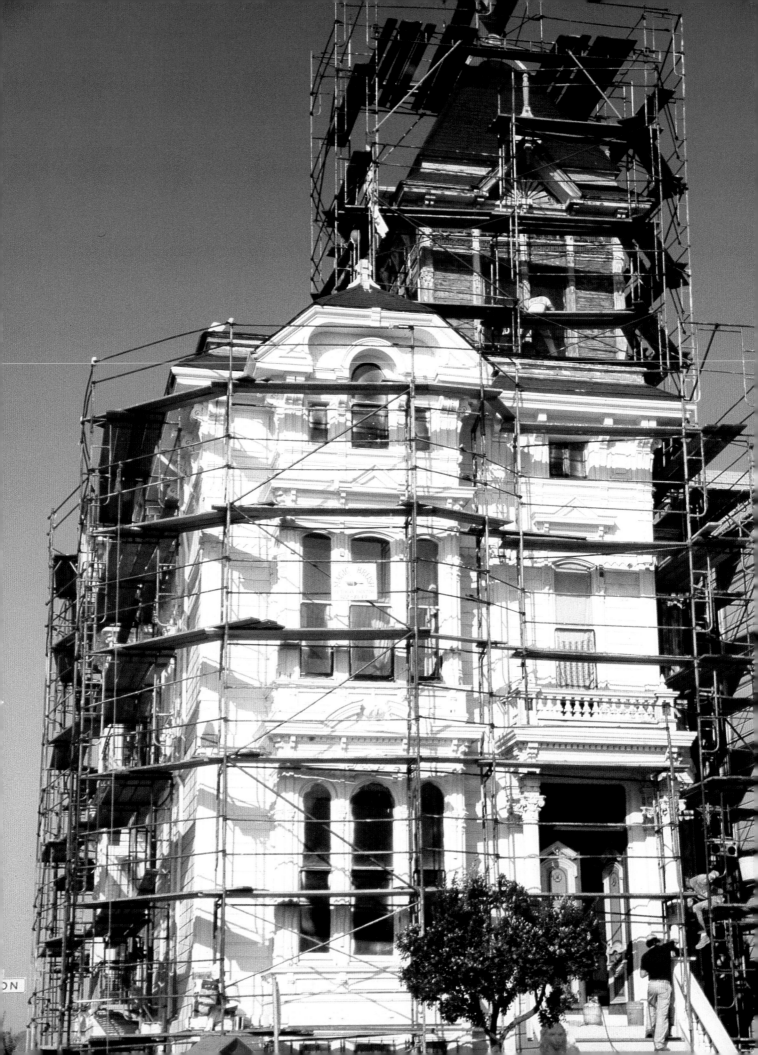

A Sample Job

Before you choose a color designer and painter, you may want to follow the history of a paint job in San Francisco. Robert Dufort of Magic Brush, Inc. took 365 workdays to paint the Westerfield House at 1198 Fulton (one of the stars of *Painted Ladies*), a large, historically important, four-sided, towered, eclectic villa. The proposal for the work took sixteen hours, including research, writing, and meetings with the owners.

After the initial prep work, torching, sanding, and scraping, a list of recommendations for gutter and dry rot repair, carpentry, replacement of lost or missing trim, millwork, and sheet metal, was presented, along with estimates of time and expense. It took sixty workdays (one person's work in an eight-hour day) for the torching, fifty-five for the scraping, sanding, etc., and sixty-five workdays for the repair work. Thirty-five workdays of priming were followed by fifty workdays of caulking and puttying. A second priming on torched and repaired areas took twenty workdays. Wire brushing of the wrought iron on the building, stairs, railways, and crown went quickly.

The scaffolding for this job cost $16,000 figured at the rate of $9,000 a month to rent, one-third of that for each additional month, with no charge for rainy days. One hundred and twenty gallons of acrylic/latex primer was used, and one hundred gallons of 100 percent acrylic finish coat.

The colors were tested on a small section of the building after the first priming. Dufort then made a detailed pencil marking of each section, showing color placement for the painters to follow. Six colors, plus gold-leaf accents, were applied from top to bottom. The finish coating took eighty workdays. The southern and western sides and the tower needed two finish coats. Usually, paint was sprayed on, then brushed in while still wet. This technique is much faster and just as good as applying the paint solely by hand. First the trim was sprayed on to cover the angles and bits, then the flat body areas were sprayed on. The line where two colors met was cut-in by hand, as were "holidays" or thin spots. Accent colors were then applied. Note that only 25 percent of the time was for finish painting.

Dufort planned this job to last ten to fifteen years, although he suggests a repainting in eight to ten years which, with a bit of spot torching and a few repairs, will cost half the price of this job. A big celebration finished the job with style.

Designing It Yourself

First think about where your house is—the neighborhood, the weather, the surrounding gardens or houses. What style of Victorian is it, and what would be appropriate? Look at the house from the curb. What makes it different? Special? What draws the eye positively or negatively? Is there a unique ornament that should be highlighted with color?

Decide whether you will opt for a historic approach or a contemporary approach that, to San Francisco colorist Jill Pilaroscia "gleans the best techniques from the past and combines them with imaginative solutions such as exterior stenciling, trompe l'oeil, and faux finishing." Choose color palettes you already like, perhaps from those inside the house, in your wardrobe, or on favorite rugs or fabrics. See what others have done and which houses make you glad to see them, which do not.

Take note of what cannot be changed, like foundation masonry, or a slate or shingled roof. The roof can be an important part of the total look and its color counts as part of the color scheme. The roof can be painted, textured, or patterned.

Does your castle have a stained-glass window with colors that could be reflected in the exterior paint?

To map out the colors of your house, trace the outlines of an enlarged black and white photo on a plain piece of white paper. Do one for each side of the house, and perhaps others for specially detailed sections. This is your personal paint-by-numbers sheet. Study the photo and the tracing.

The act of tracing gives you a real feeling for your house. It's a practice paint session. Notice the cornices, the bands of pattern, the doors and windows. You may discover molding you have never really noticed before. Separate out the main areas: body, trim, windows, gables, repeating details. What stands out? What is your favorite area or detail? What do you like best? Least?

Some color designers suggest taking dozens of 3-by-5-inch glossy color prints of the house, both distance and detail shots, to study every surface, every detail. Bob Buckter takes up to twenty photos of the house, focusing on each part of the facade, from dentils to doorway.

Don't color in your tracing. It's just not possible to duplicate the 1,600 colors available from the paint store. Instead, shade the drawings with a pencil, so you can determine light to dark values. This will tell you how many shades and hues you are aiming for.

Identify how many colors you want, and where they will be used, then number them on your drawing. The body color, the most important, is usually labeled #1. Number 2 could become the architectural or trim color: the eaves, the vertical battens on either end of the house. The zinger or accent colors for the house's accessories—the moldings, dentils, spindles, gingerbread, shutters, railings, and front door—become #3, #4, and #5.

View your color chips in different lights. Check sample color charts in natural light. Viewing the charts in open shade or an overcast sky will give you the truest color. View each color separately against a piece of white paper, not when they are next to each other on a chip card or in a fan-deck. Then isolate the chips together on light and dark backgrounds. Check each pairing individually. Be sure they correspond to the dark and light values of your black and white tracings.

Buy small samples of the paint and paint a section of the house to see how they harmonize. Live with it awhile to see how they look in different lights. The cautious citizens of one town in the Midwest "lived with" their samples for a year before finishing the job, but we don't suggest this. You might make two tests, one on the shady side of the house, another on the sunny side.

Denny Wilson, a color designer in Orange, California, who learned about color from a Disney Studio artist, sometimes paints different sides of a house different shades, so that they will all look the same in the differing light.

Remember that colors on large areas will be brighter than the same colors on small areas. And remember to talk to neighbors, paint stores, or color consultants for ideas and hints.

Light colors reflect ultraviolet light and heat, which makes them more durable, and they make areas appear larger. Dark colors absorb ultraviolet light and heat, so they fade more quickly. Because they appear to recede, they can create a sense of drama.

A wonderful lady in Boston painted her home in traditional Victorian colors, much to the perturbation of the neighbors. One remarked to her, "I can understand the gold, and I even like the red and green, but did you *have* to paint the window sashes black?"

One man might think that window sashes are too small an area to worry about, but black sashes make the windows recede, while white sashes pop out and can look out of place on a Victorian. Sash colors were always important in the nineteenth century. Luckily, storm-window manufacturers are discovering that the silver of aluminum does not enhance a Queen Anne beauty.

In the June 1986 issue of *Old-House Journal,* San Franciscan Jill Pilaroscia listed six criteria for a harmonious paint job: balance, rhythm, interaction, skeletal outline, durability, and accent.

A well-balanced color arrangement will have visual unity with color distributed evenly, top to bottom. The repetition of color juxtapositions creates a pleasing rhythm. Strong accent colors on small expanses will fade gracefully. Jill feels that accents on undersurfaces can add surprise and create surface texture. Using trim colors to create the skeletal structure for the building defines and unifies its architectural elements.

When one color touches another, it can accentuate or drain the other color. For example, white makes the color next to it less strong, while gray touching red makes the red appear redder, and the gray then takes on a reddish cast.

When you know what you want and perhaps feel that the job should be entrusted to a professional, choose a custom painter who knows and likes Victorians. Denver colorist James Martin feels that you have to love these buildings to paint them well. Too low a bid may mean a poor job. References are important, and personal compatibility is crucial.

A Plaque of Your Own

Before you finish, you may want to put your house on the National Historic Register. It can be a great source of pride and can be a financial aid. To see if this is a possibility, ask yourself the following questions: Is your house architecturally or historically significant? Did a famous person or prominent citizen design the house or live in it? Is it the best example of a certain style of architecture in your neighborhood? Was it the first in the area to have a modern improvement such as electricity? Leaded glass windows, fireplaces, and gingerbread are additional ammunition; modern improvements are not.

Work with the people at your State Historic Register before tackling the National. Your city or state preservationist will be delighted to help fill in the multitude of forms and can direct you to researchers or mapmakers. If your house is in a National Historic District, then it automatically qualifies for the National Register. Likewise, if you qualify for your State Historic Register, then there's a chance you can be on the National Historic Register. After that, you will be eligible for tax incentives, rebates, and matching and government restoration grants.

You have to pay for your own plaque, but you will know that your preservation efforts will never be violated by future owners. And you will know that your Painted Lady, a triumph of art and architecture, will endure.

Resources

Organizations

Advice about your Victorian is easy to find. In addition to hundreds of local historical societies or organizations like San Francisco's Victorian Alliance and the Foundation for San Francisco's Architectural Heritage, every state has a *chapeau* (That's French for SHPO—State Historic Preservation Office). Cities with planning departments have preservation officers.

The two national organizations interested in Victorians are:

National Trust for Historic Preservation
1785 Massachusetts Avenue
Washington, D. C. 20036
(202) 673-4000
Regional offices are located in Boston, Mass., Charleston, S.C., Chicago, Ill., Denver, Colo., Philadelphia, Pa., and San Francisco, Cal.

Victorian Society of America
East Washington Square
Philadelphia, Pa. 19106
(215) 627-4252
The Society has chapters in Atlanta, Ga., Austin, Tex., Baltimore, Md., Boston, Mass., Brighton, N.J., Cape May, N.J., Chicago, Ill., Cincinnati, O., Denver, Colo., Des Moines, Ia., Evansville-New Harmony, Ind., Honolulu, Hawaii, Hudson River Valley, N.Y., Kansas, Michigan, Milwaukee, Wis., Minneapolis, Minn., Montclair, N.J., Nashville, Tenn., New York, N.Y., North Carolina, Ohio River Valley, Portland, Ore., San Francisco, Cal., Syracuse, N.Y., Toledo, O., Washington, D. C., Williamsburg, Va., Wilmington, Del., Wichita, Ka. Headquarters of the chapters may vary so contact the Philadelphia office for the current address.

Magazines

Early American Life
Historical Times, Inc.
2245 Kohn Road, P.O. Box 8200
Harrisburg, Pa. 17105-8200
1-800-435-9610

Historic Preservation
Published by the National Trust for Historic Preservation
1785 Massachusetts Avenue, N.W.
Washington, D. C. 20036
(202) 673-4000

Old-House Journal
69A Seventh Avenue
Brooklyn, N.Y. 11217
(718) 636-4514

Victorian Homes
3600 Renovator's Old Mill
Millers Falls, Mass. 01349
(413) 659-3785
Editorial offices:
550 7th Street
Brooklyn, N.Y. 11215
(718) 499-5789

Books

American Life Foundation
Box 349
Watkins Glen, N.Y. 14891
John Crosby Freeman's American Life Foundation is a non-profit, educational institution specializing in the acquisition and dissemination of knowledge through publications. Open to the study of all aspects of American life, it is especially interested in the relationships of things and ideas and how the social functions of artifacts from the past relate to those of today. Recently, it has been republishing many nineteenth-century stylebooks about architecture and the decorative arts to assist old-house owners. Write for the catalog: *How to Become a Victorian Lover in Three Quick Steps.*

Color Consultants

Don Buckter
1862 Lakeshore
Los Angeles, Cal. 90026
(213) 663-8990

Foster Meagher
15118 No. Courtney
Los Angeles, Cal. 90046
(213) 874-9773

Tony Canaletich
San Francisco Renaissance
213 Richardson Drive
Mill Valley, Cal. 94941
(415) 921-5197

Bob Buckter
3877 20th Street
San Francisco, Cal. 94114
(415) 922-7444

Robert DuFort
Magic Brush, Inc.
2616 21st Street
San Francisco, Cal. 94114
(415) 922-8649

Butch Kardum
210 San Jose
San Francisco, Cal. 94110
(415) 824-1623

Jill Pilaroscia
Architectural Color
220 Eureka Street
San Francisco, Cal. 94114
(415) 285-4544

Doni Tunheim
123 Green Street
Santa Cruz, Cal. 95060
(408) 426-4115

Roger Moyer
Aspen Painting
P.O. Box 20123
Aspen, Colo. 81612
(303) 925-2248

Jim Weber
Aspen Quality Painting
18184 Highway 82
Aspen, Colo. 81611
(303) 923-5234

James Martin
The Color People
1672 Madison
S. Denver, Colo. 80206
(303) 388-8686

James F. Jereb
Aesthetic Painting
1116 W. Berry Avenue
Chicago, Ill. 60657
(312) 327-6567

David Irvin, Architects
22½ N. Main
Fort Scott, Kansas 66701
(316) 223-2564

Lou and Annette Conti
Kalamazoo House
447 W. South Street
Kalamazoo, Mich. 49007
(616) 343-5426

Classic Painters
621 E. 27th Street
Minneapolis, Minn. 55407
(612) 871-3816

Susan Moore
451 Marshall Avenue
Minneapolis, Minn. 55414
(612) 224-0840

Neil Hiedeman
690 Dayton Avenue
St. Paul, Minn. 55104
(612) 224-8324

Joe Adamo
Victorian Artist
1615 Carroll Street
St. Louis, Mo. 63111
(314) 421-0998

Herbert Kramer
Cape May Paint Co.
1001 Lafayette Street
Cape May, N. J. 08204
(609) 884-2233

Michael Foglia
Housescapes by Michael
100 Baynes
Buffalo, N.Y. 14213
(716) 886-7728

John Crosby Freeman
1601 Sheridan Lane
Norristown, Pa. 19404
(215) 539-3010

John Lough
1012B Wright
Heritage Painting
Milwaukee, Wis. 53212
(414) 562-5553

Bill McCluskey
Landmark Painting
2221A North Humboldt Avenue
Milwaukee, Wis. 53212
(414) 372-9545

Mike Lyster
612 Elmwood Ave.
Oshkosh, Wis. 54901
(414) 426-0321

Suppliers

Bruce Bradbury
and Paul Duscherer
Bradbury & Bradbury Wallpapers
P. O. Box 155
Benicia, Cal. 94510
(707) 746-1900

John Burrows
Victorian Design Merchant
P. O. Box 418 Cathedral Sta.
Boston, Mass. 02128
(617) 451-1982

Notes on the Photographs

When Michael and Elizabeth first offered me the job of photographing the houses for *Daughters of Painted Ladies*, I jumped at the chance. As with most photographers, my dream assignment has always been to travel around the country doing what I love to do. Taking the photographs for *Daughters* was truly an adventure and, as with all great adventures, it was filled with new places, new people, and new experiences.

With all of my equipment packed into my trusty Subaru Brat I left Oakland, California, in August 1986 on a 21,000-mile, 84-day, 44-state odyssey. Although Michael and Elizabeth had supplied me with information as to which way the houses faced so I could plan which time of day to be there, no one could predict what the weather would be like. However, it was decided that the Pacific Northwest would be best photographed in late summer when the heavy fog that frequently envelops the area would probably be light. Colorado was photographed in early September, the Midwest during the remainder of September, and New England during the first part of October when the fall colors would be at their peak. The remainder of October was reserved for the South, more for my own comfort than anything else. Central and southern California were photographed during the Indian summer month of November.

All of the photographs were taken with a Sinar F 4 x 5 view camera. Although a view camera is certainly cumbersome, there really is no other way to take consistently good architectural photographs. Besides the perspective control offered by a view camera, it disciplines the photographer to take extra care in composition, exposure, and filtration. I carried a full complement of lenses from extreme wide angle to telephoto. The two workhorses were a 180mm Symmar that offered excellent rendition of the houses when I was able to back far enough away, and a 120mm SW Nikkor when wires and foliage forced me to move in tighter. The 120mm Nikkor has incredible coverage power (it will actually cover an 8 x 10) and very low distortion. I also used a 135mm Zeiss Planar, 90mm Schneider Super Angulon, 65mm SW Nikkor and a 14-inch Ektar. The 65mm and 90mm were used when I had to compromise some distortion to get around the wires, trees, and when the space to photograph in was very tight. The 14-inch Ektar was used for detail shots. The biggest challenge in producing the correct colors in the photographs was the use of color filters. Since I could not wait around for the absolute best lighting conditions, I had to use color-correction filters. Combined with Kodak Ektachrome 100 film I was very pleased with the results. When photographing in bright sunlight, I used a 1A or 1B filter. During cloudy conditions or for backlit houses I used a slightly warmer 2A or 2B filter. During times of heavy overcast skies, I used an 81A filter.

Perhaps the most anxiety-producing part of a job like this was not really knowing how the photographs had turned out until I returned. Rather than having to live with that kind of pressure I had the pleasure of using the services of California Photo Service of Emeryville, California. When I took a photograph, I would also take a 4 x 5 Polaroid. The Polaroids along with the exposed film were sent via Federal Express to California Photo. The film would arrive the next morning and I would call later that day to check the results. The Polaroids were then matched with the transparencies and sent on to Michael and Elizabeth. The entire staff of California Photo took an active interest in all aspects of the job and are to be commended for going to great lengths to help make *Daughters of Painted Ladies* a beautiful book.

Being on the road alone for that long a time had the prospect of getting to me after a while, but it never happened because I kept in touch with friends by phone. Since I believe that nothing is ever accomplished entirely without help and support from people who care about you, I would like to thank Richard Ambro, Suzanne Arca, Stan Archacki, Andrea Bersson, Doug Boilesen, Mark Davis, Christina Del Villar, Norm Fisher, Susan Fisher, Laverne Fisher, Barbara Hall, John Hartman, Judy Houck, Laura Ihrig, Joan Kiley, Michael Larsen, Shawn Moss, Elizabeth Pomada, Linette Reilly, Claire Smolik, Del Woodall, and Michael Yates for being there when I needed them. Special thanks also go to HP.

DOUGLAS KEISTER

Authors' Biographies

Elizabeth Pomada and Michael Larsen worked in publishing in New York before emigrating to San Francisco, where they started their literary agency and consulting service for writers in 1972. They created *California Publicity Outlets* (1972), rechristened *Metro California Media* and still published annually, and *Painted Ladies: San Francisco's Resplendent Victorians* (1978), now in its eleventh printing.

Elizabeth wrote *Places to Go With Children in Northern California* (Chronicle Books), now in its fifth revision, and also writes articles on food, culture, and travel. Writer's Digest Books published Michael's books: *How to Write a Book Proposal* (1985) and *Literary Agents: How to Get and Work with the Right One for You* (1986). With Doug Keister, Michael and Elizabeth are collaborating on *Painted Ladies Revisited: San Francisco's Resplendent Victorians Ten Years Later.*

Ever since finding some discarded but unused Kodak chemicals in a neighbor's garbage can in 1964, Douglas Keister has been involved with the world of photography. After his early training in Nebraska, he moved to California in 1969. His photographs, done primarily in the larger 4 x 5 and 8 x 10 formats, have appeared in numerous publications and are also owned by collectors. His book *Driftwood Whimsy: The Sculptures of the Emeryville Mudflats* was published by California Photo Service (1985). Keister lives in Oakland, California, and works as a commercial, advertising, and architectural photographer.

Bibliography

Books

Arrowsmith, James. *How to Wallpaper Your Victorian House*. A facsimile of James Arrowsmith's *Paper-Hanger's Companion*, 1856. Watkins Glen, N.Y.: The American Life Foundation, 1978.

Barber, George F. *George F. Barber's Cottage Souvenir Number Two*. With a new Introduction by Michael A. Tomlan. Watkins Glen, N.Y.: The American Life Foundation, 1982.

Bishop, Robert, and Patricia Coblentz. *The World of Antiques, Art, and Architecture in Victorian America*. New York, N.Y.: E.P. Dutton, 1979.

Business Research Bureau, University of South Dakota, and The Historic Preservation Center. *Historic Sites of South Dakota: A Guidebook*. Sioux Falls, S.D.: Historic Preservation Center, 1980.

Calhoun, William G. *Fort Scott: A Pictorial History*. Historic Preservation Association of Bourbon County, Inc.,Fort Scott, Ka., 1981.

Clark, Rosalind. *Architecture Oregon Style*. Portland, Ore.: Professional Book Center, 1983.

Cleaveland, Henry W., Samuel D. Backus, and William Backus. *Village and Farm Cottages: A Victorian Stylebook of 1856*. With a new Introduction by David Schuyler. Watkins Glen, N.Y.: The American Life Foundation, 1982.

Cromie, Alice. *Restored America: The Preserved Towns, Villages and Historic City Districts of the United States and Canada*. New York, N.Y.: American Legacy Press, 1979.

Cudworth, Marsha. *Victorian Holidays: Self-Guided Architectural Tours Cape May, N.J.* New York, N.Y.: Lady Raspberry Press, 1985.

Dietz & Co. *Victorian Lighting. The Dietz Catalog of 1860*. Watkins Glen, N.Y.: The American Life Foundation, 1982.

Dresser, Christopher. *The Art of Decorative Design*. Watkins Glen, N.Y.: The American Life Foundation, 1977.

Ferro, Maximilian L. *How to Love and Care For Your Old Building in New Bedford*. Prepared for the City of New Bedford, Mass., 1977.

Florin, Lambert. *Victorian West*. Seattle, Wash.: Superior Pub., 1978.

Gabriel, Ralph Henry, ed. *The Pageant of America: A Pictorial History of the United States Volume XIII*. Talbot Faulkner Hamlin, *The American Spirit in Architecture*. New Haven, Conn.: Yale University Press, 1976.

Gillon, Edmund V., Jr., and Clay Lancaster. *Victorian Houses: A Treasury of Lesser-Known Examples*. New York, N.Y.: Dover Publications, 1973.

Jackson, Hal, with Ted Loring, Jr. *A Guide to the Architecture and Landscape of Eureka*. Eureka, Ca.: Hal Jackson, 1983.

Jacox, Helen P., and Eugene B. Kleinhans, Jr. *Thousand Island Park: One Hundred Years and Then Some*. A Centennial Year History. Thousand Island Park, N.Y.: The Centennial Book Project, 1975.

Labine, Clem, and Carolyn Flaherty. *The Old-House Journal Compendium* Woodstock, N.Y.: The Overlook Press, 1980.

Lancaster, Clay. *Architectural Follies in America or Hammer Saw-Tooth and Nail*. Rutland, Vt.: Charles E. Tuttle Co., 1960.

Landmarks Heritage Preservation Commission. *A Comprehensive Program for Historic Preservation in Omaha*. Omaha, Neb.: Omaha City Planning Department, 1980.

Maass, John. *The Gingerbread Age: A View of Victorian America*. New York, N.Y.: Bramhall House, 1957.

Maddex, Diane. *Architects Make Zigzags: Looking at Architecture from A to Z*. Washington, D.C.: Preservation Press, National Trust for Historic Preservation of the United States, 1986.

Mitchell, Eugene, comp. *American Victoriana: Floor Plans and Renderings from the Gilded Age*. San Francisco, Cal.: Chronicle Books, 1979.

Moss, Roger W. *Century of Color: Exterior Decoration for American Buildings 1820–1920*. Watkins Glen, N.Y.: The American Life Foundation, 1981.

———, and Gail Caskey Winkler. *Victorian Exterior Decoration: How To Paint Your Nineteenth-Century American House Historically*. New York, N.Y.: Henry Holt, 1987.

Muthesius, Stefan, *The High Victorian Movement in Architecture 1850–1870*. London: Routledge, Kegan & Paul, 1972.

Norwich, John Julius. *Great Architecture of the World*. New York, N.Y.: Random House, in Association with American Heritage Publishing Co., 1975.

Reece, Daphne. *Historic Houses of California*. San Francisco, Ca.: Chronicle Books, 1983.

———, *Historic Houses of the Pacific Northwest*. San Francisco Ca.: Chronicle Books, 1985.

Scully. Vincent. *The Rise of American Architecture: The American House from Thomas Jefferson to Frank Lloyd Wright*. New York, N.Y.: Praeger Publishers and the Metropolitan Museum of Art, 1970.

Sinclair, Peg B. *Victorious Victorians: A Guide to the Major Architectural Styles*. Photographs by Taylor B. Lewis. Text by Peg B. Sinclair. New York, N.Y.: Holt, Rinehart & Winston, 1985.

Tuthill, William B. *Late Victorian Interiors and Interior Details*. A facsimile of Wm. B. Tuthill's *Interiors and Interior Details*, 1882. Introduction by John Crosby Freeman. Watkins Glen, N.Y.: The American Life Foundation, 1984.

Von Normann, Bob. *Victorian Eureka and Ferndale: The Elegant Ladies of the North Coast*. Redcrest, Ca.: FVN Inc., 1986.

Waldhorn, Judith Lynch, and Sally B. Woodbridge. *Victoria's Legacy: Tours of San Francisco Bay Area Architecture*. San Francisco, Ca.: 101 Productions, 1978.

Zimmerman, H. Russell. *The Heritage Guidebook: Landmarks and Historical Sites in Southeastern Wisconsin*. Milwaukee, Wis.: Heritage Banks, 1978.

Periodicals

The Old-House Journal. April 1981; May 1982; January–February 1984; March 1984; August–September 1985; April 1986; May 1986.

Victorian Homes. Spring 1981; Fall 1982; Fall 1983; Winter 1983; Spring 1984; Summer 1984; Fall 1985; Winter 1985; Spring 1986; Winter 1986; Summer 1986.